Bernard Williams

Philosophy Now

Series Editor: John Shand

This is a fresh and vital series of new introductions to today's most read, discussed and important philosophers. Combining rigorous analysis with authoritative exposition, each book gives a clear, comprehensive and enthralling access to the ideas of those philosophers who have made a truly fundamental and original contribution to the subject. Together the volumes comprise a remarkable gallery of the thinkers who have been at the forefront of philosophical ideas.

Published

Donald Davidson
Marc Joseph

Nelson Goodman
Daniel Cohnitz & Marcus Rossberg

Saul Kripke
G. W. Fitch

David Lewis
Daniel Nolan

John McDowell
Tim Thornton

Hilary Putnam
Maximilian de Gaynesford

Wilfrid Sellars
Willem A. deVries

Bernard Williams
Mark P. Jenkins

Forthcoming

David Armstrong
Stephen Mumford

Thomas Nagel
Alan Thomas

John Rawls
Catherine Audard

Peter Strawson
Clifford Brown

Bernard Williams

Mark P. Jenkins

McGill-Queen's University Press
Montreal & Kingston · Ithaca

ISBN-13: 978-0-7735-3179-6 ISBN-10: 0-7735-3179-3 (bound)
ISBN-13: 978-0-7735-3180-2 ISBN-10: 0-7735-3180-7 (pbk.)

Legal deposit third quarter 2006
Bibliothèque nationale du Québec

Published simultaneously outside North America
by Acumen Publishing Limited

McGill-Queen's University Press acknowledges the financial support of the Government of Canada through the Book Publishing Development Program (BPIDP) for its activities.

Library and Archives Canada Cataloguing in Publication

Jenkins, Mark P., 1957-
Bernard Williams / Mark P. Jenkins.

Includes bibliographical references and index.
ISBN-13: 978-0-7735-3179-6 ISBN-10: 0-7735-3179-3 (bound)
ISBN-13: 978-0-7735-3180-2 ISBN-10: 0-7735-3180-7 (pbk.)

1. Williams, Bernard, 1929- I. Title.

B1674.W496J46 2006 192 C2006-902314-X

Typeset by Newgen Imaging Systems (P) Ltd, Chennai, India.
Printed and bound by Cromwell Press, Trowbridge.

In memory of my grandfather, Alden W. Johnson

Contents

Acknowledgements

Were I obliged to thank all those who have urged me, undoubtedly with my best interests at heart, to "just sit down and write the damn thing", these acknowledgements might easily rival the ensuing chapters in length. As it is, I confine my gratitude here to those whose extraordinary generosity – with assistance or accommodation or criticism or encouragement – merits special mention. For assistance, I thank John Shand, Peggy Burge, Adrian Moore, Lauren Lepow and, especially, Chris Jason and Sue Hadden. For accommodation, I thank John Finney, Jonathan Cohen, Patricia Churchland and, especially, Pippin Schupbach. For criticism, I thank Patrick Frierson, Chad Flanders and an anonymous reader for the publisher. For encouragement, I thank Sarah Warren. For all four, I thank Julie Nelson Christoph, Paul Loeb, Robert Pippin, Candace Vogler and, especially, Marya Schechtman. Finally, although many know how difficult it can be to finish a book, few know how difficult it can be for a surfer. For amazing patience over an embarrassingly long period of time, I thank Steven Gerrard at Acumen. No one here mentioned, of course, bears the slightest responsibility for the book's defects; besides, as Nelson Goodman once said, "obvious inadequacies are for the convenience of critics."

Chapter 1

Introduction: "Against the shortsighted"

According to his long-time friend and fellow philosopher Thomas Nagel, "Bernard Williams once posed the awkward question, What is the point of doing philosophy if you're not extraordinarily good at it?" (Nagel 1995a: 10). The idea seems to be that whereas the brilliant thinkers of, say, chemistry and physics require thought-corroborating minions, philosophy's brightest lights require few, if any, to reflect their glory: underlabourers need not apply. Nagel continues: "If you're not extraordinary, what you do in philosophy will be either unoriginal (and therefore unnecessary) or inadequately supported (and therefore useless). More likely, it will be both unoriginal and wrong" (*ibid.*). By such measures, Williams clearly counts as extraordinary (as does Nagel, for that matter), and this book documents that extraordinariness by presenting in detail both Williams's substantial original contributions to contemporary philosophy and their supporting arguments.

Nietzsche poses a different question. In *Human, All Too Human*, he asks "shortsighted" readers: "Do you think this work must be fragmentary because I give it to you (and have to give it to you) in fragments?" (Nietzsche 1986: 243). Williams might well ask this same question in connection with his own work, giving, of course, the same emphatic, if implicit, negative reply. In fact, Williams *did* suggest this very passage as a fitting epigraph for his life's work (personal conversation: 13 November 1996). Still, readers might be forgiven, at least initially, for seeing Williams's contributions to contemporary philosophy as all too fragmentary, addressing, as they do, a vast array of areas, periods and problems in philosophy, most notably in ethics, where his views on a host of issues – metaphysical, political, epistemological, practical, psychological, historical – in a variety of voices – sceptical, critical, constructive, by turns positive and pessimistic – have proven especially influential. But neither the number nor the scope of these contributions should prevent readers, shortsighted or otherwise, from detecting and appreciating three overlapping convictions that testify to Williams's importance, his extraordinariness, as a philosopher, even as they defend against charges that his fragments must be fragmentary. What is more, these convictions come fortuitously linked to a prodigious talent on near constant display.

Williams's first guiding conviction insists that philosophy, especially moral philosophy, is only as valuable or plausible or accurate as the psychology it incorporates. In this insistence he bears a torch famously lit by G. E. M. Anscombe's claim in "Modern Moral Philosophy" that "it is not profitable for us at present to do moral philosophy ... until we have an adequate philosophy of psychology, in which we are conspicuously lacking" (Anscombe 1997: 26). Indeed, much of Williams work over the years, as the following chapters will demonstrate, can best be understood as developing and refining an underlying psychological picture adequate to the various tasks of philosophical analysis. Two examples from his earliest writings on ethics make this point clear. First, in "A Critique of Utilitarianism", Williams questions consequentialism's reliance on "the notion of *negative responsibility*: that if I am ever responsible for anything, then I must be just as responsible for things that I allow or fail to prevent, as I am for things that I myself ... bring about" (Williams 1973a: 95). The problem, ultimately traced to blind faith in impartiality, arises for Williams because negative responsibility as a philosophical doctrine rings false to certain features of human psychology; for instance, that when it comes to feeling responsible one's own actions tend to possess special salience relative to the actions of others. And, as Williams goes on to argue, privileging personal agency over impersonal outcomes "is an idea closely connected with the value of integrity" (*ibid.*: 99). Utilitarianism, integrity and related issues are discussed in Chapter 3.

A second example of getting the psychology right as a precondition of philosophical progress comes from Williams's well known paper "Ethical Consistency" and the following insight: "Moral conflicts are neither systematically avoidable, nor all soluble without remainder" (Williams 1973e: 179). Once again, Williams sees psychological reality undermining philosophical fantasy. In this case, taken up in Chapter 4, the possible persistence of an emotional "remainder" in the form of regret, despite one's having done the right thing, calls into question the tenability of moral theories inclined to characterize such "agent-regret" as irrational, most particularly Kant's. These examples also illustrate Williams's advocacy of what he calls "realistic" moral psychology (see Chapter 7), based loosely on Nietzsche's penchant for explaining moral phenomena in terms of less moral phenomena, or in terms of "what an experienced, honest, subtle, and unoptimistic interpreter might make of human behaviour elsewhere" (Williams 1995f: 68). In fact, the phrase "decent philosophy demands realistic psychology" neatly sums up Williams's first conviction.

William's second sweeping conviction also reflects Nietzsche's influence, in the idea that philosophy, and here not just moral philosophy, is only as valuable or plausible or accurate as the historical sense it incorporates; not a sense for stale or static or "one damned thing after another" history, however, but a sense for history in the spirit of genealogy, which, in its Nietzschean guise, Williams describes as a mixture of "history, phenomenology, 'realistic' psychology, and conceptual interpretation" (Williams 1995f: 75n12). Of course, this emphasis on genealogy is not meant to downplay Williams's more straightforward contributions to the history of philosophy, perhaps most notably his work on Descartes (Williams 1978a). But the conviction at hand has less to do with getting the past right as the past, and much more to do with getting the past right as the present, as it assumes altered, less easily recognizable forms, infusing and influencing contemporary philosophical concerns. It is not just that forgetting invites repeating, although the legacy of a number of philosophical disputes does seem to confirm Santayana, but that, for Williams, contemporary philosophical problems, of ethical objectivity or moral motivation, say, can only be properly approached as palimpsests, with an appreciation of philosophy's past scribblings essential to efforts at improving its present veneer.

Shame and Necessity, in many ways Williams's masterpiece, well exemplifies this commitment to the importance of history for philosophy, as it argues that those who see discontinuities between Greek and current conceptions of responsibility, agency and emotion must be blind to the fact that the ancient conceptions have been not so much replaced as covered up, in most cases by an insidious Kantian wallpaper of duty and obligation. Insisting that "if we can come to understand the ethical concepts of the Greeks, we shall recognize them in ourselves", Williams suggests that such understanding depends on an understanding of Greek epic poetry and, especially, tragic drama (Williams 1993b: 10). In a somewhat similar vein, Williams's more recent *Truth and Truthfulness* invokes, sometimes even invents, the past in an attempt to illuminate the present, in this case bringing not Nietzschean, but "vindicatory", genealogy to bear on the following question: "Can the notions of truth and truthfulness be intellectually stabilized, in such a way that what we understand about truth and our chances of arriving at it can be made to fit with our need for truthfulness" (Williams 2002: 3). Genealogy – vindicatory, Nietzschean or otherwise – is discussed in Chapter 7, in connection with Williams's views on ethical naturalism. Important for present purposes is simply recognizing its usefulness, in as much as our philosophical ideas turn out to be "a complex deposit of many different traditions and social forces ... [which] have themselves been shaped by self-conscious representations of that history" (*ibid.*: 20).

According to Williams, the more successful this task of conceptual archaeology, of unearthing this complex deposit, the more it "is likely to reveal a radical contingency in our current ethical conceptions" (*ibid.*). So we reach his third conviction, that philosophy is only valuable or plausible or accurate to the extent that it acknowledges radical contingency in the world and takes to heart the implications of that contingency for its own ambitions. Embracing contingency in this context need imply no more than rejecting the sort of necessity associated with one-size-fits-all teleologies and explanatory schemes of, say, ethical progress or truth, such necessity being belied by the manifest plurality and incommensurability of values, not to mention the inevitability and significance of tragedy in life. Like his great friend Isaiah Berlin, Williams "warns us against the deep error of supposing that all goods, all virtues, all ideals are compatible, and that what is desirable can ultimately be united into a harmonious whole without loss" (Williams 1978b: xvi). In fact, much of Williams's vaunted scepticism about ethical theory can be seen as rooted in scepticism about any "necessary expectation that the world of ideas and practices in which we find ourselves should conceptually hang together, or form one homogeneous ethical whole" (Williams 1995i: 139). Hence also comes Williams's affinity for Greek tragedy, which, in his view, "precisely refuses to present human beings who are ideally in harmony with their world, and has no room for a world that, if it were understood well enough, could instruct us how to be in harmony with it" (Williams 1993b: 164). Williams's recurrent emphasis on the elusiveness of harmony underscores his repeated emphasis on the prevalence of contingency and the importance of this fact for philosophical understanding.

These three interlocking convictions, then, involving philosophy's need to develop and deploy a sufficiently sophisticated psychology, to appreciate the continued relevance of its own history and to acknowledge fully just how much contingency infects that history, affects that psychology and effects those problems called philosophical, inform the chapters that follow. Ordered along very rough chronological lines, these chapters focus on personal identity, utilitarianism, Kantian ethical theory, practical reason, truth and objectivity and the ancient world.

Williams's three guiding lights certainly deserve attention in their own right; however, it is really only when placed in the service of an amazing talent that they prove truly illuminating. This talent amounts to an almost uncanny ability, on display from his very earliest writings, to grow bountiful philosophical crops in allegedly infertile soil. Not surprisingly, this knack for rejuvenating exhausted fields by applying new and imaginative approaches and ideas characterizes many of Williams's best known, most influential papers. Take, for instance, "Internal and External Reasons" (Williams 1981b), the focus of much of Chapter 5, which continues to generate steady comment after more than two decades. This paper essentially revivifies David Hume's insistence on necessarily relating the explanation and justification of action, moral or otherwise, to an agent's existing motivations. Although Williams takes himself to modify substantially Hume's own necessary conditions for what counts as a reason for action, such modification simply points up another successful harvest from seeds innovatively sown in otherwise familiar acreage. Arguably the single best display of this talent occurs in connection with Williams's success in reanimating the plausibility of a bodily or otherwise physical criterion of personal identity, thus challenging Lockean or neo-Lockean orthodoxy. This challenge, clearly his first major contribution to contemporary philosophy, is considered in Chapter 2, which, while not intended to be anything like a comprehensive survey of this exceedingly complex and still actively debated philosophical topic, underscores this talent for rehabilitating derelict intellectual properties, a talent going no small distance towards explaining Williams's prominence in so many different areas of philosophy. But before we turn to personal identity, three final introductory issues need to be noted briefly.

First, the chapters that follow, although designed to be read serially, can also be profitably pursued as one-off treatments of their respective topics; that is, little in later chapters presupposes material from earlier ones. Readers, then, with a targeted interest in Williams's views on, say, practical reason, may wish to skip his views on personal identity, which is not at all to say that no interesting connections exist between those topics, but simply to acknowledge that the book's readers, as well as the uses they may wish to make of it, will be varied.

Secondly, as suggested above, and as so many of the ensuing topics illustrate, this book often takes Williams's most significant contributions to involve not as much the formulation of new philosophical positions reflecting some clear advance, however defined, over previous views, as the destabilization of previous views sufficient to encourage scads of other philosophers to engage in vital new approaches. Of course, as one might expect, not some insignificant portion of that activity aims at destabilizing Williams's own position. Here is the point: while the goal of the book is to render Williams's views as fairly, accurately and clearly as possible, the views of a select few of his contemporaries cannot be, and have not been, ignored, most especially the views of those who have engaged and challenged Williams at almost every turn, at an extremely high level of rigour and sophistication. A number of philosophers fit this bill, but a few stand out in particular (e.g. John McDowell, Christine Korsgaard, Martha Nussbaum), and when their analyses seem particularly illuminating or useful, they are presented alongside Williams's own.

Thirdly, and finally, Williams died in June 2003. Since then, and after this book was largely complete, three new edited collections of Williams's philosophical essays have appeared, and perhaps a word here is warranted concerning the contents of those collections and this book's relation to them. The three volumes vary by editor, theme, the degree to which Williams foresaw them in something like their present form and, most importantly for present purposes, the amount of hitherto unpublished material they contain. Only one of them, *In the Beginning Was the Deed: Realism and Moralism in Political Argument* (Williams 2005), edited by Geoffrey Hawthorn, contains any significant amount of new material, new both in the sense of never having been published (several of the pieces are lectures) and in the sense of presenting new or expanded views, in this case views largely concerned with questions of political legitimacy and the modern liberal state. Two things must be said about this new material: first, it is undoubtedly important; secondly, the chapters that follow do not take account of it.

By contrast, of the forty-two essays that make up the remaining two collections, all but four have been previously published, albeit often somewhat obscurely. *The Sense of the Past* (Williams 2006b), edited by Myles Burnyeat, although apparently largely planned by Williams himself, and pertaining to historical themes and personages, ancient and modern, contains only two new pieces among its twenty-five entries. Such duplication notwithstanding, Burnyeat's introduction, replete with priceless reminiscence, should be compulsory reading for anyone interested in tracing certain lines of philosophical influence leading both to and away from Williams. *Philosophy as a Humanistic Discipline* (Williams 2006a), edited by A. W. Moore, likewise contains just two new essays among those that not only engage more contemporary philosophical issues, but, indeed, memorably reflect upon contemporary philosophy itself. It can be claimed with some confidence, then, that these latter two volumes, or rather their contents, have been duly considered in what follows.

Chapter 2

Personal identity

Introduction

Personal identity as a modern philosophical problem concerns attempts to specify necessary and sufficient conditions for re-identifying persons over time; that is, it involves specifying the conditions under which a person at time $t + 1$ may be said to be the same person as at some earlier time t. Standard histories of philosophy trace the modern formulation and initial solution of this problem to Locke's ideas regarding the connected nature of consciousness, a connectedness cashed out in terms of memory. What makes a person now the same person as at some earlier time is current consciousness of, the ability consciously to remember, that earlier time, or as Locke himself puts it: "as far as this consciousness can be extended backwards to any past Action or Thought, so far reaches the Identity of that *Person*; it is the same *self* now it was then" (Locke 1975: 335). For Locke, then, personal identity depends exclusively upon certain psychological relations obtaining, which is simultaneously to insist that personal identity does not depend on any physical relations obtaining. The continuation of a person owes everything to the continuation of the mind (or soul) and nothing to the continuation of the body.

If anything links otherwise disparate theorizers about personal identity over more than three centuries it may be their penchant for often fanciful, at times downright bizarre, thought experiments. Even Locke contributes a few in support of his psychological criterion, of which probably the best known involves a body-switch between a prince and a cobbler, purporting to illustrate the difference between *persons* and *men*: "For should the Soul of a Prince, carrying with it the consciousness of the Prince's past life, enter and inform the body of a Cobler as soon as deserted by his own Soul, everyone sees he would be the same Person with the Prince, accountable only for the Prince's Actions: But who would say it was the same Man?" (Locke 1975: 340). Here it becomes clear that, for Locke, whether something is or is not the same man depends on whether or not that something possesses the same body, whereas "whatever has the consciousness of present and past Actions, is the same Person to whom they both belong" (*ibid.*). Here the discussion of personhood acquires a distinctively forensic flavour, explicitly linking issues of identity and responsibility.

Locke's criterion of personal identity in terms of memory and the connectedness of consciousness attracted considerable critical attention, of course, with two particularly noteworthy arguments being advanced against it. The first argument, associated with Joseph Butler, finds Locke's account circular, in as much as "consciousness of personal identity presupposes, and therefore cannot constitute, personal identity" (Butler, in Perry 1975b: 100). Just exactly what Butler means here and just exactly how vulnerable Locke's particular account may be to his charge remain disputed matters of historical interpretation, but one seemingly natural way of fleshing out an accusation of circularity against Locke involves the thought that, in so far as the very concept of memory relies upon a person at time $t + 1$ recalling the experience of that same person at some earlier time t, it relies upon a notion of personal identity and so cannot be used to define it. The second argument, associated with Thomas Reid, finds Locke's account vulnerable to a seeming disconnect between its implicit transitivity and the foibles of memory. Reid suggests that a "brave officer" might have been flogged as a boy, captured an enemy flag as a young man and been made a general at an advanced age. Certainly, in so far as the young man remembers being flogged and the old man remembers capturing the flag, the old man must, "if there be any truth in logic", be the same person as the boy (Reid, in Perry 1975b: 114–15). But it seems perfectly plausible to suppose that the old man possesses no memory of being flogged and so, according to Locke, would not be the same person as the boy. "Therefore", Reid concludes, "the general is, and at the same time is not, the same person with him who was flogged at school" (*ibid.*: 115), an absurd conclusion, and thus a formidable challenge to Locke.

Again, nothing like an authoritative treatment of the history of the problem of personal identity is here intended (for excellent accounts, differing in scope and emphasis, see Perry 1975a; Martin & Barresi 2002a; and especially Noonan 1991). Suffice it to say that more or less satisfactory solutions have been proposed to the problems identified by Butler and Reid, perhaps most notably in the latter case, in terms of continuity, rather than simple connectedness, of memory, or in terms of what Derek Parfit calls, in easily the most provocative contemporary book on the subject, "an overlapping chain of experience-memories" (Parfit 1984: 205). The point here is simply that Lockean or neo-Lockean accounts of personal identity in terms of certain psychological relations holding over time remained philosophical orthodoxy until Williams shook things up, in "Personal Identity and Individuation", with his famous argument, based on the possibility of reduplication, "that the omission of the body takes away all content from the idea of personal *identity*" (Williams 1973g: 10). In point of fact, such psychological accounts may well remain orthodoxy to this day (see Olson 1997: 11–21), but, if they do, they must have somehow met the challenge Williams's essay poses.

Reduplication

The challenge posed by Williams's paper comes out in the following thought experiment. Suppose a man named Charles claims the life history of Guy Fawkes, or at least the life history of Fawkes prior to his execution in 1606 for conspiring to blow up Parliament for the Catholic cause: "Not only do all Charles' memory-claims that can be checked fit the pattern of Fawkes' life as known to historians, but others that cannot be checked are plausible, provide explanations of unexplained facts, and so on" (Williams 1973g: 7–8). As Williams sees it, the temptation to say that Charles is now Fawkes "is very strong" (*ibid.*: 8). And, of course, such strength derives from certain psychological features Charles/Fawkes displays; that is, from Charles effectively satisfying Locke's psychological criterion of personal identity.

At this point, however, Williams points out that "If it is logically possible that Charles should undergo the changes described, then it is logically possible that some other man should simultaneously undergo the same changes; e.g. that both Charles and his brother Robert should be found in this condition" (*ibid.*). Needless to say, adds Williams,

> They cannot both be Guy Fawkes; if they were, Guy Fawkes would be in two places at once, which is absurd. Moreover, if they were

> identical with Guy Fawkes, they would be identical with each other, which is also absurd. Hence we could not say that they were both identical with Guy Fawkes. . . . So it would be best, if anything, to say that both had mysteriously become like Guy Fawkes, clairvoyantly knew about him, or something like this. If this would be the best description of each of the two, why would it not be the best description of Charles if Charles alone were changed?
>
> (*Ibid*.: 8–9)

One of the paper's key aims, clearly in evidence here, involves distinguishing between identity and "exact similarity", with Charles perhaps displaying the latter relation *vis-à-vis* Fawkes, but not the former (although, in fact, Williams appears fairly sceptical regarding the notion of exact similarity when it comes to memories, as opposed to bodies). But, of course, the main aim of the paper, as of the thought experiment, is "to show that bodily identity is always a necessary condition of personal identity" (*ibid*.: 1).

The guiding principle underlying Williams's reduplication argument may be characterized in one of two ways. First, whether or not Charles has become Fawkes cannot depend on whether or not rival candidates exist; that is, on whether or not others also claim to be Fawkes, such that if no rival candidate exists Charles is Fawkes, but that if a rival candidate emerges the matter becomes (at best) indeterminate. As Williams explains, in an article meant to clarify his position:

> The principle of my argument is, very roughly put, that identity is a one–one relation, and that no principle can be a criterion of identity for things of type *T* if it relies only on what is logically a one–many or many–many relation between things of type *T*. What is wrong with the supposed criterion of identity for persons which relies only on memory claims is just that ". . . being disposed to make sincere memory claims which exactly fit the life of . . ." is not a one–one, but a many–one relation, and hence cannot possibly be adequate in logic to constitute a criterion of identity.
>
> (Williams 1973c: 21)

As Robert's appearance on the scene changes the Charles/Fawkes situation from one–one to many–one, so it calls into question memory as a sufficient condition of identity.

One may also take Williams's guiding principle a second way, as claiming that questions of identity must be settled in terms of intrinsic relations; extrinsic factors, such as, in Williams's example, the existence of Robert, may not impinge, which is just to say, once more, "that the question whether a certain person in the future, let us call him Y, is the same person present now, X, cannot be a question of whether Y is merely the *best candidate* available at the time for being X" (Williams 1982a: 32). Whether or not relations of identity hold between X and Y can only be a function of intrinsic relations between X and Y. Again, Williams believes his reduplication argument undermines Lockean-style accounts that take psychological continuity in terms of memory as a sufficient condition for personal identity, and so provides critical room for bodily or spatiotemporal continuity as a necessary condition, most naturally in terms of the brain. But, as Richard Swinburne, himself more than happy to embrace the implications of Williams's argument for his own preferred dualist agenda, points out, "any brain theory is also open to the duplication objection" (Swinburne 1984: 14).

The problem for Williams here, if indeed it is a problem, stems from the possibility of brain fission, given the anatomical reality that human brains consist of two hemispheres that may, at least theoretically, be surgically split and transplanted, with each maintaining more or less similar and more or less pre-surgical levels of functioning. Again, Swinburne: "There are no logical difficulties in supposing that we could transplant one of P_1's hemispheres into one skull from which a brain had been removed, and another hemisphere into another such skull. . . . If these transplants took . . . [e]ach of the resulting persons would then be good candidates for being P_1" (*Ibid.*: 14–15; and see, generally, Nagel 1979a). In any case, as Swinburne cannot resist adding, this surgical scenario "is certainly more likely to occur than the Guy Fawkes story told by Williams!" (Swinburne 1984: 15). Although the continuation of the brain may now seem, in the light of Williams's attack on purely psychological accounts, a welcome and necessary bodily condition on personal identity, it appears vulnerable to similar concerns regarding the possibility of many–one or extrinsic relations.

To his credit, Williams appreciates this vulnerability, although not (immediately) in terms of brain bisection:

> It is possible to imagine a man splitting, amoeba-like, into two simulacra of himself. If this happened, it must of course follow from my original argument that it would not be reasonable to say that either of the resultant men was identical with the original one: they could not both be, because they are not identical with each other, and it would not be reasonable to choose one rather than the

> other to be identical with the original. Hence it would seem that by my requirements, not even spatio-temporal continuity would serve as a criterion of identity.
>
> (Williams 1973c: 23; compare Williams 1973b: 77)

Williams, however, resists this conclusion, arguing that "There is a vital difference between this sort of reduplication, with the criterion of spatio-temporal continuity, and the other sorts of case" (Williams 1973c: 24). Appreciating this vital difference requires appreciating the superior possibilities afforded by bodily cases for charting causal chains of identity or, put another way, requires appreciating the extent to which "a thorough application of the [spatiotemporal] criterion would itself reveal the existence of the reduplication situation, and so enable us to answer (negatively) the original identity question" (*ibid.*). Charles and Robert sharing a brain presents a very different scenario, Williams believes, from Charles and Robert sharing memories.

In "Are Persons Bodies?" Williams endeavours to make his position plain:

> The reduplication problem arises if a supposed criterion of identity allows there to be two distinct items, *B* and *C*, each of which satisfies the criterion in just the way that it would if the other did not exist. But this is not so with bodily continuity; what is true of *B* when it is in the ordinary way continuous is just not the same as what is true of it when, together with *C*, it has been produced from *A* by fission. (Williams 1973b: 77–8)

At least at this point in the discussion, it does appear relatively straightforward that when Charles and his brother Robert both claim to be Guy Fawkes, and when the standard for assessing their claims and determining their identity depends on their reported memories, there is nothing to choose between them. And since two people cannot both be identical with a third, Williams is correct to see the reduplication of Fawkes's memories as proof that a purely psychological criterion cannot be sufficient to answer questions of personal identity. But now add a bodily component to the story, such that, say, Charles's brain containing Fawkes's memories is split, with one hemisphere remaining in Charles and the other hemisphere transplanted into Robert's skull, from which his own complete brain has been previously removed. In this case, Williams seems to think a determinate negative answer can be given on the question of identity, in as much as a thorough investigation into the history of both claimants to Fawkes's identity will uncover the brain surgery that led to the two single-hemisphered selves. Since "in a case of fission ... the resultant items are not, in the strict sense, spatio-temporally continuous with the original", neither post-surgery Charles nor post-surgery Robert can be identical with pre-surgery Charles (Williams 1973c: 24). In as much as Williams believes the reduplication argument makes bodily continuity a necessary condition of personal identity, and in as much as Williams believes that fission cases fail to preserve bodily continuity, and in as much as Williams believes that fission cases cannot help but be uncovered by historical investigation, Williams believes that the bare possibility of bodily or brain reduplication does not have the same malign consequences for a spatiotemporal criterion of personal identity as memory reduplication does for the psychological criterion.

Williams's case for the superior resistance of accounts of personal identity requiring bodily continuity to threats posed by reduplication has been challenged on a number of grounds (see, for example, Perry 1976, a valuable review of Williams's papers on personal identity; Noonan 1991: 150–2). For one thing, it may not be obvious that a split-brained Charles fails to cross the threshold set by Williams for problematic reduplication. Remember Williams's claim that, when it comes to bodily continuity, "what is true of *B* when it is in the ordinary way continuous with *A* is just not the same as what is true of it when, taken together with *C*, it has been produced from *A* by fission" (Williams 1973b: 78). Perhaps one might challenge Williams here to spell out just exactly what is no longer true of post-surgery Charles that was true of pre-surgery Charles. Presumably he would simply point to post-surgery Charles being a literal half-brain, but it is hard, at least theoretically, to see just what Charles's half-brained status falsifies of his previous whole-brained self. Williams concludes, however, "that this sort of [fission] case, because of its special nature, does not tell against my general position; which is that in order to serve as a criterion of identity, a principle must provide what I have called a one–one relation and not a one–many relation" (Williams 1973c: 25; see Perry 1976: 425–8). And, in any event, the aim here is less to develop and critique Williams's arguments on personal identity than to support Harold Noonan's claim, in his authoritative treatment of personal identity, that "[Williams's reduplication] argument transformed subsequent discussion of the problem and led philosophers to the formulation of positions which were wholly new" (Noonan 1991: 149). The next section considers one of Williams's most memorable papers,

"The Self and the Future", and its own doubts about psychological continuity as a sufficient condition for personal identity.

A *risky* choice

Just what role intuition ought to play in philosophical argument is a complex and controversial question. Some philosophers believe intuition to be of almost no account, whereas others believe that intuitions should be preserved at virtually any cost; still others take philosophy's primary task as being reconciling or seeking some sort of equilibrium between rational argument and intuition, privileging neither (see Williams 1995j for a discussion of more technical notions of intuition, especially in ethics). Whatever one's view, all can agree that conflicting intuitions frequently indicate philosophical issues or problems needing attention. Moreover, all can agree that exposing, even inventing, cases or circumstances that prod such conflicting intuitions can be of immense philosophical value. This is precisely what Williams's masterful "The Self and the Future" succeeds in doing, prompting conflicting intuitions regarding "what matters in survival", and so what counts for personal identity, from what he ingeniously presents as essentially the same case or set of circumstances.

"Suppose that there were some process to which two persons, *A* and *B*, could be subjected as a result of which they might be said – question-beggingly – to have *exchanged* bodies" (Williams 1973i: 46). So begins "The Self and the Future" and so begins the description of a hypothetical experimental procedure at the foundation of two very differently described cases, designed to elicit two very different, indeed, mutually opposed, conclusions about the nature of personal identity. The first of these, which, as John Perry rightly maintains, "puts the case for the possibility of bodily transfer about as effectively as it has been put" (Perry 1976: 418), goes like this. First, "suppose it were possible to extract information from a man's brain and store it in a device while his brain was repaired, or even renewed, the information then being replaced. ... Hence we can imagine ... information extracted into such devices from *A*'s and *B*'s brains and replaced in the other brain" (Williams 1973i: 47). So far, so good: a technology exists whereby the contents of brains, call them psychologies (some amalgam of memory and character), can be extracted, stored and either replaced or transplanted elsewhere.

Of particular philosophical interest is what this technology might reveal about personal identity. Suppose *A* and *B* retain their bodies while swapping psychologies. Is the resultant person with *A*'s body (still) *A*? Or does *A* now occupy *B*'s body; that is, is *B* now *A*? The latter result would seem to validate psychological continuity as a sufficient condition of personal identity, and Williams, in an attempt to settle the matter definitively, offers the following thought experiment:

> We take two persons, *A* and *B*, who are going to have the [body exchange/psychology swap] process carried out on them. ... We further announce that one of the two resultant persons, the *A*-body-person and the *B*-body-person, is going after the experiment to be given $100,000, while the other is going to be tortured. We then ask each of *A* and *B* to choose which treatment should be dealt out to which of the persons who will emerge from the experiment, the choice to be made (if it can be) on selfish grounds.
> (Williams 1973i: 48)

There is nothing like the prospect of immediate pain to focus one's intuitions, and Williams suggests that both *A* and *B* will choose that the money follow their psychologies; that is, *A* prefers that the *B*-body-person will receive the money and the *A*-body-person be tortured, whereas *B* prefers that the *A*-body-person will get rich and the *B*-body-person will get pain. Moreover, such choices indicate that "'changing bodies' was indeed a good description of the outcome" (*ibid.*). Williams concludes "that to care about what happens to me in the future is not necessarily to care about what happens to this body (the one I now have)" (*ibid.*: 49), going even further to say that "the only rational thing to do, confronted with such an experiment, would be to identify oneself with one's memories, and so forth, and not with one's body" (*ibid.*: 51). Who one is seems not to depend on whose body one occupies. The psychological criterion appears alive and well.

Now, however, Williams asks the reader to "consider something apparently different", a second scenario, albeit one still dependent on the experimental technology of memory extraction, storage, replacement and exchange:

> Someone in whose power I am tells me that I am going to be tortured tomorrow. ... He adds that when the time comes, I shall not remember being told that this was going to happen to me, since shortly before the torture something else would be done to me which will make me forget the announcement. ... He then adds

> that my forgetting the announcement will be only part of a larger process: when the moment of torture comes, I shall not remember any of the things I am now in a position to remember. ... He now further adds that at the moment of torture I shall not only not remember the things I am now in a position to remember, but will have a different set of impressions of my past, quite different from the memories I now have ... [T]he person in charge add[s] lastly that the impressions of my past with which I shall be equipped on the eve of torture will exactly fit the past of another person now living, and that I shall acquire these impressions by (for instance) information now in his brain being copied into mine.
> (Williams 1973i: 52)

Williams quite sensibly reports that, when initially informed of his impending torture, "I am frightened and look forward to tomorrow in great apprehension" (*ibid.*). The big question here concerns whether any of the additional information provided to him should or would mitigate his fear.

Williams thinks not. If anything, subsequent information might actually intensify his apprehension. For example, to the prospect of acquiring some other person's memories just prior to being tortured, Williams responds: "Fear, surely, would still be the proper reaction: and not because one did not know what was going to happen, but because in one vital respect at least one did know what was going to happen – torture, which one can indeed expect to happen to oneself, and to be preceded by certain mental derangements as well" (*ibid.*). And Williams re-emphasizes this point: "the predictions of the man in charge provide a double ground of horror: at the prospect of torture, and at the prospect of the change in character and in impressions of the past that will precede it" (*ibid.*: 54–5). A "positively straightforward" principle grounds the analysis here: "one's fears can extend to future pain whatever psychological changes precede it" (*ibid.*: 63), as Williams insists that "Physical pain ... is absolutely minimally dependent on character and belief. No amount of change in my character and beliefs would seem to affect substantially the nastiness of tortures applied to me; correspondingly, no degree of predicted change can unseat the fear of torture which, together with those changes, is predicted for me" (*ibid.*: 54). But if one's fear of pain and torture truly proves indifferent to the promise of radical psychological rearrangement, then perhaps what makes for the same person at a later time is something other than, or at least something in addition to, one's psychology. Bodily continuity as a necessary condition for personal identity seems, then, the unmistakable moral of this second story, just as psychological continuity as a sufficient condition of personal identity appears the unmistakable moral of the first. Yet, as Williams quite unforgettably argues, *the two stories are essentially the same*, which leaves things, to say the least, "totally mysterious" (*ibid*.: 52).

According to Williams, the second case "is of course merely one side, differently represented, of the transaction which we considered before; and it represents it as a perfectly hateful prospect, while the previous considerations represented it as something one should rationally, perhaps even cheerfully, choose out of the options there presented" (*ibid*.: 52–3). Admittedly, two factors distinguish the story's second telling from the first, but Williams believes neither to be of sufficient weight to explain away the stories' disparate interpretations. The first thing different about the second case is the "not very neutral" way in which the experimenter puts the case in the second-person singular – "'you', the man in charge persistently says" (*ibid*.: 53) – whereas the first case presents the upcoming events in (arguably) less emotionally charged third-person terms. Yet would a more neutral characterization really render the prospect of torture any less fearful? Williams thinks not.

The second difference is that in the latter case the second person, the psychology donor, occupies a much more incidental role than in the former case, being alluded to solely as the source of the transplanted memories and not also as, for example, the recipient of an exchange himself, not to mention the recipient of $100,000. "But", Williams wonders, "why *should* he mention this man and what is going to happen to him?" After all, "My selfish concern is to be told what is going to happen to me, and now I know: torture, preceded by changes in character, brain operations, changes in impressions of the past" (*ibid*.: 55). As such, Williams feels confident in offering an unequivocal "surely not" to the following question: "when we look at these two differences of presentation, can we really convince ourselves that the second presentation is wrong or misleading, thus leaving the road open to the first version which at the time seemed so convincing?" (*ibid*.: 53). And so he remains puzzled, given that "there are two presentations of the imagined experiment and the choice associated with it, each of which carries conviction, and which lead to contrary conclusions" (*ibid*.: 61), and each of which contains no little risk.

It should be clear that when Williams rejects the relevance of another person in the second case above, he basically invokes, indeed, he basically restates, the principle advanced earlier in support of his reduplication argument, what Noonan calls "the Only x and y principle", whereby the identity of a later person y with some earlier person x can only depend upon relations between x and y, and cannot be influenced by facts involving some third person z (see Noonan 1991: 16). As to justifying the crucial claim that no proposed changes in psychology appear sufficient to dispel one's fear of torture, what might be called his pain principle, Williams (1973i: 55–6) basically challenges the reader to pick a point in the experiment, now somewhat redescribed and rendered schematically, at which it would no longer make sense for *A* to expect pain:

(i) *A* is subjected to an operation that produces total amnesia.
(ii) Amnesia is produced in *A*, and other interference leads to certain changes in his character.
(iii) Changes in his character are produced, and at the same time certain illusory "memory" beliefs are induced in him: these are of a quite fictitious kind and do not fit the life of any actual person.
(iv) The same as (iii), except that both the character traits and the "memory" impressions are designed to be appropriate to another actual person, *B*.
(v) The same as (iv), except that the result is produced by putting the information into *A* from the brain of *B*, by a method that leaves *B* the same as he was before.
(vi) The same as (v), but *B* is not left the same, since a similar operation is conducted in the reverse direction.

Williams's by now familiar claim is that neither amnesia nor a new character and memories, no matter how acquired, ought to stem *A*'s fears of imminent torture. Indeed, he suggests something of a corollary to the pain principle: "If [*A*'s] fears can, as it were, reach through the change, it seems a mere trimming how the change is in fact induced" (*ibid.*: 57). Korsgaard interestingly critiques Williams's focus on pain, given what she sees as the relatively tenuous link between what it is to experience pain and what it is to be some particular person: "Although it is true that there is an important way in which my physical pains seem to happen to *me* and to no one else, it is also true that they seem to have less to do with who I am (which *person* I am) than almost any other psychic events" (Korsgaard 1996b: 394n36). Korsgaard's remarks reflect, among other things, dissatisfaction at the pre-eminence of minimal re-indentification criteria in discussions of personal identity to the exclusion of more substantial notions of selfhood, about which more will be said in the next section (see also, importantly, Schechtman, 1996).

Perry, in his aforementioned review, raises an equally intriguing complaint as regards the role that fear of pain plays in Williams's second experiment. Lamenting a certain vagueness in just what *A* is led to expect, particularly as far as amnesia goes, Perry memorably suggests that the procedure that seems best to capture Williams's actual experimental designs in the article is a "brain zap", whereby "The information in the brain is destroyed", such that "Efforts to trigger the disposition to remember would be silly, because the dispositions are not there" (Perry 1976: 421). If this is right, then Perry believes that the procedure might just as well be characterized as involving the complete removal of *A*'s brain. But if such a characterization truly appears warranted, then, Perry concludes, Williams has misdescribed the situation, in as much as the appropriate fear in this case would be no longer of torture, but of death: "When it is not clear that [*A*'s] brain will be zapped, he fears torture. When that is clear, but he is left to assume the worst about the survival of the information in his brain, he fears death, or perhaps doesn't know what to fear" (*ibid.*: 422). Of course it might make considerable difference were *A* informed, as per (vi) above, that he can expect that his own psychology will be transplanted into *B*'s zapped brain, yet this constitutes precisely the sort of information that Williams deems irrelevant to *A*'s predicament. If Perry is right, however, and it makes sense to ascribe the prospect of imminent death, rather than torture, to *A*, not only will *A*'s fear fail to "reach through" stages (i)–(vi), but the information conveyed to *A* in (vi) could be construed as literally lifesaving, at least as long as what matters in survival remains, as in Williams's original case, psychological continuity.

Nothing like a truly detailed account of Williams's own writings on personal identity is here intended, let alone even a partial consideration of reactions by others. Still, it may be useful to add just a little more flesh to Noonan's earlier quoted observation that Williams's work on personal identity provoked "wholly new" approaches to the subject. That is, after all, perhaps the dominant contention of this book: that not only the problem of personal identity but also other philosophical topics were re-oriented or reconceived or simply revitalized by Williams's work. Focusing for a moment, then, solely on the reduplication argument, since it plays a significant role, as shown above, throughout Williams's account, and assuming, despite Williams's protest, that both psychological and bodily accounts of personal identity succumb to worries regarding the logical possibility of reduplication, a few key responses may be noted.

To begin with, and to be honest, one of these responses is anything but new. Swinburne, for instance, takes Williams's reduplication argument to lend credence to the view "that personal identity is something ultimate, unanalysable in terms of such observable and experienceable phenomena as bodily continuity and continuity of memory" (Swinburne 1984: 26), a view that he admits dates back some 250 years. Resisting Williams's case for a necessary bodily role in addressing questions of re-identification, Swinburne endorses "stuff of another kind, immaterial stuff", while claiming "that persons are made of normal bodily matter and of this immaterial stuff but that it is the continuity of the latter which provides that continuity over time which is necessary for the identity of the person over time" (*ibid.*: 27). Needless to say, no small irony surrounds immaterialists like Swinburne taking strength from an argument designed expressly to further the materialist cause.

No doubt Robert Nozick's "closest continuer theory" better represents the kind of thing Noonan had in mind by a "wholly new" formulation in response to Williams's work. Whereas Williams takes the possibility of memory reduplication (the possibility of, say, Robert coming on to the scene in his Guy Fawkes's example) to threaten accounts of psychological continuity, and others have taken the possibility of bodily reduplication (the possibility of, say, brain fission) additionally to threaten spatiotemporal accounts, Nozick introduces his own necessary condition for identity as a direct response to Williams's puzzle cases: "y at t_2 is the same person as x at t_1 only if, first, y's properties at t_2 stem from, grow out of, are causally dependent on x's properties at t_1 and, second, there is no other z at t_2 that stands in a closer (or as close) relation to x at t_1 than y at t_2 does" (Nozick 1981: 36–7). Nozick, then, straightforwardly rejects Williams's one–many principle – that whether someone is the same as some earlier person can only depend only on relations intrinsic to those two – by insisting on the potential relevance of extrinsic factors in the form of other candidates. In fact, Nozick presumably believes that precisely the relevance of extrinsic factors explains the dramatically conflicting intuitions that so frustrate Williams in "The Self and the Future".

In the first case, the explicit inclusion of *B* from the outset provides a valuable point of reference against which to assess *A*'s possible continuity conditions, allowing *A* to differentiate memory retention as of primary concern. In the second case, by contrast, with no clear rival candidate for *A*'s identity, it proves extremely difficult to envision pain affecting anyone but *A*, and so extremely difficult to see why *A*'s diminishing psychological connectedness should diminish *A*'s fear. Of course, using Nozick's criterion to account for our disparate responses is not quite the same thing as using it to solve Williams's puzzle. Perhaps the presence or absence of rival candidates does affect perceptions of identity, but that fails to settle Williams's issue of whether psychological or spatiotemporal considerations should be paramount in determining identity. Nozick appears to concede this point when he says "The closest continuer theory helps to sort out and structure the issues . . . [I]t does not, by itself, tell which dimension or weighted sum of dimensions determines closeness; rather, it is a schema into which such details can be filled" (Nozick 1981: 33). But regardless of how best to interpret this disclaimer or of the exact scope of Nozick's ambitions, his rejection of the "Only *x* and *y*" principle remains, for Williams, a philosophical non-starter (see Williams 1982a).

Many other examples might be cited in support of Noonan's claim regarding Williams's influence on subsequent theorizing (e.g. Perry 1972; Lewis 1983b, c; Unger 1990). Certainly, however, no discussion of responses to the issues posed by Williams's seminal papers on personal identity, however cursory, would be complete without at least mentioning Parfit's ambitious and multifaceted *Reasons and Persons*, which just might contain more thought experiments than any other book in the history of philosophy. There Parfit famously argues, first, that personal identity may be essentially indeterminate, and, secondly, that identity *per se* is not what actually matters in survival; that is, that identity is not the source of that special concern that people have for their futures. Instead, what matters is psychological continuity and connectedness by virtually any means (see Parfit 1984: especially Chapters 10–12; for helpful summaries of Parfit's main claims, see Kolak & Martin 1991: 172–5; Shoemaker 1997). Of particular interest here, however, is simply the extent to which Parfit's first principle point regarding indeterminacy may be seen as a direct response to Williams's "The Self and the Future".

Wielding the Sorites paradox to dramatic effect, Parfit re-imagines Williams's second case, in which the persistence of *A*'s apprehension in the face of dramatic psychological reconfiguration seems to underwrite a necessary bodily criterion for personal identity, in terms of a "psychological spectrum" along which lie different cases featuring varying degrees of psychological connectedness over time; in other words, the spectrum begins with a case in which a person at time t_2 possesses the same physical and psychological characteristics as at time t_1 (say, same brain, same memories) and ends with a case in which the physical, but absolutely none of the psychological, characteristics remain the same (say, same brain, different or no memories). To Parfit, the far end of the spectrum perfectly represents the denouement of Williams's second case in "The Self and the Future" and, in the context of the psychological spectrum, Williams's argument would go as follows: since personal identity must be determinate at any given point, and since no point along the spectrum apparently marks a psychological sacrifice sufficient to undermine *A*'s identity and since at the far end of the spectrum absolutely no psychological continuity remains, then a purely psychological criterion for personal identity cannot be correct (see Parfit 1984: 231–3).

To this "psychological spectrum" interpretation of Williams's argument, Parfit opposes a "combined spectrum", reflecting degrees of both physical and psychological connectedness, beginning with himself at one end (Parfit's brain, Parfit's psychology) and ending with a completely different person, Greta Garbo, at the other (Garbo's brain and psychology). Of course the great philosopher and the great actress may be easily distinguished towards either end of the spectrum, where they will share few or no cells and few or no memories: in no way is Greta Garbo the same person as Derek Parfit. But matters become progressively murkier towards the centre, as "between neighbouring cases in this Spectrum the differences are trivial" (*ibid.*: 239). Challenging readers to locate some one point along the spectrum where he effectively dies and Garbo comes to exist, Parfit concludes that determinacy of identity cannot be assumed and, in so far as Williams's case against psychological continuity assumes such determinacy, it fails.

In Parfit's view, then, the plausibility of Williams's second case depends upon the implausibility of undermining *A*'s identity, given the reasonableness of the demand for a determinate answer across the spectrum to the question *A* or *not-A*? As the reasonableness of that demand evaporates, so does any necessity that *A* remain *A*, and so, therefore, does Williams's support for a necessary bodily criterion. And as far as the reduplication argument goes more generally, where Swinburne applauds its threats to materialist identity conditions as a boon to dualism, and Nozick responds by proposing ways to sort out, rather than simply reject, the argument's multiple candidates, Parfit takes the ultimate indeterminacy of identity to make Williams's concerns regarding the possibility of reduplication largely beside the point. Although Williams may be correct that two later persons *B* and *C* cannot both be identical with some earlier person *A*, despite being psychologically continuous, in Parfit's view one need not, as with Williams, reject both *B* and *C*, nor, with Nozick, attempt to choose between them; instead one may see both as bearing the only relations to *A* that ultimately matter, psychological connectedness and continuity.

Conclusion

According to Raymond Martin and John Barresi's helpful introduction to their excellent anthology of contemporary work on the subject, "the evolution of Western theorizing about the self and personal identity can seem to divide neatly into three phases: from Plato to Locke, from Locke to the late 1960s, and from the late 1960s to the present" (Martin & Barresi 2002a: 1). They further point to three important developments characterizing the latest period: first, the proliferation of many–one or extrinsic views of personal identity; secondly, rising scepticism about the claim that identity is what really matters in survival; and, thirdly, increased support for viewing persons as four-dimensional time-slices or "aggregates of momentary person-stages" (*ibid*.: 1–4). Now, the first thing worth noting, although perhaps obvious enough from the previous two sections, is that Williams explicitly or implicitly resists each of these moves, a resistance that seems to place him squarely in the second, Lockean, phase of history. After all, not only does his reduplication argument depend on the intrinsicality and determinacy of identity relations, but, as discussed below, Williams also resists at least Parfit's conclusions based upon a logic of "successive selves". However, the second thing worth noting dwarfs the first in importance: a decent case can be made for viewing each of these three developments as a reaction to what might be termed Williams's reproblematizing of the problem of personal identity, thus making his papers vital events in, even something of a condition for, the transition to the third, post-Lockean, phase of theorizing.

One important feature distinguishing Parfit from the pack is that in addition to analysing meticulously the problem of personal identity, he eagerly develops the ethical implications of that analysis; in a word, he changes the subject from metaphysical to moral personhood. No one should be surprised to learn, then, that the conversation between Williams and Parfit extends beyond the critique in *Reasons and Persons* of "The Self and the Future", for perhaps no other contemporary philosopher has become better associated, and deservedly so, with plumbing the depths of moral personhood than Williams. In rejecting the all-or-nothing view of personal identity, Parfit cites dramatic variation in degrees of psychological connectedness, so dramatic, in fact, that he feels warranted in referring to "successive selves" in those cases "When the connections have been markedly reduced – when there has been a significant change of character, or style of life, or of beliefs and ideals" (Parfit 1984: 304–5). Such talk seems seriously to threaten the concept of unity of agency over time and, moreover, to raise one particular moral theory above its rivals:

> If we cease to believe that persons are separately existing entities, and come to believe that the unity of a life involves no more than the various relations between the experiences in this life, it becomes more plausible to become more concerned about the quality of experiences, and less concerned about whose experiences they are. This gives some support to the Utilitarian view.
>
> (*Ibid.*: 346)

This view, that "It becomes more plausible, when thinking morally, to focus less upon the person, the subject of experiences, and instead to focus more upon the experiences themselves" (*ibid.*: 341), Williams flatly rejects. Indeed, as the next two chapters document, there may be few positions with which Williams would more strongly disagree. So, for example, a section of Williams's well known "Persons, Character and Morality" responds to Parfit's views on moral personhood, themselves at least partially engendered by Williams's earlier views on metaphysical personhood. This does not get it quite right, however, for Williams might actually agree, does agree in fact, that morality seems to demand just the sort of impersonality Parfit sees as naturally flowing from his conception of persons, but then, Williams believes, so much the worse for morality.

Chapter 3

Critique of utilitarianism

Introduction

The very last line of "A Critique of Utilitarianism", Williams's frequently reprinted companion piece to J. J. C. Smart's "An Outline of a System of Utilitarian Ethics", prophesies of utilitarianism: "The day cannot be too far off in which we hear no more of it" (Williams 1973a: 150). Ironically, however, the significant impact of this essay's attack ensured that we would, in the ensuing decades, hear much more of it. And attack seems not too strong a word, as Williams pursues the "breaking point of utilitarian thought" (*ibid.*: 114). Furthermore, while it is true that Williams comes to regret "an excess of polemical assertiveness" in his reply to Smart, he never abandons its constituent claims (Williams 1995h: 211). This chapter examines those claims, as well as others, which may be principally summarized as follows: that act (or what Williams calls "direct") utilitarianism alienates moral agents from both their actions and their feelings, and in so doing undermines their integrity; that rule (or what Williams calls "indirect") utilitarianism relies on an untenable division between theory and practice; and, finally, in a claim crucial to appreciating Williams's overall take on ethical life, "that for utilitarianism, tragedy is impossible" (Williams 1972: 86).

"Utilitarianism", according to Williams, "is the most ambitious of extant ethical theories" (Williams 1985: 92). Just what Williams means by an ethical theory, and whether what Williams means by an ethical theory captures what most philosophers mean by an ethical theory, turn out to be fairly contentious issues, ones that will occupy us in the next chapter, in connection with Williams's more general assault on "the morality system". For now, let us grant Williams's own, possibly tendentious, definition from *Ethics and the Limits of Philosophy*: "An ethical theory is a theoretical account of what ethical thought and practice are, which account either implies a general test for the correctness of basic ethical beliefs and principles or else implies that there cannot be such a test" (*ibid.*: 72). Viewed against this definition, utilitarianism's ambitiousness stems from the comprehensiveness and conclusiveness with which it both stakes out the good and identifies the right.

Utilitarianism "takes facts of individual welfare as the basic subject matter of ethical thought" (*ibid.*: 75), seeing "as primary the idea of producing the best possible state of affairs", these understood "in terms of people's happiness or their getting what they want or prefer" (*ibid.*: 16). In his first book, *Morality: An Introduction to Ethics*, Williams outlines four putative attractions of utilitarianism as an ethical theory:

> First, it is non-transcendental, and makes no appeal outside human life, in particular not to religious considerations. ... Second, its basic good, happiness, seems minimally problematical: however much people differ, surely they at least all want to be happy, and aiming at as much happiness as possible must surely, whatever else gives way, be a reasonable aim. ... Its third attraction is that moral issues can, in principle, be determined by empirical calculation of consequences. Moral thought becomes empirical. ... Fourth, utilitarianism provides a common currency of moral thought: the different concerns of different parties, and the different sorts of claims acting on one party, can all be cashed (in principle) in terms of happiness. (Williams 1972: 83–5)

Only the first of these features, utilitarianism's mundaneness, completely escapes Williams's critique. The second and fourth, happiness as both common end and common currency, come under sustained attack. As for the third, although Williams does insist that utilitarianism "involves serious technical difficulties as well as deep conceptual ones", it is probably fair to say that only the latter truly absorb his attention (*ibid.*: 81).

As mentioned, Williams distinguishes between act- and rule-, or direct and indirect, utilitarianism: "The term *direct* I use ... to mean that the consequential value which is the concern of morality is attached directly to particular actions, rather than to rules or practices under which decisions are taken without further reference to consequences; the latter sort of view is *indirect* consequentialism" (Williams 1973a: 81). Here Williams deliberately runs together the species, utilitarianism, and its genus, consequentialism, justifying this benign conflation with the claim that "some undesirable features of utilitarianism follow from its general consequentialist structure" (*ibid.*). Without a doubt, Williams's best known arguments against utilitarianism take act-utilitarianism as their target.

In fact, Williams believes rule-utilitarianism to be fundamentally unstable, teetering on incoherency, for at least the following reason:

> If calculation has already been made, and the consequences of breaking the rule are found better than those of keeping it; then certainly no considerations about the disutility of calculation could upset that result. And, indeed, it is very difficult to see how anything, for a consistent utilitarian, could upset that result. Whatever the general utility of having a certain rule, if one has actually reached the point of seeing that the utility of breaking it on a certain occasion is greater than that of following it, then surely it would be pure irrationality not to break it? [*sic*]
>
> (Williams 1972: 93–4)

Rule-utilitarianism will be looked at below in connection with the important ethical issue of transparency. For now it is enough to note that Williams never abandons his early conviction that "forms of utilitarianism which help themselves too liberally to the resources of indirectness lose their utilitarian rationale and end up as vanishingly forms of utilitarianism at all" (Williams 1973a: 81). It is best to begin, then, with Williams's most famous, many would say infamous, argument against utilitarianism, one that created quite a stir, about which Williams himself seems somewhat circumspect: "It turned out that I had invented something called the 'integrity objection' to Utilitarianism, and had started a discussion on the question of how, if at all, that objection might be met" (Williams 1995h: 211).

Integrity: actions

In his sustained sceptical analysis of ethical theory, *Ethics and the Limits of Philosophy*, Williams approvingly cites John Findlay's claim that "the separateness of persons [is] the basic fact for morals" (Williams 1985: 88). But if Findlay is right, then utilitarianism would seem to be in a very bad way from the outset, for, at least as Williams sees it, the separateness of persons is not a fact, basic or otherwise, recognized by the theory. Moreover, Williams, through a series of inferential steps, ultimately links this inattention to separateness, this failure to acknowledge sufficiently each individual's unique, personal point of view, this "agglomerative indifference" (Williams, 1981b: 4), this insistence that " 'it's me' can never in itself be a morally comprehensible reason" (Williams 1973a: 96), with utilitarianism's incapacity to accommodate integrity as a value (see Flanagan 1991: 58–9).

The charge that utilitarianism somehow ignores the separateness of persons is certainly not original with Williams. W. D. Ross, for example, in *The Right and the Good*, observes that:

> If the only duty is to produce the maximum of good, the question who is to have the good – whether it is myself, or my benefactor, or a person to whom I have made a promise to confer that good on him, or a mere fellow man to whom I stand in no special relation – should make no difference to my having a duty to produce that good. But we are all in fact sure it makes a vast difference.
>
> (Ross 1930: 22)

And at just about the time when Williams himself begins considering the issue, John Rawls, echoing Ross, remarks that "The striking feature of the utilitarian view of justice is that it does not matter, except indirectly, how the sum of satisfactions is distributed among individuals" (Rawls 1971: 26). Furthermore, Rawls cries foul at the notion of applying to society a theory best suited to desire satisfaction at the individual level, famously concluding that "Utilitarianism does not takes seriously the distinction between persons" (*ibid.*: 27). But whereas Ross and Rawls focus on limitations associated with the *distribution* of utilitarian welfare sums, Williams emphasizes limitations concerning their *production*. Here the idea is that utilitarianism fails to appreciate the importance of just who produces the consequences, a failure he ultimately attributes to utilitarianism's "notion of *negative responsibility*" (Williams 1973a: 95).

According to Williams, a distinctive feature of utilitarianism, with distinctive implications, is the leading role it assigns to states of affairs:

> What matters is what states of affairs the world contains, and so what matters with respect to a given action is what comes about

> if it is done, and what comes about if it is not done, and those are questions not intrinsically affected by the nature of the causal linkage, in particular by whether the outcome is partly produced by other agents. (*Ibid.*: 95)

At any given time, some action or combination of actions, understood as so many "causal levers", will guarantee optimal consequences. That someone pulls the right levers and so effects the desired action or combination of actions is crucial. Just who actually does the pulling is largely irrelevant: "As a Utilitarian agent I am just the representative of the satisfaction system who happens to be near certain causal levers at a certain time" (Williams 1981f: 4). And this indifference to the particular circumstances of agency is, Williams feels, closely related to utilitarianism's doctrine of negative responsibility: "that if I am ever responsible for anything, then I must be just as responsible for things that I allow or fail to prevent, as I am for things that I myself ... bring about" (Williams 1973a: 95). But, Williams objects, the doctrine of negative responsibility violates our deeply held conviction that individual, personal agency, that who actually acts or pulls the lever, makes, as Ross might say, a vast difference. Utilitarianism "cuts out ... a consideration involving the idea ... that each of us is specially responsible for what he does, rather than for what other people do", and, as will become clear, Williams believes that "This is an idea closely connected with the value of integrity" (*ibid.*: 99).

In an effort to elucidate this connection, Williams introduces two examples, whose protagonists, George and Jim, have become household names in contemporary moral philosophy. Before we turn to them, however, it is worth noting that, from the outset, Williams appears somewhat apprehensive about just how these examples will be interpreted, volunteering that "the aim is not just to offer or elicit moral intuitions against which utilitarianism can be tested ... rather, the aim of the examples and their discussion ... is to lead into reflections which might show up in greater depth what would be involved in living with these ideas" (*ibid.*: 78). Moreover, Williams, eventually seeing his earlier apprehension as warranted, reaffirms that "If the stories of George and Jim have a resonance, it is not the sound of a principle being dented by an intuition" (Williams 1995h: 211). Still, in fairness to his interpreters, distinguishing dents via intuition from dents via reflection may not be nearly as easy as Williams imagines. As one interpreter laments of George and Jim: "It is clear that Williams' examples have *force*, though it is not obvious just what their force is" (Davis 1980: 19).

George, a recent chemistry PhD, cannot find a job. Readers are told that George is sickly, that he is deeply attached to his wife, that he has small children and that both his marriage and children suffer from strain imposed by his wife's full-time work. A job offer comes George's way: research chemist in a biological and chemical warfare laboratory. However, deeply opposed to chemical and biological warfare, George refuses the position. He is asked to reconsider. After all, the position will be filled regardless; in fact, if George turns it down, the job will go to someone who positively revels in the possibilities of better dying through chemistry. Furthermore, his wife does not share his scruples. In these circumstances, Williams asks, what should George do?

Jim takes a wrong turn on a South American botanical expedition and lands in a prickly situation. He arrives in a small town just as twenty randomly chosen Indians are about to be gunned down as a bloody warning to would-be government protesters. However, the captain supervising the execution offers Jim a "guest's privilege" of shooting an Indian himself. If Jim accepts, the remaining nineteen will be released. If Jim declines, all twenty Indians will be shot. We are told that heroics on Jim's part, commandeering the captain's gun, say, would prove futile and that both onlookers and, more importantly, those about to be killed urge Jim to accept. In these circumstances, Williams asks, what should Jim do?

Williams believes that utilitarians will think the correct resolution of both cases obvious: take the job and shoot an Indian. But Williams himself thinks neither case obvious. In fact, he thinks the utilitarian simply wrong in George's case and, even if right in Jim's, not obviously so, for in each case the utilitarian response effectively "makes integrity as a value more or less unintelligible" (Williams 1973a: 99). Conducting chemical and biological weapons research would violate George's integrity, while shooting an Indian might violate Jim's, with integrity here meaning, for Williams, no more and no less than "a particular person's sticking by what that person regards as ethically necessary or worthwhile" (Williams 1995h: 213). More to the point, "the reason why utilitarianism cannot understand integrity is that it cannot coherently describe the relations between a man's projects and his actions" (Williams 1973a: 100). With this sentence Williams assigns "project-talk" a leading role in his overall critique of ethical theory.

One's projects go a long way towards defining one's character. Examples of projects include:

> The obvious kind of desire for things for oneself, one's family, one's friends, including basics necessities of life, and in more relaxed circumstances, objects of taste. Or there may be pursuits or interests of an intellectual, cultural or creative character. … Beyond these, someone may have projects connected with his support of some cause. … Or there may be projects which flow from some more general disposition towards human conduct and character.
>
> (*Ibid.*: 110–11)

Participation in certain projects, "those with which one is more deeply and extensively involved and identified" (*ibid.*: 116), engenders "commitments": "One can be committed to such things as a person, a cause, an institution, a career, one's own genius, or the pursuit of danger" (*ibid.*: 112). Williams gives Zionism and, with a nod towards George, opposition to chemical and biological warfare as examples of projects, and also includes attachments to friends and family. Such projects go some way towards filling the "vast hole" utilitarianism digs "in the range of human desires, between egoistic inclination and necessities at one end, and impersonally benevolent happiness-management at the other" (*ibid.*: 112); in other words, projects need be neither selfish nor sanctimonious.

The importance of projects and commitments stems not so much from their content, as from their role in shaping character, in constituting the self, in providing nothing less than reasons to live. As Williams puts it, "my present projects are the condition of my existence, in the sense that unless I am propelled forward by the conatus of desire, project and interest, it is unclear why I should go on at all" (Williams 1981f: 12). Quite simply, if perhaps somewhat melodramatically, projects confer meaning, or at least represent a necessary condition for the possibility of a meaningful life: no projects, no meaning. It seems only fair, then, to expect utilitarianism to honour whatever meaning a life possesses by respecting its projects. Instead, Williams believes, utilitarianism alienates agents from their actions, and so from their projects, and so from themselves. And although Thomas Nagel suggests that "It's a claim few people could make without bluffing", caricaturing Williams's view here as "If I have to serve the greatest good of the greatest number … I might as well be dead" (Nagel 1995c: 170), Williams appears decidedly in earnest.

We have already examined Williams's claim that utilitarianism, with its doctrine of negative responsibility, tends to depreciate individual agency by calling on people to pull or to refrain from pulling various causal levers without caring about the individual projects of those to whom such levers may be attached. Utilitarianism assigns a welfare coefficient to the satisfaction of each agent's projects and, having done so, concludes that the utilitarian calculus now fairly values all agents' interests. If the calculus determines that the maximization of welfare requires the discontinuation of someone's personal project, so as not to interfere with others pursuing theirs, so much the worse for that one agent.

It all goes back to utilitarianism's preoccupation with states of affairs. But, Williams now asks, "how can a man, as a utilitarian agent, come to regard as one satisfaction among others, and a dispensable one, a project or attitude round which he has built his life, just because someone else's projects have so structured the causal scene that that is how the utilitarian sum comes out?" (Williams 1973a: 116). In a passage unrivalled among his writings for sheer rhetorical energy, Williams rejects any suggestion that utilitarianism might accurately value projects constitutive of identity. Instead, in misvaluing them it threatens them, and in threatening them, utilitarianism breeds alienation:

> It is absurd to demand from such a man, when the sums come in from the utilitarian network which the projects of others have in part determined, that he should just step away from his own project and decision and acknowledge the decision which utilitarian calculation requires. It is to alienate him in a real sense from his actions and the source of his action in his own convictions. It is to make him into a channel between the input of everyone's projects, including his own, and an output of optimific decision; but this is to neglect the extent to which his actions and his decisions have to be seen as the actions and decisions which flow from the projects and attitudes with which he is most closely identified.
>
> (*Ibid.*: 116–17)

According to Williams, by subverting the capacity to act from the projects and commitments that define agents as persons, utilitarianism subverts their integrity. And not only is their integrity with regard to actions vulnerable to utilitarian calculation, but their integrity with regard to feelings as well.

Integrity: feelings

Utilitarianism compromises integrity by alienating agents from their feelings, particularly "in circumstances where there are strong reasons ... for doing something which one finds morally distasteful, and against which one has a strong personal commitment" (Williams 1981k: 40). Actions do not, of course, take place in a psychological or emotional vacuum, and Williams's focus here is on the way utilitarianism accommodates, or fails to accommodate, the intense feelings of someone like Jim, called upon by circumstance and the utilitarian calculus to kill a man. Williams's point is not, or not just, that Jim's "feelings might seem to be of very little weight compared with the other things that are at stake", but concerns "a powerful and recognizable appeal that can be made on this point: as that a refusal by Jim to do what he has been invited to do would be a kind of self-indulgent squeamishness" (Williams 1973a: 102). Such an appeal constitutes "a familiar, and it must be said a powerful, weapon of utilitarianism" (*ibid.*), a weapon Williams investigates twice: first, in his response to Smart, as part of his overall "integrity objection", and then again, almost a decade later, as a stand-alone phenomenon, in "Utilitarianism and Moral Self-indulgence".

In "A Critique of Utilitarianism", Williams begins by observing that, from the utilitarian point of view, an agent's integrity, Jim's, for instance, is *not* threatened in cases where he "feels bad ... *because he thinks he has done the wrong thing*", and this for a very simple reason (Williams 1973a: 101): "if the balance of outcomes was as it appeared to be ... then he has not (from the utilitarian point of view) done the wrong thing" (*ibid.*). It is not that Jim cannot feel bad at the time of decision, but that such feelings have already been taken into consideration by the utilitarian calculus and, given that calculus's verdict as to the rightness of Jim's killing one Indian to save nineteen, any subsequent bad feelings are (again, from the utilitarian point of view) irrational, a point to which we return later in this chapter in connection with regret. So just what does the charge of moral squeamishness or moral self-indulgence amount to, and what exactly is its connection with integrity?

Having initially described the appeal or accusation as a powerful weapon for utilitarianism, Williams hedges somewhat:

> One must be clear, though, about what [the charge of self-indulgence] can and cannot accomplish. The most it can do, so far

> as I can see, is to invite one to consider how seriously, and for what reasons, one feels that what one is invited to do is (in these circumstances) wrong, and in particular, to consider that question from the utilitarian point of view. When the agent is not seeing the situation from the utilitarian point of view, the appeal cannot force him to do so; and if he does come round to seeing it from a utilitarian point of view, there is virtually nothing left for the appeal to do.
> (*Ibid*.: 102)

In one sense, then, attempting to impugn the feelings of the agent with a charge of moral squeamishness means attempting to manipulate the agent into a utilitarian deliberative framework, an attempt that may or may not succeed.

For Williams, however, the real question is: are unpleasant feelings merely unpleasant experiences amenable to calculative appraisal or something more, something deeper? Suppose Jim refuses to shoot the Indian. The utilitarian maintains that Jim's feelings are (or would be) just unpleasant experiences, certainly to be credited, but of no special account relative to considerations of overall welfare maximization, and that resisting the utilitarian conclusion in deference to those feelings displays self-indulgence. But assuming that Jim looks at the matter from a non-utilitarian point of view, he may see his feelings as not merely unpleasant experiences, but as nothing less than expressions of right and wrong, indicative of what he can and cannot do. And this is where integrity comes in:

> The reason why the squeamishness appeal can be very unsettling, and one can be unnerved by the suggestion of self-indulgence in going against utilitarian considerations, is not that we are utilitarians who are uncertain what utilitarian value to attach to our moral feelings, but that we are partly at least not utilitarians, and cannot regard our moral feelings merely as objects of utilitarian value. Because our moral relation to the world is partly given by such feelings, and by a sense of what we can or cannot "live with", to come to regard those feelings from a purely utilitarian point of view, that is to say, as happening outside one's moral self, is to lose a sense of one's moral identity; to lose, in the most literal way, one's integrity. At this point utilitarianism alienates one from one's moral feelings. (Williams 1973a: 103–4)

Remember Williams's characterization of utilitarianism's seemingly boundless ambition to reduce all ethical phenomena, including feelings, to a common currency of welfare maximization. Yet one may well be reluctant or unable to endorse this goal, and in demanding cooperation, utilitarianism exhibits once more its inability to do justice to the value of integrity, or so Williams maintains in "A Critique of Utilitarianism".

In his later essay "Utilitarianism and Moral Self-indulgence" Williams appears less concerned with how to accommodate feelings of squeamishness and more interested in the actual content of the charge of self-indulgence. Whereas he had earlier discussed the threat to integrity posed by utilitarianism's failure to portray unpleasant feelings in any light but that of the impartial satisfaction of collectively determined interests, Williams now addresses the charge of self-indulgence itself. Of course, as just discussed, Williams believes the charge, put forth in terms of squeamishness, tantamount to a coercive invitation to utilitarian deliberation. But what lies at the heart of the charge?

It is important to recognize that at no point does Williams deny the reality of moral self-indulgence, nor does he claim that it occurs only as a bogus concept in some noxious rhetorical strategy whereby utilitarians browbeat non-utilitarians into altering their method of ethical analysis. (Interestingly, on this picture, the utilitarian winds up something like the external reasons theorist – see Chapter 5 – trying, as Williams sees it, to bluff the agent into deliberating in a manner contrary to his existing dispositions.) What Williams does deny, however, is any necessary connection between manifestations of integrity, especially in situations where utilitarian considerations come to be overridden, and moral self-indulgence.

Williams believes that "When the agent's refusal takes the particular form of saying that while others, no doubt, will bring evil about, at least it will not come about through *him*, the charge may handily take the form of saying that the agent takes a possessive attitude towards his own virtue" (Williams 1981k: 40). Moreover, this charge "of being concerned with his own integrity or purity or virtue at others' expense ... imputes a specific kind of *motive*" (*ibid.*: 44), and it is this motive, Williams claims, that lies at the heart of the charge. He identifies this motive with an ethically suspect "reflexive concern", according to which "what the agent cares about is not so much other people, as himself caring about other people" (*ibid.*: 45). Suppose Jim refuses to shoot an Indian. Whether or not his refusal amounts to self-indulgence depends upon whether

> he had substituted for a thought about what is needed, a thought which focuses disproportionately upon the expression of his own

> disposition, and that he derives pleasure from the thought that his disposition will have been expressed – rather than deriving pleasure, as the agent who is not self-indulgent may, from the thought of how things will be if he acts in a certain way, that way being (though he may not think this) the expression of a disposition. (*Ibid*.: 47)

For Williams, moral self-indulgence "involves a reversal at a line ... fundamental to any morality or indeed sane life at all, between self-concern and other-concern; it involves a misdirection not just of attention, though that is true too, but genuinely of concern" (*ibid*.). But would Jim, then, displaying integrity by refusing the captain's invitation, lest his actions violate his conviction that killing an innocent person is always murder regardless of circumstances, fairly invite the charge of self-indulgence? Would George, assuming he sticks to his (quite metaphorical) guns and displays integrity by turning down the weapons job, merit the charge of self-indulgence? Not unless integrity figures as a motive in their deliberations, something Williams, interestingly, finds conceptually impossible.

Although Williams agrees that integrity is "an admirable human property", it is not for that reason "a disposition which itself yields motivations" (*ibid*.: 49). On this line of thought, "one who displays integrity acts from those dispositions which are most deeply his, and has also the virtues that enable him to do that" (*ibid*.). It is those virtues, whatever they are, and not integrity itself, which succeed in motivating the agent. We attribute integrity to those who stand up for what they believe in or who exhibit the courage of their convictions. Integrity is a compliment we pay in the light of certain (other) elements of character. George, for example, does not act *from* integrity in refusing the job (if he does); instead he acts from some amalgam of compassion or reverence or honour. As Williams notes some years later: "Reflections on one's own integrity are unappealing in any case, but integrity as a supposed *criterion* of action seems seriously confused as well, for what will the integrity be *to*?" (Williams 1995h: 212). Integrity, then, involves a capacity to act in accordance with one's projects and commitments, such projects and commitments featuring disparate virtues and dispositions, such virtues and dispositions providing motivational punch.

The mistake the utilitarian makes in levelling an accusation of moral self-indulgence involves counting integrity as a virtue in the first place.

But, having made this mistake, Williams believes that the ensuing charge of moral self-indulgence is quite understandable:

> For if [integrity] is regarded as a motive, it is hard to reconstruct its representation in thought except in the objectionable reflexive way: the thought would have to be about oneself and one's character, and of the suspect kind. If integrity had to be provided with a characteristic thought, there would be nothing for the thought to be about except oneself – but there is no such characteristic thought, only the thoughts associated with the projects, in carrying out which a man may display his integrity.
> (Williams 1981k: 49)

Therefore, once the utilitarian comes to appreciate that, say, Jim or George only acts *with* integrity in the process of acting *from* ingrained ethical dispositions emanating from, as we have seen, identity-conferring projects and commitments, the charge of moral self-indulgence loses much, if not all, of its force.

Still, Williams wonders, "what of the thought 'not through me'?" (*ibid.*: 50). Surely this thought is both reflexive and intimately bound up with the notion of integrity. This is true, but Williams, in keeping with his earlier discussion, denies that "not through me" constitutes a motivation:

> The thought [i.e. "not through me"] . . . is not in itself a motivating thought, and those words do not express any distinctive motivation. It is not merely that they do not on all occasions express some one motivation. Rather, they do not, in themselves, express any motivation at all: if one is motivated not to do it oneself, then there is some (other) motive one has for not doing it. (*Ibid.*)

Although Jim's rationale for refusing to kill an Indian might seem to be "not through me", fully spelled out it must really be something like, "Killing an innocent person is always murder whatever the circumstances and I am, thank you very much, no murderer." In other words, although "not through Jim" initially appears tantamount to an appeal to integrity as a motivation, on closer inspection the motivation, and ultimately any display of integrity, relies on invoking something like the ignominy of murder and, however tacitly, Jim's disposition to abhor and refrain from ignominious acts.

Williams, then, describes utilitarians advancing the charge of moral self-indulgence in two different ways: either as an accusation of squeamishness, of "being overcome with unstructured moral feeling" (Williams 1981k: 52), intended to prod – in effect, shame – the agent into utilitarian thinking; or as an accusation of unseemly reflexivity in the form of a self-conscious appeal to one's own integrity as a motive for action, an accusation undermined, Williams argues, by integrity's motivational inertness. In denigrating feelings and attributing false motives, Williams finds further proof "that utilitarianism cannot hope to make sense, at any serious level, of integrity" (Williams 1973a: 82). In fact, although it might seem natural to suppose utilitarianism the "unique enemy of moral self-indulgence" (after all, Williams asks, "isn't utilitarianism just the expression of concern for everyone, among whom self is outnumbered by others?"), Williams points out that "the distinction between other-concern and self-concern is in no way the same thing as the distinction between utilitarian and non-utilitarian" (Williams 1981k: 49). In the end, utilitarian motives are just as susceptible to corruption by excessive reflexivity and self-concern as any other form of ethical deliberation, although in such cases the issue of integrity will rarely if ever arise, having been rendered more or less unintelligible, in Williams's view, by utilitarianism itself.

Government House utilitarianism

Speaking of indirect or rule-utilitarianism in *Ethics and the Limits of Philosophy*, Williams laments the "deeply uneasy gap or dislocation in this type of theory, between the spirit of the theory itself and the spirit it supposedly justifies", a gap indirect utilitarians would span by invoking a distinction between theory and practice (Williams 1985: 108). On the one hand, indirect utilitarianism as a practice relies on the cultivation of certain ethical dispositions and habits – that is, certain tendencies to follow ethical rules – by agents who regard those very habits and dispositions as largely justified in virtue of their intrinsic value. As Williams says, "The dispositions help to form the character of an agent who has them, and they will do the job the theory has given them only if the agent does not see his character purely instrumentally, but sees the world from the point of view of that character" (*ibid.*). Indeed, the success of the indirect scheme depends upon agents regarding themselves as acting in character. On the other hand, of course, indirect utilitarianism as a theory justifies the formation of such characters with reference to a higher- or second-order goal of overall welfare maximization. Thus the disconnect between what agents take to be their motives and what their motives *really* are, testifying to the fact that "Critical thinking, itself utilitarian, can reach the conclusion . . . that one does not maximize utility by thinking, most of the time, as a utilitarian" (*ibid.*: 107). The first casualty of this disconnect is transparency.

In the light of this disconnect and failure in transparency, Williams labels indirect utilitarianism "Government House utilitarianism", invoking "the important colonialist connections of utilitarianism" or, in a word, its paternalism (*ibid.*: 108). According to Williams, indirect utilitarianism's distinction between theory and practice "determined two classes of people, one of them a class of theorists who could responsibly handle the utilitarian justification of non-utilitarian dispositions, the other a class who unreflectively deployed those dispositions" (*ibid.*). As such, "Government House utilitarianism is indifferent to the values of social transparency" (*ibid.*: 109). Just as the whys and wherefores of African or Indian policy were not to be entrusted to native populations by their European bwanas and sahibs (naturally for their own good), so the framers of utilitarian social organization and policy try to enhance efficiency and effectiveness by sparing most agents reflective considerations of a utilitarian kind. Instead, whatever dispositions utilitarianism may require are inculcated through a process of education and internalization, their justification to all appearances self-contained.

Now, however, in these more progressive (or at least more sensitive) times, nothing as crude as the analogy between an enlightened governing class and an ignorant governed class will do. Accordingly, "Current versions of indirect utilitarianism . . . usually identify the distinction between theory and practice in psychological rather than social terms" (*ibid.*: 109). Williams here has in mind, and means to differentiate between, more classical versions of indirect utilitarianism such as Henry Sidgwick's and relatively contemporary versions such as R. M. Hare's (see, for example, Sidgwick 1981; Hare 1952, 1981). Theory and practice now come apart intrapersonally rather than interpersonally, not at a distance, but at a point, in so far as indirect utilitarians "distinguish between the *time* of theorizing and *time* of practice, and use Bishop Butler's notion of the 'cool hour' in which the philosophically disposed moralist reflects on his own principles and practice" (Williams 1985: 109). Unfortunately, Williams reports, "There are equally severe difficulties with this version" (*ibid.*).

Whereas Government House utilitarianism appears unpalatable when viewed as an interpersonal, sociopolitical phenomenon, it proves just as implausible, Williams believes, as an intrapersonal, psychological phenomenon, and this owing to deep facts about psychological organization and the human capacity for willed ignorance. Where formerly agents were seen to act ethically from dispositions ultimately justified by a utilitarian rationale of which they were unaware, now agents still act according to their dispositions, but in some sense both knowing and not knowing the extent to which such dispositions are valuable only instrumentally, in the service of utilitarianism. The basic idea involves reflectively and theoretically endorsing the cultivation of certain ethical dispositions, valuable from a utilitarian point of view, and then somehow realizing those dispositions in practice, but unreflectively, without benefit or burden of their utilitarian justification, and this, once again, because sometimes the goals of utilitarianism are best served by avoiding explicit utilitarian reasoning. The problem, in Williams's view, arises because "Any such picture makes, in some degree, a Platonic assumption that the reflective agent as theorist can make himself independent from the life and character he is examining" (*ibid.*: 110). But it is a point repeatedly emphasized throughout Williams's writings that such independence represents a chimera, albeit a chimera of perennial philosophical allure.

In an extended consideration of Sidgwick's philosophy, Williams identifies the chief obstacle faced by ethical models relying on an intrapsychic bifurcation of theory and practice:

> The difficulty is . . . that the moral dispositions, and indeed other loyalties and commitments, have a certain depth or thickness: they cannot simply be regarded, least of all by their possessor, just as devices for generating actions or states of affairs. Such dispositions and commitments will characteristically be what gives one's life some meaning, and gives one some reason for living it; they can be said, to varying degrees and variously over time, to contribute to one's practical or moral identity. There is simply no conceivable exercise that consists in stepping completely outside myself and from that point of view evaluating *in toto* the dispositions, projects, and affections that constitute the substance of my own life.
>
> (Williams 1995g: 169–70)

Once again the notion of personal projects and their role in constituting identity comes to the fore; indeed, the notions of integrity and the meaning of life are never far from Williams's mind, as the demands of indirect utilitarianism conceivably compromise the wholeness and satisfactions of a transparent practical agency. These moves towards abstraction and theoretical disengagement Williams finds particularly, even pathologically, demanding in moral theories of a Kantian stripe, as the next chapter will show. But, by way of preview, it may be worth considering a most general lesson Williams draws from his discussion of Government House utilitarianism: "there is no coherent ethical theory" (*ibid.*: 171).

Williams's lesson stems from what an ethical theory is being asked to do. According to Williams, an ethical theory

> will always run into some version of the fundamental difficulty that the practice of life, and hence also an adequate theory of that practice, will require the recognition of what I have called deep dispositions; but at the same time the abstract and impersonal view that is required if the theory is to be genuinely a *theory* cannot be satisfactorily understood in relation to the depth and necessity of those dispositions. Thus the theory will remain, in one way or another, in an incoherent relation to practice. But if ethical theory is anything, then it must stand in close and explicable relation to practice, because that is the kind of theory it would have to be.
>
> (*Ibid.*: 171)

An ethical theory can never do what it sets out to do because ethical practice, that which the theory sets out to capture, consists in just the sort of activity, for example, the pursuit of personal projects, that resists capture by theory. Just as Williams indicts act-utilitarianism for its inability properly to weigh or even to acknowledge the sort of projects and commitments that infuse one's life with meaning, so he sees rule-utilitarianism, with its forced separation of deliberation and justification, as similarly misrepresenting, if not similarly threatening, those same projects and commitments.

Regret, tragedy and incommensurability

To this point the charges Williams levels against utilitarianism, however different in detail, share at least this feature: that utilitarianism at best fails to acknowledge and at worst intentionally subverts the crucial relationship between agents and the projects and commitments through which they express their identity and imbue their lives with meaning. Whether alienating agents from their actions, compromising their feelings or partitioning their psyches, utilitarianism threatens their integrity in at least three ways: act-utilitarianism's "agglomerative indifference" indiscriminately overwhelms the personal point of view; act-utilitarianism's calculative elegance ignores the decided inelegance of much moral feeling; and rule-utilitarianism's artificial separation of theory and practice places unrealistic demands on psychic organization. Interestingly, however, the problematic features Williams identifies – the indifference, the calculatedness, the artificiality – appear related as symptoms of a more general malady diagnosed quite early in his career: "But what [the utilitarian] is bound to do . . . is to regard as an indisputable general aim of moral thought, the reduction of conflict, the elimination wherever possible of value conflicts without remainder" (Williams 1972: 86). And this pursuit of conflict elimination becomes philosophically pathological precisely because it ignores, in Williams's view, two inescapable features of the ethical landscape: the phenomenon of regret and the plurality and incommensurability of values.

Williams's observations on regret and its importance as a test of the ability of a moral theory like utilitarianism to capture adequately certain essential aspects of ethical life date to one of his earliest, if not the earliest, papers on ethics, "Ethical Consistency", in which he first recognizes the philosophical importance of, as we might say, "the 'ought' not taken": "It seems to me a fundamental criticism of many ethical theories that their accounts of moral conflict and its resolution do not do justice to the facts of regret and related considerations: basically because they eliminate from the scene the *ought* that is not acted upon" (Williams 1973e: 175). According to cognitivist theories, moral claims represent factual assertions admitting of truth and falsity. In cases of moral conflict, it becomes "just a question of which of the conflicting *ought* statements is true, and they cannot both be true, to decide correctly for one of them must be to be rid of error with respect to the other" (*ibid.*). Similarly for utilitarianism, resolving a moral conflict between two alternative courses of action means resolving factual questions as to which of them will produce the greatest utility or least disutility. Once decided, one alternative represents the right thing to do, the other the wrong thing. And here is the point: it would be senseless to regret not having done the wrong thing, yet such regrets occur all the time.

Recalling utilitarianism's claim to provide a common currency of moral thought in terms of happiness, Williams summarizes the issue:

> This provision, importantly, has the consequence that a certain kind of conflict, well-known to some other moral outlooks, is

> impossible – the conflict, that is to say, of two claims which are both valid and irreconcilable. Under some other systems, a man may come to a situation in which (as it seems to him) whatever he does involves doing something wrong. For utilitarianism, this is impossible. The various claims he may feel on him can be brought to the common measure of the Greatest Happiness Principle, and there can be no coherent idea of a right or wrong thing to do, other than what is, or is not, *the best thing to do on the whole*. . . . As against this, many people can recognize the thought that a certain course of action is, indeed, the best thing to do on the whole in the circumstances, but that doing it involves doing something wrong. This is a thought which for utilitarianism must, I think, ultimately be incoherent. (Williams 1972: 85)

For Williams, "moral conflicts are in two different senses ineliminable. In a particular case, it may be that neither of the *ought*'s is eliminable. Further, the tendency of such conflicts to occur may itself be ineliminable" (Williams 1973e: 179). If neither ought is eliminable, yet utilitarianism insists on suppressing one of them, and if it would be appropriate to experience regret in the face of the eliminated alternative, yet utilitarianism leaves the agent no room for such sentiment, then utilitarianism as a moral theory has once more failed to capture the reality of ethical experience.

Two points deserve passing mention. First, one sees here something of a precursor to Williams's much discussed bifurcation of science and ethics in his rejection of ethical cognitivism and the notion that ought statements parallel statements of belief, in particular by possessing truth value (see especially Williams 1985: Chapter 8). Take the key sentence from "Ethical Consistency": "I reach the conclusion that a moral conflict shares with a conflict of desires, but not with a conflict of beliefs, the feature that to end it in decision is not necessarily to eliminate one of the conflicting items: the item that was not acted upon may, for instance, persist as regret" (Williams 1973e: 179). Such regret in the face of ethical conflict suggests to Williams a difference in kind; just how deep a difference, a complex question as it turns out, is considered in Chapter 6.

Secondly, it may be helpful to note a distinction between the sort of regret arising in cases of ethical conflict and another "particularly important species of regret", which Williams discusses at some length in his seminal essay "Moral Luck" (1981c: 27). This latter sort Williams calls "agent-regret", regret at the prospect that one might have acted otherwise and thus forestalled some undesirable outcome, specifically in cases where no question exists but that the agent did in fact act ethically: for example, a driver's regret at killing a child who ran into the street without looking. Williams's point, or one of his points, concerns what he sees as the futility of insisting, as certain theorists will be sure to do, on the non-moral nature of such regret, a point bound up with the following question, to be taken up in the next chapter: "how important is morality in the narrow sense as contrasted with a wider sense of the ethical?" (Williams 1995f: 255).

The phenomenon of regret illustrates a clear tension between utilitarianism's ambition to establish a single right course of action in any ethical predicament and Williams's insistence that "Moral conflicts are neither systematically avoidable, nor all soluble without remainder" (Williams 1973e: 179). This tension, moreover, clouds our appreciation and understanding of those ethical situations Williams calls "tragic". In tragic situations, those concerning, say, Antigone and her brother, or Agammemnon and his daughter, or, for that matter, Jim and the Indians,

> an agent can justifiably think that whatever he does will be wrong: that there are conflicting moral requirements, and that neither of them succeeds in overriding or outweighing the other. In this case, though it can actually emerge from deliberation that one of the courses of action is the one that, all things considered, one had better take, it is, and it remains, true that each of the courses of action is morally required, and at a level which means that, whatever he does, the agent will have reason to feel regret at the deepest level. (Williams 1981a: 74)

Utilitarianism makes tragedy impossible by eliminating the moral requirement accompanying one of the courses of action, and so also, in a push for psychological parsimony, by eliminating any cause for regret as long as one acts to maximize utility. Again, the familiar culprit from Williams's point of view remains utilitarianism's demand that happiness assume the role of common currency in any economy of deliberation. That tragedy of this sort is not only endemic to moral life, but crucial to understanding it, has much to do with the way such situations present ethical demands as at once independent of our control, yet uncannily the product of who we are and how we live, a connection to be explored in Chapter 7. But such tragic situations may advertise something besides the implausibility of happiness as a common currency of utilitarian value; they may advertise the implausibility of any common value at all. They may advertise the incommensurability of value.

Much of Williams's thought on the issue of incommensurable values, indeed on the issue of values generally, appears to owe much to his long-time friendship with Isaiah Berlin. At the very least, Williams's characterization of Berlin's views could easily capture his own:

> Again and again ... Berlin warns us against the deep error of supposing that all goods, all virtues, all ideals are compatible, and that what is desirable can ultimately be united into a harmonious whole without loss. This is not the platitude that in an imperfect world not all the things we recognise as good are in practice compatible. It is rather that we have no coherent conception of a world without loss, that goods conflict by their very nature, and that there can be no incontestable scheme for harmonizing them.
>
> (Williams 1978b: xvi)

As we have seen, Williams certainly finds utilitarian schemes for harmonization contestable.

Williams's most cogent analysis of claims regarding incommensurability occurs in his essay "Conflicts of Values", according to which "the claim that values are incommensurable does say something true and important. In fact, it says more than one thing" (Williams 1981a: 77). As Williams sees it, a claim that values are incommensurable might be equivalent to any of the following:

(1) There is no one currency in terms of which each conflict of values can be resolved.
(2) It is not true that for each conflict of values, there is some value, independent of any of the conflicting values, that can be appealed to in order to resolve that conflict.
(3) It is not true that for each conflict of values, there is some value that can be appealed to (independent or not) in order rationally to resolve that conflict.
(4) No conflict of values can ever be rationally resolved.

Of the four, only the last strikes Williams as "too despairing" (*ibid.*). Of course, the first three involve just the sort of denial Williams himself makes concerning utilitarianism's aspiration to adjudicate all ethical conflict in terms of the maximization of some one value. After all, "The most basic version of the idea that utility provides a universal currency is that all values are versions or applications in some way of utility, and in this sense the claim that all values are incommensurable of course rejects the idea of a universal currency" (*ibid*.: 78). The acceptance of incommensurability and the rejection of utilitarianism are, for Williams, of a piece.

Williams does allow that he cannot dismiss out of hand the "Utopian theorist of ideology", someone who maintains that "what needs to be transcended is present society, and that in some better condition conflict will be reduced, and false values discarded" (*ibid*.: 80). But he insists that the Utopian can agree with him here and now "that the enterprise of trying to reduce our conflicts, and to legislate to remove moral uncertainty, by constructing a philosophical *ethical theory* (in the sense of systematizing moral belief) is a misguided one" (*ibid*.). If, as so many of Williams's examples show, and as the prevalence of regret and tragedy in everyday life appears to affirm, "conflict among our values is not necessarily pathological, ... it must be a mistake to regard a need to eliminate conflict as a purely rational demand, of the kind that applies to a theoretical system" (*ibid*.: 81). Utilitarianism, then, as perhaps the dominant theoretical system of ethics in the world today, must be mistaken.

Conclusion

By way of conclusion, consider once more the four major attractions of utilitarianism identified by Williams in *Morality*: (a) utilitarianism makes no transcendental appeal; (b) utilitarianism, in happiness, features a plausible basic good; (c) utilitarianism's results achieve empirical status; (d) utilitarianism, in happiness, provides a common currency of moral thought. It should now be clear just how superficial and elusive, with the exception of (a), Williams finds these attractions, particularly (b) and (d). Williams's critique of (d), happiness as a common currency, focusing on utilitarianism's failed attempts to solve moral conflicts without remainder and its inability to countenance a plurality of (potentially incommensurable) values, has just been reviewed. It is one thing to take happiness for a "minimally problematical" basic good (Williams 1972: 83) and quite another to believe, not as much that it represents the only value, as that happiness is, as Williams says, "homogeneous", by which he means that all other values end up being "just versions of it" (Williams 1981a: 78).

As to (c), Williams certainly recognizes the allure of what "has always been found by many one of the most gratifying features of utilitarianism", namely that ethical deliberation becomes, especially "on matters of public policy, a matter of social science" (Williams 1972: 85). However, and perhaps not surprisingly, Williams appears anything but convinced that utilitarianism's penchant for exactness and calculation deserves uncritical praise. For one thing, in its drive to make ethical decisions algorithmic, utilitarianism fails to appreciate the existence of, let alone to differentiate between, two distinct categories of proposed action: the empirically conceivable and the morally conceivable. There may be, Williams suggests, "certain situations so monstrous that the idea that the processes of moral rationality could yield an answer in them is insane: they are situations which so transcend in enormity the human business of moral deliberation that from a moral point of view it cannot matter any more what happens" (Williams 1973a: 92). Williams's point seems to be that utilitarian welfare summing, scientific or not, is at once too blunt and too refined. It is too blunt to the extent that virtually every conceivable situation becomes grist for its calculative mill; it is too refined to the extent that virtually every conceivable situation at least pretends to calculative precision. As Williams puts it in one of the most acerbic remarks to appear anywhere in his writings: "making the best of a bad job is one of [utilitarianism's] maxims, and it will have something to say even on the difference between massacring seven million, and massacring seven million and one" (*ibid.*: 93). Utilitarianism's social scientific empiricism is one attraction Williams finds easy to resist.

Revisiting (b), and the claim that happiness constitutes an uncontroversial final end, Williams's reservations on this point concern not as much the end itself as utilitarianism's crude licensing of any and all means to achieve it. Here occur familiar worries about utilitarianism's emphasis on states of affairs, its doctrine of negative responsibility, its neglect of the personal point of view and (thus) its inability to appreciate integrity as a value. Or, putting the matter somewhat differently, it is not utilitarianism's embrace of happiness as a final end that bothers Williams, but the structure of utilitarianism, which tends not only to ignore, but to alienate individuals from, just the sorts of projects, commitments, ideals and relationships that are necessary for, even constitutive of, that happiness. Illegitimate demands of impartiality impinging not just on agency, but on personhood itself, mark utilitarianism's most fatal attraction. But just how specific or uniquely applicable to utilitarianism is this – perhaps Williams's most devastating – criticism?

Remember that such criticism ultimately amounts to the charge that utilitarianism fails to leave sufficient room for, or grant sufficient weight to, the personal point of view; indeed, just this insufficiency grounds Williams's integrity objection. However, in a book not incidentally aimed at crafting a form of utilitarianism better able to accommodate some of Williams's concerns, Samuel Scheffler maintains that "if the objection from integrity is interpreted as an objection to the in-principle dispensability of the agent's projects, then it must be regarded as a criticism of almost all non-egoistic theories, and not as an objection to which utilitarianism is distinctly vulnerable" (Scheffler 1994: 8–9). One might claim, after all, that utilitarianism's emphasis on impartiality, rather than uniquely defining it, merely satisfies a prime criterion of virtually any moral theory. In a similar vein, David Brink argues that "The worries that the importance of the personal point of view raises can be viewed not as *moral worries* but as *worries about morality*. … These are worries about the justification or supremacy of moral demands, not about the correctness of a utilitarian account of morality" (Brink 1986: 432–3). In so far as utilitarian calculation successfully captures the moral worth of personal projects, any complaint Williams might have about its demands should more accurately be directed towards the demands of morality period. Any move to privilege the personal point of view may indeed run foul of, say, utilitarianism's emphasis on states of affairs, but, again, seemingly any moral theory will include some mechanism by which to dampen that privilege, and should anyone – should Williams – really conclude, so much the worse for any moral theory?

As a matter of fact, not only is Williams ready to rule out, as the following chapters will show, the possibility of any satisfactory moral theory, eventually indicting as utilitarianism's co-conspirators various alternatives inspired by Kant and Aristotle, he stands ready to rule out morality itself. But, then, morality for Williams ends up possessing a fairly narrow meaning. Setting a major theme in *Ethics and the Limits of Philosophy*, Williams differentiates morality and ethics, suggesting that "the word 'morality' has by now taken on a more distinctive content, and I am going to suggest that morality should be understood as a particular development of the ethical, one that has special significance in modern Western culture" (Williams 1985: 6). Chapter 4 investigates this development and its significance. Why should Williams view morality as "the peculiar institution" (*ibid*.: 174)? Moreover, Chapter 4 investigates, or begins to investigate, not only Williams's distinction between morality and ethics, but also the potentially much more significant distinction between the moral and the non-moral. Invoking some of the same sentiments underlying his critique of utilitarianism, he explains: "I have wanted to ask a prior question, about what the distinction between the 'moral' and the 'non-moral' is supposed to do for us; and I have suggested that considerations of the moral kind make sense only if they are related to other reasons for action that human beings use, and generally to their desires, needs and projects" (Williams 1993a: xiii). Never has Williams invested a question – what is the value to us or what is the importance to us of our distinction between the moral and the non-moral? – with greater weight.

Chapter 4

Critique of the morality system

Introduction

Turning from Williams's multi-front assault on utilitarianism, this chapter considers a similarly variegated attack on a perhaps less familiar, but no less formidable, target, the "morality system". This latter confrontation takes place on contested conceptual territory, occupied, at least in part, by two ungainly contrasts and a dense legacy. The contrasts are between theory and anti-theory, and between morality and ethics. The legacy is Kant's. Just how this pair of distinctions and this legacy interact is a complex matter. It could be argued, for example, that, for Williams, only one distinction truly exists, in as much as either his scepticism towards morality collapses into scepticism towards theory, or his endorsement of ethics amounts to an anti-theoretical approach to the conduct of life. Moreover, it might be claimed that, equivalent or not, the distinctions between theory and anti-theory and between morality and ethics, or at least Williams's preferences concerning them, naturally fall out from a certain interpretation of Kantian ethical theory. As such, something needs to be said, by way of introduction, about the way Williams maps out and orients himself towards this conceptual territory: towards ethical theory, towards ethics itself and towards Kant.

According to the editors of a valuable collection on the subject, "Anti-theorists reject normative theory as unnecessary, undesirable, or impossible, and usually for all three reasons" (Clarke & Simpson 1989: 3). So described, Williams certainly counts as a full-blown anti-theorist. Despite avoiding the term "anti-theory" in his own writing, he consistently maintains not only that moral philosophy "has received more over-general and over-simplified systematization, while inviting it less, than virtually any other part of philosophy", but that "There is no reason why moral philosophy . . . should yield any interesting self-contained theory at all" (Williams 1972: xx–xxi). As mentioned in the previous chapter, Williams's best known definition of ethical theory occurs in *Ethics and the Limits of Philosophy*, a definition distinguished by its demand for "a general test for the correctness of basic ethical beliefs" (Williams 1985: 72). A slightly earlier passage may give some idea of just what such a general test amounts to: "There cannot be any very interesting, tidy or self-contained theory of what morality is, nor, despite the vigorous activities of some present practitioners, can there be an ethical theory, in the sense of a philosophical structure, which, together with some degree of empirical fact, will yield a decision procedure for moral reasoning" (Williams 1981i: ix–x). For Williams, then, this "general test" or "decision procedure" marks the critical component in any ethical theory, some mechanism by which to determine, given any concrete practical situation, one's moral course of action.

Such a requirement seems plausibly met, as Chapter 3 suggests, by utilitarianism, in both its direct and indirect forms. In the one case, morally right action becomes a matter of calculating consequences, in the other, it becomes a matter of adhering to rules; but in either case a preset, action-guiding procedure exists for the agent to follow. Things may not be as straightforward, however, with other candidate theories. For example, in a spirited defence of ethical theory, Nussbaum points out that Rawls's holistic, coherentist process of justification via reflective equilibrium eschews any single test or decision procedure for ethical correctness, yet Williams's discussion of *A Theory of Justice* in *Ethics and the Limits of Philosophy* plainly takes Rawls to be promoting an ethical theory (Nussbaum 2000: 233; see Williams 1985: Chapters 5 and 6). And matters are perhaps even more complicated in the case of Kant, in many ways both Rawls's forebear and Williams's arch-nemesis.

As will become evident, for Williams, "Kant's account presents great difficulties and obscurities", of which the most prominent may be a dissociation between situated moral actor and impartial deliberating agent, a dissociation sufficient to render suspect the possibility of a viable decision procedure constructed along Kantian lines (Williams 1985: 64). This is not to say that Kant fails to satisfy Williams's more relaxed criteria for "a positive ethical theory", in as much as, for example, the *Groundwork* "combines views on what ethical thought is and how it should be conducted, with substantive consequences of conducting it in that way" (*ibid.*: 74), but to say that Williams sees Kant's hallmark views as less representative of *ethics*, and more reflective of *morality*, "understood as a particular development of the ethical, one that has a special significance in modern Western culture" (*ibid.*: 6). Morality (as in "morality system", a key trope of *Ethics and the Limits of Philosophy*) "peculiarly emphasizes certain ethical notions rather than others ... and it has some peculiar presuppositions" (*ibid.*). These notions and presuppositions, peculiar or otherwise, involve what Williams laments as, for the most part, distinctively Kantian views concerning abstractness and impartiality, obligation and blame, moral purity and resistance to luck. In fact, "It is specifically *morality* that Kant introduces" (*ibid.*: 55). Furthermore, Williams's criticism of some of these notions and presuppositions forms what may be viewed as a modestly retooled integrity objection, this time to Kantian theory, rather than utilitarianism.

It may be worth noting that Williams's critique of Kantian moral theory appears to be almost totally disengaged from Kant's texts. Although he is certainly no stranger to sophisticated philosophical exegesis (e.g. Williams 1978a, 1980, 1997), references to and discussion of particular passages from Kant rarely appear in Williams's writings. For instance, not one of his (arguably) three most important papers bearing on Kant's moral philosophy ("Morality and the Emotions", "Persons, Character and Morality", "Moral Luck") contains a single reference to any specific work by Kant. And even *Ethics and the Limits of Philosophy*, with its sustained scepticism regarding Kant's legacy in ethics, refers to Kant's writings only in sporadic endnotes. Now, much of the reason for Kant's conspicuous absence is no doubt tied to the conspicuous presence in Williams's work of prominent contemporary philosophers of Kantian bent, Kantian epigones or proxies, if you will, with whom Williams is very much engaged, philosophers such as Nagel, Rawls and Alan Gewirth, to name just three. Still, one cannot deny that Williams's indictment of morality impugns, first and foremost, Kant himself, holding, as it does, that "The philosopher who has given the purest, deepest, and most thorough representation of morality is Kant" (Williams 1985: 174). Williams does, therefore, open himself up to objections based on perceived inadequacies in his reading of Kant, objections that have not failed to materialize.

Barbara Herman, in particular, importantly takes Williams to task for his mistreatment of Kant, especially a failure to appreciate the resourcefulness of Kantian theory in addressing just the sorts of challenges his critique poses. She takes those challenges to be basically three, and each of the next three sections considers one of them. First, Williams complains that Kantian morality "insists on dominion over even our most basic projects and intimate commitments, demanding a degree of attachment to morality that alienates us from ourselves and what we value" (Herman 1993a: 24). This complaint roughly amounts to Williams's integrity objection to Kantianism. Second (again, this is Herman interpreting Williams interpreting Kant), Kantian morality "leads to an estrangement from and devaluation of our emotions, especially in the rejection of emotions as morally valued motives" (*ibid.*). This criticism initially appears in one of Williams's earliest published papers, "Morality and the Emotions". Finally, "Kantian morality often demands that we care about the wrong thing – about morality – and not about the object of our action and natural concern" (Herman 1993a: 24). This third charge is perhaps best explored in connection with Williams's well known formulation "one thought too many", from "Persons, Character and Morality". Following discussion of these three issues (integrity, emotions, "one thought too many"), the chapter continues with a consideration of the "morality system", and concludes with an analysis of Williams's wide-ranging, widely read and, at least potentially, widely misunderstood paper "Moral Luck".

It is clear that Williams prefers anti-theory to theory: "I am more than ever convinced that what [moral philosophy] does not need is a theory of its own" (Williams 1981i: ix). But one must appreciate his views on the limitations of Kantian theory to understand fully this preference. It is equally clear that he prefers ethics to morality, believing the latter something "we should treat with a special skepticism" (Williams 1985: 6). But, again, fully appreciating this scepticism towards morality depends upon grasping Williams's scepticism towards Kant's theoretical ambitions. Thus this chapter, in some respects piecemeal, incorporating a number of distinguishable complaints concerning the limitations of contemporary ethical philosophy, maintains unity through the formidable role played by Kant's influence at every turn.

Integrity (again)

In Chapter 3, "ground projects" came to the fore, threatened by the "agglomerative indifference" of utilitarianism; that is, threatened by utilitarianism's focus on the maximization of overall welfare, at the potential expense of an agent's identity-conferring commitments or ideals or plans, which, as we saw, Williams takes to be "the condition of [one's] existence, in the sense that unless [one is] propelled forward by the conatus of desire, project and interest, it is unclear why [one] should go on at all" (Williams 1981f: 12). Whether taken literally or not, such claims stress the separateness of persons, while privileging the personal point of view, a point of view that, in one sense, utilitarianism accounts for, at least to the extent that some quantum of utility, indicating some value of the project to the agent, becomes assigned in the overall utilitarian calculus, but that, in another and deeper sense, it ignores, in that such projects, given what Williams at one point calls their "categorical" nature, inherently resist methods of utilitarian valuation. Again, this simply reflects the fact that "one's pattern of interests, desires and projects not only provide the reason for an interest in what happens within the horizon of one's future, but also constitute the conditions of there being such a future at all" (*ibid.*: 11). For Williams, in sacrificing agents' ground projects, utilitarianism undermines not only their identity, but also, quite straightforwardly, their integrity.

After making the above case in "A Critique of Utilitarianism", Williams moves, in "Persons, Character and Morality", to consider whether and in what ways Kantian theory might succeed where utilitarianism fails. At first glance, prospects look good. After all, Kantianism, in favouring intentions over consequences as a measure of moral worth, appears, admirably, to focus on the agent. But such optimism proves short-lived:

> The Kantian outlook emphasizes something like the separateness of agents, and in that sense makes less of an abstraction than Utilitarianism does.... But now the question arises, of whether the honourable instincts of Kantianism to defend the individuality of individuals against the agglomerative indifference of Utilitarianism can in fact be effective granted the impoverished and abstract character of persons as moral agents which the Kantian view seems to impose ... [I]t is a real question, whether the conception of the individual provided by Kantian theories is enough to yield what is wanted, even by the Kantians; let alone enough for others who, while equally rejecting Utilitarianism, want to allow more room than Kantianism can allow for the importance of individual character and personal relations in moral experience.
>
> (Williams 1981f: 4–5)

Plainly the culprit here is the impoverishment and abstraction Williams sees accompanying the adoption of any perspective impartial enough to permit Kantian universalization in accordance with the categorical imperative.

Here a two-standpoints interpretation of Kant's theory seems at least tacitly accepted, whereby actions (more accurately, the maxims thereof) proposed from the standpoint of particular individuals require something like the stamp of moral approval from another, more impartial standpoint. The categorical imperative, then, becomes the conduit linking the two standpoints, through which the action is endorsed (or not) as morally permissible, in virtue of being an action anyone in similar circumstances might perform. But in as much as Kantian impartiality fails to represent adequately the importance of the sort of identity-conferring, character-infusing personal projects that Williams emphasizes in his critique of utilitarianism, integrity becomes threatened once more.

Maintaining that "The Kantian emphasis on moral impartiality ... provid[es] ultimately too slim a sense in which projects are mine at all" (Williams 1981f: 12), Williams wonders: "How can an *I* that has taken on the perspective of impartiality be left with enough identity to live a life that respects its own interests?" (Williams 1985: 69). Of course, for Williams, it cannot, and he provides this summary of his disappointed expectations for Kantianism:

> A man who has such a ground project will be required by Utilitarianism to give up what it requires in a given case just if that conflicts with what he is required to do as an impersonal utility-maximizer when all the causally relevant considerations are in. But the Kantian, who can do rather better than that, still cannot do well enough. For impartial morality, if the conflict really does arise, must be required to win; and that cannot necessarily be a reasonable demand on the agent. There can come a time at which it is quite unreasonable for a man to give up, in the name of the impartial good ordering of the world of moral agents, something which is a condition of his having any interest in being around in that world at all. (Williams 1981f: 14)

This last claim (and certainly its tone), almost an ultimatum really, regarding the reasonableness or unreasonableness of impartial demands, is becoming all too familiar, as will shortly become apparent, to some of Williams's critics. Suffice it to say, this passage stakes out an area of no small controversy regarding the legitimacy of demands imposed by moral theories committed to impartiality, which makes it, as many philosophers have recognized (e.g. Davis 1980; Flanagan 1991; Herman 1993a; Scheffler 1994), a controversy regarding virtually any moral theory.

Williams's appeal to integrity and to the sanctity of the personal point of view, his rejection of the Kantian insistence on abstracting from an identity formed by personal projects and on adopting an impartial perspective, characterizes a more general rejection of Kantian morality as unconditional. Although it might appear that the particularities of personal projects, and hence the building blocks of identity and integrity, can be preserved within Kantian theory, at least provided a sufficiently fine-grained formulation of maxims, the real threat emerges when those projects are deemed morally impermissible, as Herman well recognizes:

> Williams is not misreading Kantian morality here. It does involve a requirement that one be prepared to set aside one's deepest projects if they require impermissible actions. The question is whether a moral agent committed to morality in this way would have his integrity as a person threatened. ... For morality to respect the conditions of character (one's integrity as a person), it must respect the agent's attachments to his projects in a way that permits his actions to be the expression of those attachments. Kantian morality, understood as a morality of limits, can do this. What it cannot do is honor *unconditional attachments*. ... Indeed, given the possibility of grossly immoral projects or vile actions taken for the sake of morally neutral projects, it does not seem rational to want it otherwise. (Herman 1993a: 39)

The point for Williams is simple: regardless of their content, if one's projects truly confer identity, by giving them up one gives up one's self, a sacrifice no moral theory can require. But the rejoinder by Herman (and many others) is equally simple: any moral theory worth the name must require the sacrifice of immoral projects, identity-conferring or otherwise. Indeed, Herman's teacher, John Rawls, speaks to this point in *A Theory of Justice*: "Now of course the virtues of integrity are virtues, and among the excellences of free persons. Yet while necessary, they are not sufficient; for their definition allows for almost any content" (Rawls 1971: 519). Morality trumps integrity.

In rejecting Kant's abstract requirement of universalization, or at least its overridingness, Williams apparently sees himself connecting with some common-sense intuition privileging the personal over the impartial. But the existence of any such intuition may be questionable at best. Nussbaum argues, for example,

> that the demand to see our situation from a point of view external to our own is a demand that arises within the ordinary point of view on ethical matters. Often we feel that we are too self-focused; even small children soon acquire the idea of a fair division of good things, and criticize those who think only of their own goals and projects. The idea that a division should be impartial, made as if from the point of view of no particular individual, is more common on the playground (and at the family dinner table) than in politics. . . . Williams is surely shortchanging a part of ordinary life when he represents the non-theoretical agent as immured within a personal perspective on the world. (Nussbaum 2000: 243)

Now, just how loudly the manners of small children speak against Williams's views may be hard to gauge, but surely Nussbaum is on to something, if only that, in so far as Iris Murdoch is right to claim that "In the moral life the enemy is the fat relentless ego", Williams's views may seem an inadequate bulwark against the enemy (Murdoch 1970b: 52).

Others appear similarly sceptical about resisting the dictates of an impartial perspective. Indeed, where Williams sees gains to selfhood in the form of integrity, Peter Railton sees potential losses in the form of autonomy:

> Bernard Williams has emphasized that many of us have developed certain "ground projects" that give shape and meaning to our lives, and has drawn attention to the damage an individual may suffer if he is alienated from his ground projects by being forced to look at them as potentially overridable by moral considerations. But against this it may be urged that it is crucial for autonomy that one hold one's commitments up for inspection – even one's ground projects. Our ground projects are formed in our youth, in a particular family, class, or cultural background. It may be alienating or even disorienting to call these into question, but to fail to do so is to lose autonomy. (Railton 1988: 107)

In fairness to Williams, however, it does seem that his notion of projects includes an element of reflective endorsement sufficient to prevent just the sort of bad consciousness to which Railton alludes, albeit one that may fall short of strict impartiality. For the most part, ground projects confer identity in an exercise, rather than an abdication, of personal autonomy: one makes one's projects one's own. In any case, as Williams puts it in "Morality and the Emotions", taken up next,

> There are indeed human activities and relations in which impartiality and consistency are very much the point. But to raise on these notions a model of all moral relations is, just as Kant said it was, to make us each into a Supreme Legislator; a fantasy which represents, not the moral ideal, but the deification of man.
>
> (Williams 1973f: 226)

Rest assured that whatever constitutes Williams's moral ideal, assuming such a thing even makes sense within his overall scheme of ethical life, it will be eminently mundane, firmly tied to the specifications and capacities of human psychology and social organization.

Morality and emotions

As noted in Chapter 1, many of Williams's most significant and enduring contributions to philosophy have had less to do with inventing narrow arguments, and more to do with unearthing broad themes. Confessing a "widening doubt" about "morality" in the preface to *Moral Luck*, he reports that "It is this doubt, as well as skepticism about the powers of moral or ethical theory, which has led me to try and find out – often by the crude method of prodding it – which parts of moral thought seem to be actually alive, before trying to design any elegant physiology for it" (Williams 1981i: x). Certainly one moribund part of moral thought prodded by Williams, one now remarkably resuscitated, owing in no small measure to his efforts, concerns the nature and role of emotions, not only in practical deliberation, but in moral psychology generally. Given the deluge of philosophical theorizing about the emotions in recent years, one may be forgiven for not realizing just how ignored the topic was in moral philosophy when (and arguably until) Williams turned his attention to it in 1965. Moreover, according to Williams's diagnosis, such ignorance was hardly innocent, but instead largely motivated by "a combination of two things – a rather simple view of the emotions, and a deeply Kantian view of morality" (Williams 1973f: 207). Remember, however, in considering Williams's appraisal of this combination, that it is as much the very fact of his appraisal that merits appreciation as the particulars thereof.

Quite simply, Williams believes that any systematic account of morality that fails to acknowledge the significant role emotions play in our ideas of both good lives and right actions inevitably falsifies that account. So,

> It is time, finally to face up to Kant. For, if one is going to suggest that those things that a man does as an expression of certain emotions, can contribute to our view of him as a moral agent; if, further, one is going to say ... that one's conception of an admirable human being implies that he should be disposed to certain kinds of emotional response, and not to others; one has to try and answer the very powerful claim of Kant that this is impossible.
> (Williams 1973f: 225–6)

When Williams takes on "Morality, the Peculiar Institution", in Chapter 10 of *Ethics and the Limits of Philosophy*, he observes that although Kant is without question the *éminence grise* of the morality system, "morality is not an invention of philosophers. It is the outlook, or, incoherently, part of the outlook, of almost all of us" (Williams 1985: 175). In a similar vein, it is not that Kant invents the notion of an emotionless ethical life, any more than he invents, as we will see, that of an ethical life immune to luck, but that he pushes these notions – our notions – to extremes whose absurdity, according to Williams, is rivalled only by their purported metaphysical justifications. But what grounds could possibly be given for denying the relevance of emotions to ethical well-being?

As Williams reads Kant there are three; that is, there are three noteworthy "objections to the idea that any emotionally governed action by a man can contribute to our assessment of him as a moral agent – or be a contribution, as Kant put it, to his moral worth" (Williams 1973f: 226). First, emotions are too "capricious" to serve as reliable guides to moral conduct. At bottom, this objection goes, actions guided by emotions are fundamentally irrational, to be distinguished from rational acts undertaken in accordance with firm principle. Rejecting outright what he takes to be Kant's "moral woodenness or even insolence in this blank regard for consistency", Williams argues that the contribution of emotions to moral life need not be an all or nothing thing. More to the point, Kant's view of emotion seems overly simplistic, as it is "certainly false" to suggest "that there is no way of adjusting one's emotional response in the light of other considerations, of applying some sense of proportion, without abandoning emotional motivation altogether" (*ibid.*).

Second, Kant holds that, in so far as emotions tend simply to assail us, to come unbidden, they expose once more their irrational roots and their unfitness as guides to moral action. For Kant, moral action must be autonomous, if any is, and emotions must be heteronomous, if anything is. Obviously, this subject of freely chosen action leaves, as Williams well recognizes, "everything to be said", and he contents himself with making two "suggestions" (*ibid.*: 227). In the first place, the idea that involuntary emotions are somehow external to and parasitic on voluntary rational decision needs rethinking: "that people decide to adopt their moral principles is a myth". Supporting this suggestion is a neat piece of moral psychology eloquently expressed (and not for the last time): "We see a man's genuine convictions as coming from somewhere deeper in him than [his decision]; and by what is only an apparent paradox, what we see as coming from deeper in him, he – that is, the deciding "he" – may see as coming from outside him. So it is with the emotions" (*ibid.*; compare Williams 1985: 191). If nothing else, we see here Williams's characteristic appeal for a moral philosophy adequate to the phenomenon, in this case the emotions.

His second suggestion Williams terms "banal", but that hardly does justice to its formulation, which may come closer than any other to capturing, again quite eloquently, all of his reservations concerning Kantian (and not just Kantian) moral theory. To the idea that a recipient of moral kindness would be better off if the kind action were motivated by adherence to principle, rather than by emotion, or, in more Kantian terms, if the action were truly to possess moral worth, Williams responds: "He may have needed, not the benefits of universal law, but some human gesture" (Williams 1973f: 227). And should such gestures prove to be in some sense non-moral, "it just shows", and here is one of Williams's most enduring themes, "that people place other sorts of value on human conduct besides moral value" (*ibid.*), a theme to be more fully explored in the following three sections and, indeed, throughout the book.

Finally, Kant holds that since people naturally differ in their emotional make-up, it would be wrong to base moral worth on these fortuitously distributed features of personality, or, in Williams's words, it would be "both logically incompatible with the notion of *the moral*, and also in some ultimate sense hideously unfair" (*ibid.*: 228). To this point Williams responds with a sweeping indictment of Kant, at once, and quite characteristically, philosophical, psychological and anthropological, which bears quoting at length for the insight it gives into his nascent, yet fast coalescing, scepticism towards any conception of the ethical whose reach, descriptive or prescriptive, exceeds its grasp of empirical fact:

> Here it is essential to keep in mind two facts about Kant. One is that his work contains the working out to the very end of that thought ... that moral worth must be separated from any natural advantage whatsoever, which, consistently pursued by Kant, leads to the conclusion that the source of moral thought and action must be located outside the empirically conditioned self. The second fact to be remembered, at the same time, is that Kant's work is in this respect a shattering failure, and the transcendental psychology to which it leads is, where not unintelligible, certainly false. No human characteristic which is relevant to degrees of moral esteem can escape being an empirical characteristic, subject to empirical conditions, psychological history and individual variation, whether it be sensitivity, persistence, imaginativeness, intelligence, good sense; or sympathetic feeling; or strength of will. (*Ibid*.: 228)

Of course, the sentence beginning "No human characteristic which is relevant to degrees of moral esteem can escape being an empirical characteristic" could serve as a rallying cry for ethical naturalism, the often frustratingly vague agenda in contemporary philosophy, to which, nonetheless, Williams has made substantial and, for the most part, far from vague contributions. However, the sentence beginning "Kant's work in this respect is a shattering failure" has hardly gone unchallenged.

Ultimately, Williams rejects Kant's strict privileging of acts done from a motive of duty, meaning, roughly, acts done from a willingness to conform to rational principle, over those done from any other motivation, emotional, say, seen as an instance of, at best, non-rational inclination. If moral actions must be pure, then emotions cannot be part of the Kantian story of morality, which makes the Kantian story of morality, as far as Williams is concerned, a fairy tale. But philosophers have taken Williams to task for painting far too crude a picture of the place of emotions in Kant's ethics, claiming that he fails to appreciate the extent to which moral principle plays a "regulative role" (Baron 1995: 127) or acts as a "limiting condition" (Herman 1993a: 31).

Williams accuses Kant of being too black and white on the subject of moral motivation, but in fact, say his critics, it is Kant who has the more nuanced view.

According to Herman, Kant's notion of duty, captured in the form of the categorical imperative, should be seen not, or not necessarily, as a motivational force unto itself, but as a higher-order check on the moral permissibility of actions, regardless of their occurrent motivation. What actions must be is morally permissible, what they need not be is motivated by the very fact of their permissibility. Herman summarizes her view:

> Thus, in the case of bringing aid to someone in need, it would be quite ordinary for the action of the normal moral agent to be overdetermined: he might act from the emotion-based desire to help (meeting the other's need would then be the direct object of his action), *and* he would act from the motive of duty (the permissibility of what he was doing would be a necessary condition of his acting to help). . . . If the claim against the motive of duty was that whenever it was present and effective in controlling the way someone acts it excludes the influence of emotions as motives, or makes the agent unable to respond to the need of another, when the motive of duty functions as a limiting condition neither of these claims against it are valid. (Herman 1993a: 31–2)

Williams might be forgiven a bit of déjà vu. For here Herman's analysis seems strikingly parallel to her earlier assertions of unconditionality and overridingness: "The Kantian argument is that at the limit, where conflict with morality is serious and unavoidable, morality must win" (*ibid.*: 40). However, Herman's Kantian account, in requiring that emotions be chaperoned by moral principle, denigrates, to Williams's mind, a legitimate moral motivation of considerable maturity, needing no accompaniment. And this (still) far from settled issue of whether or not moral actions need be accompanied by moral principles is at the heart of Williams's well known analysis of a certain hypothetical sinking ship.

"One thought too many"

If Williams's integrity objection focuses on the danger posed by moral theory in terms of alienation from ourselves, from the projects and commitments that define our characters and so reflect who we most deeply are, his relatively brief discussion of a passage by Charles Fried, at the very end of "Persons, Character and Morality", highlights a similar danger, now posed in terms of alienation from others, those with whom we find ourselves most deeply engaged. Suppose, the story goes, the ship is sinking and a man may, with equal expenditure of effort, save one, but only one, of two people, one of whom is his wife. Moral theorists, suggests Williams, will search for a justification for the man's action. Perhaps a utilitarian might invoke the welfare-maximizing consequences of a preference for spouses over strangers in emergencies. A Kantian, on the other hand, might claim that the action of wife-saving in such circumstances (suitably represented in a maxim, of course) is ruled morally permissible by the categorical imperative. For Williams, however, any such justification presents "one thought too many".

Instead of an appeal to abstract principle, Williams suggests that "it might have been hoped by some (for instance, by his wife) that his motivating thought, fully spelled out, would be the thought that it was his wife and that in situations of this kind it is permissible to save one's wife" (Williams 1981f: 18). Notwithstanding Marcia Baron's pointed observation that the wife's hopes in this case are of dubious moral relevance (Baron 1995: 138), Williams clearly finds moves to justify the action impartially – say, by formulating a principle according to which any husband in similar circumstances ought save his wife rather than someone else – ludicrous, yet typical, even definitive, of Kantian theory. He concludes his discussion by observing that "somewhere (and if not in this case, where?) one reaches the necessity that such things as deep attachments to other persons will express themselves in the world in ways which cannot at the same time embody the impartial view, and that they also run the risk of offending against it" (Williams 1981f: 18). In short: "some situations lie beyond justification" (*ibid.*).

Williams's "one thought too many" objection to impartial, especially Kantian, moral theory may represent a rare case among his writings in which ensuing criticism has managed to quell further discussion of the issue, or at least discussion in the same terms. In any event, Williams never returns to Fried's case. This is not because of, once again, Herman's defence of Kant in language that, as we have seen, for Williams is tantamount to capitulation: "What the Kantian requires is only that he not view his desire to save his wife as an *unconditionally* valid reason" (Herman 1993a: 42); and not because of legitimate doubts in the philosophy of mind concerning the possibility of isolating the content of motivating thoughts; but because Williams's discussion seems pretty clearly to run together issues, or rather moments, of motivation and justification. Scheffler nicely summarizes this concern:

> It must be said that the notion of a "motivating thought" is not altogether clear, still less so the notion of a "motivating thought, fully spelled out". Let us suppose, as seems reasonable in the context of the passage as a whole, that such a thought must be one that the man actually has, as opposed, say, to one he would have, if the justifiability of his action were challenged . . . [T]hat assumption is bound to strike most people, upon reflection, as very implausible. It is implausible to suppose that, in general, whenever one makes a favorable assessment of an act, one is committed to saying that the agent who performs the act ought to have, and ought in part to be motivated by, the thought of its permissibility.
>
> (Scheffler 1992: 21–2)

Nussbaum bluntly reinforces the point: "no ethical theory requires explicit reflection before each ethical choice" (Nussbaum 2000: 246).

Kantianism justifies right actions in so far as they are done from duty, manifest a good will and are subject to the categorical imperative. Now, it is true that Kant has been influentially interpreted as presenting the categorical imperative as very much a decision procedure in the sense Williams indicates in his definition of ethical theory (see Rawls 1989), but that it can yield a decision is not to say that it must therefore be consulted on every occasion. The question for Williams, then, should boil down not to whether Kantian theory proves ridiculous in demanding some particular thought at the time of action, a thought, moreover, both necessary and sufficient for motivation, but to whether, in requiring that actions be morally justified via alignment with impartial principle, Kantian theory threatens personal relationships to a degree that may cause us to re-evaluate our commitment to morality. And this question remains very much alive.

The morality system

Williams's war on Kantian ethics certainly seems to range widely, with battles on a number of fronts: ground projects and integrity, emotions and moral motivation, personal relations and "one thought too many". In another sense, however, the war may seem narrower, in so far as all these attacks apparently rely on a similar strategy, employing similar ammunition: the claim that Kant's signature move to impartiality, never mind exactly how achieved, carries consequences whose severity undermines the very plausibility of that move. Making room for integrity and emotions in the moral economy of the individual, then, requires disintermediation of the categorical imperative that Williams sees Kant as placing between oneself as moral agent and one's projects and commitments. Such a move ushers morality from the realm of abstract rationalizing back into the realm of concrete living. In fact, in the three attacks just considered, it is ultimately Kantian abstraction that makes for Williams's common enemy. But it is not his only enemy.

In differentiating ethics from morality at the beginning of *Ethics and the Limits of Philosophy*, Williams particularly emphasizes the extent to which the "range of considerations that falls under the notion of the ethical ... is not clearly delimited", whereas "*morality*, the special system, ... demands a sharp boundary for itself" (Williams 1985: 7). The impoverished nature of morality's conceptual resources marks a recurrent theme for Williams, as does his insistence on locating ethical and non-ethical considerations along a continuum, with the potential and, for him, not necessarily unwelcome vagueness such a picture implies. Theories, according to Williams, with Kant's as a prime example, "desire to reduce all ethical considerations to one pattern ... try[ing] to show that one or another type of ethical consideration is basic, with other types to be explained in terms of it" (*ibid.*: 16). But such a desire flies in the face of one of Williams's most hallowed views, touched on in Chapter 3 in terms of incommensurability: "We use a variety of different ethical considerations, which are genuinely different from one another, and this is what one would expect to find, if only because we are heirs to a long and complex ethical tradition, with many different religious and other social strands" (*ibid.*). Rousingly, his solid anti-reductionism comes once more to the fore: "If there is such a thing as the truth about the subject matter of ethics ... why is there any expectation that it should be simple? In particular, why should it be conceptually simple, using only one or two ethical concepts ... rather than many? Perhaps we need as many concepts to describe it as we find we need, and no fewer" (*ibid.*: 17). Certainly needed will be more than the one concept Williams finds most characterisitic of the morality system: moral obligation.

According to Williams, "Morality is distinguished by the special notion of obligation it uses and the significance it gives to it" (*ibid.*: 174). What makes this notion of obligation so special, and the system that relies on it so peculiar, can be seen in the two principles or maxims Williams associates with its deployment, both of which manifest morality's conceptual claustrophobia, its narrow, constricted focus and its aura of inescapability. One of these principles is "only an obligation can beat an obligation" (*ibid.*: 180). The other is "obligation-out, obligation-in" (*ibid.*: 181). Williams would have us reject both principles and, indeed, the morality system altogether.

It may be worth pointing out in passing that in labelling morality "the peculiar institution", Williams deliberately evokes, albeit without comment, a pervasive euphemism for the institution of slavery in the American South. Presumably there exists some connection in Williams's mind between the way slavery manages to challenge ideas of humanity and equality and compassion, yet managed to go largely unchallenged itself by Southern landowners, and the way in which morality has come to dominate our ethical consciousness, despite clearly deforming and misrepresenting moral experience. Williams sees his task throughout *Ethics and the Limits of Philosophy* (and much else besides) as broadening the realm of the ethical to reflect more accurately the multiplicity and complexity of, as he generally and not all that helpfully puts it, ethical considerations, but also, and just as importantly, as emphasizing the degree to which many of these considerations are not inherently or uniquely ethical, but become so only by degrees and in certain circumstances.

"In the morality system", says Williams, "moral obligation is expressed in one especially important kind of deliberative conclusion – a conclusion that is directed toward what to do, governed by moral reasons, and concerned with a particular situation" (Williams 1985: 174–5). So far, so good. "However", he continues, "there is a pressure within the morality system to represent every consideration that goes into deliberation and yields a particular obligation as being itself a general obligation; so if I am now under an obligation to do something that would be for the best, this will be because I have some general obligation, perhaps among others, to do what is for the best" (*ibid.*: 175). The idea seems to be that obligations in the form of deliberative conclusions must pick up their obligatory nature, their categorical or must-be-done quality, from somewhere, and where better than from some other, more general obligation. Such a move underlies, then, what Williams calls the obligation-out, obligation-in principle, "The pressure of the demand within the morality system to find a general obligation to back a particular one" (*ibid.*: 181). Although this principle may be reminiscent of that decried by Williams in his "one thought too many" reaction to Fried, where moral theorists sought at best superfluous justifications for action (e.g. one has an obligation in cases of shipwreck to save one's wife, *because* one has a more general obligation to maximize happiness in such cases), the issue may actually be broader than whether or not actions motivated by, say, natural sentiment need be covered by more theoretical considerations. What concerns Williams here seems to be the ever-tricky problem of morality's scope.

Traditionally the problem of the scope of moral obligation centres on questions such as, given that one has an obligation to, say, help those less fortunate than oneself, how broadly should the net of "those less fortunate" be cast? To whom does one actually owe help as a matter of moral obligation? To family? Family and friends? Family, friends and neighbours? All the people in the country? Featherless bipeds? Another way to frame the issue is simply: how demanding – of our time and attention and resources and conscience – does morality have a right to be? Williams summarizes his concern:

> Once the journey into more general obligations has started, we may begin to get into trouble – not just philosophical trouble, but conscience trouble – with finding room for morally indifferent actions ... [I]f we have accepted general and indeterminate obligations to further various moral objectives ... they will be waiting to provide work for idle hands, and the thought can gain a footing (I am not saying it has to) that I could be better employed than in something I am under no obligation to do, and, if I could be, then I ought to be. ... If obligation is allowed to structure ethical thought, there are several natural ways in which it can come to dominate ethical life altogether. (Williams 1985: 181–2)

Put another way, morality becomes inescapable, a thought reinforced by Williams's second principle of the morality system: only an obligation can beat an obligation.

What drives morality's proliferation of obligations is the phenomenon of blame, in the form of both social opprobrium and self-reproach, the latter understood as an internalized manifestation of the former. As Williams says, "Blame is the characteristic reaction of the morality system" (*ibid.*: 177). What he means, really, is that blame is the characteristic reaction to transgressions within the morality system, which, of course, means that blame is the characteristic reaction to obligations not met. Given the deliberative priority of a morally obligated action, and the blame attending pursuit of any non-obligatory alternatives, given, that is, what Williams calls the "stringency" of moral obligations, pressure naturally builds to see alternative possibilities as obligatory themselves, and decisively so: "Morality encourages the idea, only an obligation can beat an obligation" (*ibid.*: 180). What is the source of such new-found moral authority? Why, some more general obligation, of course, and here we witness the symbiosis between morality's two maxims. Under the morality system, non-moral considerations cannot trump moral considerations without the agent incurring blame. To avoid blame, then, hitherto non-moral motivations are transformed into moral duties, through the invocation, Williams would say invention, of ever more general obligations. Indeed, both Ross's prima facie obligations and those "fraudulent items", duties to oneself, Williams sees as ultimately unsatisfactory attempts to accommodate or adjust to the inescapability of moral obligation licensed by the morality system (*ibid.*: 182), a licence he would just as soon revoke.

How can this be done? "In order to see around the intimidating structure that morality has made out of the idea of obligation, we need an account of what obligations are when they are rightly seen as merely one kind of ethical consideration among others" (*ibid.*: 182). Forming such an account necessarily involves acknowledging something that the morality system insists on denying, indeed, is predicated on denying, but that, unless faced, prevents an honest appreciation of ourselves as creatures for whom the requirements of morality, while frequently of considerable importance, fall short of being inescapable. As Williams puts it, "Ethical life is important, but it can see that things other than itself are important" (*ibid.*: 184). However, Kant and his followers remain blind to the importance of these other things, and so many of Williams's writings can be seen as attempts both to establish the critical role non-moral, non-obligatory, non-blame-inviting deliberative considerations play in people's lives, and to emphasize their resilience in the face of moral considerations as presumptive trumps. Yes, there is such a thing as obligation, and yes, it is essential to the smooth functioning of ethical life, in as much as it is, as Williams says, "grounded in the basic issue of what people should be able to rely on" (*ibid.*: 185), and yes it will, in appropriate contexts, assume deliberative priority; that is, it will override competing deliberative claims. But considerations concerning just what people should be able to rely on, or need to be able to rely on, in order to function, even to flourish, will constitute, Williams thinks, remarkably few specific obligations, cast negatively in the form of prohibitions (do not kill, do not steal and so forth), falling far short of the sort of wide-open general obligations favoured by the morality system.

Does this mean that there are no positive obligations? Not at all: for goodness sake, save your spouse from drowning! But it means that that the obligation to save your spouse owes everything to ethical considerations, or considerations period, reflecting intimacy and commitment, immediacy and emergency, contingency and context, and nothing to, for example, all-encompassing duties of beneficence, such as might instantiate the principles of obligation-out, obligation-in and only an obligation can beat an obligation. A decade after *Ethics and the Limits of Philosophy*, Williams revisited his critique of morality:

> Against morality, I urged among other things, that obligations are never final practical conclusions, but an input into practical decision. They are only one kind of ethical input, constituting one kind of ethical consideration among others. I also made some suggestions about the kind of consideration they are, to the effect that they are one way – a way that runs through the deliberations of socialized agents – of securing the protection of important interests. (Williams 1995h: 205)

Note the emphasis: one way, but not the only way, to secure important interests, but not just ethical interests. Ultimately, the morality system intends obligation as a bulwark against the motivational efficacy of desire and self-interest, often construed in terms of hedonism and prudence, and seen as potentially, if not probably, inimical to the interests of morality, usually construed in terms of abstraction and impartiality.

One way to sum up the morality system, a very Kantian way, according to Williams, is as a demand for moral purity: purity of moral motivation in terms of an unconditioned will; purity of moral obligation in terms of ubiquity; purity of moral action in terms of an "I must" that goes all the way down; purity of moral reaction in terms of blame. But as has been shown, and will be shown in yet more detail in connection with the subject of practical reason in Chapter 5, Williams rejects the idea of moral purity at every turn: all action is conditioned; nothing necessarily privileges moral obligation; even desire may underwrite an "I must" that goes all the way down; blame is but one of many possible negative moral reactions. Once again, "[moral philosophy's] prevailing fault, in all its styles, is to impose on ethical life some immensely simple model" (Williams 1985: 127), when ethical life is anything but simple.

One important reason for the complexity of ethical life has to do with the integral role played by personal dispositions and internalized social values in forming individual character. Williams would replace morality's focus on the unconditioned moment of judgement with attention to the inherently messier moments associated with the creation and exhibition of character. However, as Williams has it, quoting Camus to nasty effect in the epigraph to *Ethics and the Limits of Philosophy*, "When one has no character, it is necessary to adopt a method" (*"Quand on n'a pas de caractère, il faut bien se donner une méthode"*). Purity of character is an obviously impossible goal; yet purity of theory, equally impossible according to Williams, remains a recognizable goal in contemporary moral philosophy. One reason the goal dies hard relates to the perceived consequences of abandoning it, which might be thought to include the unconscionable admission of luck into ethical experience. As Williams says, "The purity of morality itself represents a value ... the ideal that human existence can be ultimately just. ... The ideal of morality is a value, moral value, that transcends luck" (Williams 1985: 195). In fact, the project of accurately specifying the relation between morality and luck was to become, again with Williams's prodding, something of a cottage industry in moral philosophy.

Moral luck

Several signature issues inform Williams's seminal paper "Moral Luck", and this section devotes more attention to their exegesis than to their critique. Even so, given the philosophical fertility of the paper, worthy of a book length treatment on its own, that exegesis must be regrettably incomplete. Certainly a chapter on Kant and the morality system seems the most appropriate place to consider these issues, since Williams sees Kant as the "most rigorous exponent" of the "still powerfully influential idea that there is one basic form of value, moral value, which is immune to luck" (Williams 1981e: 22). And certainly the stakes are high, since he considers the "Kantian attempt to escape luck ... so intimate to our notion of morality ... that its failure may rather make us consider whether we should not give up that notion altogether" (*ibid.*: 23). As he puts it in a "Postscript", written close to twenty years after the original version of the paper for a valuable collection of articles on the subject (see Statman 1993), "the resistance to luck is not an ambition gratuitously tacked on to morality: it is built into it, and that is why morality is inevitably open to skeptical doubts about its capacity to fulfill this ambition" (Williams 1995e: 242). This postscript proves particularly helpful owing to the considerable complexity of, and, to be fair to a generation of readers, the considerable challenge posed by, the original. As Mary Midgley writes: "Williams's discussion is so rich, and brings together so many different kinds of skeptical argument, that it tends to overwhelm the reader" (Midgley 1984: 28). Indeed, Williams himself came to recognize various problems with the paper's presentation (not to mention its reception).

Anyone who has read even a few of Williams's papers knows that they frequently address multiple topics and may resist easy conceptual unification. "Persons, Character and Morality", for example, discussed at the beginning of this chapter, focuses not only on "one thought too many" and the susceptibility of Kantianism to integrity-style objections, but also on Parfit's work and whether or not personhood admits of scalar interpretation. "Moral Luck" presents a similarly full, but also somewhat confusing, agenda. As Williams later admits:

> The most important source of misunderstanding ... was that I raised, as I now think, three different issues at once. One was the question ... how important is morality in the narrow sense as contrasted with a wide sense of the ethical? The second question concerns the importance, for a given agent and for our view of certain agents, of the ethical even in the wide sense. ... The third question raised in the article is that of retrospective justification, and this is the widest, because it can arise beyond the ethical, in any application of practical rationality. (Williams 1995e: 244–5)

The first issue, Williams's differentiation of the narrow concerns of the morality system from those of a more broadly realized ethical domain, should be quite familiar by now, and its role in "Moral Luck" easily appreciated. In as much as the morality system, beholden to Kant's insistence on purity, can make no conceptual room for luck, while Williams's notion of the ethical can, the latter should be preferred to the former. Such familiarity and predictability seem reason enough to devote this section principally to considering Williams's second and third issues.

It may be worth remarking, however, that Williams does concede the "allure" of Kantianism's (equally, the morality system's) "solace to a sense of the world's unfairness" (Williams 1981e: 21), or the allure of, as he puts it in *Ethics and the Limits of Philosophy*, "an ideal, presented by Kant, once again, in a form that is the most unqualified and also one of the most moving ... that human existence can be ultimately just" (Williams 1985: 195). Such justice depends on particular interpretations of equality and desert, according to which morality is open to all people equally, while people deserve blame only for what is under their control. "Moral Luck" straightforwardly questions this latter claim as it relates to the process of justifying our actions, the third issue raised by Williams. Furthermore, Williams believes that the solace Kantianism offers, tantalizing though it may be, ultimately requires swallowing an unpalatable assumption: "It can offer that solace ... only if something more is granted. Even if moral value were radically unconditioned by luck, that would not be very significant if moral value were merely one kind of value among others. Rather, moral value has to possess some special, indeed supreme, kind of dignity or importance" (Williams 1981e: 21). This gets to the second question or issue Williams wants to discuss in "Moral Luck", the nature and significance of the difference, now framed in terms of importance, between the ethical and everything else. Of course, this topic has been raised before as well, and it will be raised again, so high does it rank among Williams's philosophical priorities. Not only does morality not deserve, as a matter of fact, some special status with unique deliberative priority, but people do not, according to Williams, even wish that it did; indeed, they are happier it does not.

Different philosophers have found different aspects of moral luck philosophically salient, and some of these later, alternative interests and interpretations may have at times been read back into Williams's own paper (where, after all, the term was coined), rendering it even cloudier than it might have first appeared. Given such cloudiness, it might be worthwhile, before discussing the idea of retrospective justification, arguably the most significant component of "Moral Luck", to put to the side some forms of luck that Williams is not, or not really, concerned with, all of which can be illustrated in the context of his famous discussion of Gauguin. Williams asks us to imagine (his) Gauguin as someone who "owes something to romantic conceptions of artistic creation" (Williams 1995e: 244), "a creative artist who turns away from definite and pressing human claims on him in order to live a life in which, as he supposes, he can pursue his art" (Williams 1981e: 22). It is important that (at least) Williams's Gauguin "is concerned about these claims and what is involved in their being neglected (we may suppose this to be grim), and that he nevertheless, in the face of that, opts for the other life", a life he understands "determinately under the category of realising his gifts as a painter" (*ibid.*: 23). It is even more important that "Whether he will succeed cannot, in the nature of the case, be foreseen. We are not dealing with the removal of an external obstacle to something which, once that is removed, will fairly predictably go through. Gauguin, in our story, is putting a great deal on a possibility which has not unequivocally declared itself" (*ibid.*). So just what variety of luck particularly occupies Williams in Gauguin's case?

Deservingly influential in its own right, Nagel's own "Moral Luck" was originally written as a reply to Williams's essay. In it he helpfully lays out

> roughly four ways in which the natural objects of moral assessment are disturbingly subject to luck. One is the phenomenon of constitutive luck – the kind of person you are, where this is not just a question of what you deliberately do, but of your inclinations, capacities, and temperament. Another category is luck in one's circumstances – the kind of problems and circumstances one faces. The other two have to do with the causes and effects of actions: luck in how one is determined by antecedent circumstances, and luck in the way one's actions and projects turn out.
>
> (Nagel 1979b: 28)

Ignoring for now the question of just how strongly Williams would endorse Nagel's characterization of luck's influence in ethical matters as "disturbing", it is crucial to understand that Williams's primary concern in "Moral Luck" involves only the last of the ways Nagel distinguishes.

More specifically, Williams's primary concern involves the way in which luck, infusing events representing the product of practical deliberation, can be said to justify, or to fail to justify, that deliberation. More specifically still, Williams's primary concern involves the way in which luck, infusing events representing the product of practical deliberation, can be said to determine the rationality of that deliberation. As he himself puts it:

> I want to explore and uphold the claim that … the only thing that will justify [Gauguin's] choice will be success itself. If he fails … then he did the wrong thing, not just in the sense in which that platitudinously follows, but in the sense that having done the wrong thing in those circumstances he has no basis for the

> thought that he was justified in acting as he did. If he succeeds, he does have a basis for that thought. (Williams 1981e: 23)

What clearly fascinates Williams, motivating much of "Moral Luck", is the concept of retrospective justification: "Gauguin could not do something which is thought to be essential to rationality and to the notion of justification itself, which is that one should be in a position to apply the justifying considerations at the time of the choice and in advance of knowing whether one was right" (*ibid*.: 24). In other words, what Williams proposes flies in the face of accepted views of practical deliberation, whereby assessing the rationality or irrationality of a given action depends on assessing how an agent reasons in the light of factors (e.g. beliefs, plans, addictions, desires, emotions) operative at the time of decision. By contrast, Williams suggests that the justifiability of Gauguin's decision depends on events occurring after and, importantly, because of it, and how those turn out is to some degree a matter of luck.

Of course, Gauguin must possess certain specific capacities in order for his case to come alive at all. As such, constitutive luck might seem necessarily germane to any discussion. Williams insists, however, that it is not simply luck as regards Gauguin's ability or temperament, say, that interests him, but the way Gauguin's own conception of those factors, a key input into his deliberation and decision, will be effectively vindicated or vitiated by subsequent events. "It is", Williams says, "the question of how far, and in what ways, the view that an agent retrospectively takes of himself or herself may be affected by results and not be directed simply to the ways in which he or she deliberated, before the event" (Williams 1995e: 245). It should be even clearer, then, that Williams largely ignores luck associated with Gauguin's circumstances, or what he calls "external" or "incident" luck.

Gauguin makes a decision to pursue his project of realizing his gifts as a painter, at the expense of fulfilling obligations to his family. Is such a decision rationally justified? As Williams sees it, only the unfolding of events will tell. If his project succeeds, yes. If it fails, however, whether or not justification for his decision materializes will depend upon how it fails; in particular, "It matters how intrinsic the cause of failure is to the project itself" (Williams 1981e: 25). If Gauguin becomes ill after leaving his family, so that he is unable to paint in the South Pacific, that is certainly bad luck, but of an incidental or circumstantial or external variety that cannot itself undermine the rationality of his earlier decision, cast as it was in terms of pursuing his gifts as a painter, something he has been prevented from doing. In such a case "He does not, and never will, know whether he was wrong. What would prove him wrong in his project would not just be that it failed, but that he failed" (*ibid.*). That is, what would prove him wrong is (bad) intrinsic luck, which "concentrates itself on virtually the one question of whether he is a generally gifted painter who can succeed in doing genuinely valuable work" (*ibid.*: 26). In realizing his gifts as a painter, Gauguin succeeds not only in rationally justifying his decision to pursue a painter's life in paradise, but also – there is not a better way to put it – in justifying himself. For Williams this marks no small point, for "The discussion is not in the first place directed to what we or others might say or think of these agents (though it has implications for that), but on what they can coherently think about themselves" (*ibid.*: 27). This important point, however, has not always been acknowledged or appreciated by Williams's readers.

Under the entry for "Gauguin problem" in his excellent *Oxford Dictionary of Philosophy*, Simon Blackburn writes: "Williams uses the painter Gauguin as a symbol of someone behaving rather badly (at least to his family) for the sake of art, and who is justified in the event by the successes he has achieved in that sphere" (Blackburn 1996: 153). But this is seriously ambiguous (not that Blackburn himself need be confused): justified to whom? At no point does Williams suggest that the *ex post facto* validation of Gauguin's decision as rational necessarily justifies that decision to others, least of all to his abandoned family. In fact, from the outset he is quite explicit on this point:

> One should be warned ... that, even if Gauguin can be ultimately justified, that need not provide him with any way of justifying himself to others. Thus he may have no way of bringing it about that those who suffer from his decision will have no justified ground of reproach. Even if he succeeds, he will not acquire a right that they accept what he has to say; if he fails he will not even have anything to say. (Williams 1981e: 23–4)

Clearly, then, the issue most basically concerns the possibility of self-justification in terms of the success or failure of the sorts of identity-conferring ground projects Williams first introduced in "A Critique of Utilitarianism". In cases like Gauguin's,

> The project in the interests of which the decision is made is one with which the agent is identified in such a way that if it succeeds

> his standpoint of assessment will be from a life which then derives an important part of its significance for him from that very fact; if it fails, it can, necessarily, have no such significance in his life. ... If he fails, his standpoint will be of one for whom the ground project of the decision has proved worthless. (*Ibid.*: 35)

Thus, for Williams, Gauguin's ground project, the realization of his artistic talent, amounts to no less than, as noted earlier in connection with integrity, "a condition of his having any interest in being around in [the] world at all".

Gauguin deliberates, at some point deciding that his project requires hm to abandon his family. What "Moral Luck" so provocatively argues, against standard interpretations of rational agency, is that whether or not this constitutes a rational decision on Gauguin's part admits of no definite answer at that time, depending as it does on luck, in the form of artistic success, something for which no guarantee then exists. The anti-Kantian thrust here is unmistakable. In *Ethics and the Limits of Philosophy*, Williams states that "Kant's approach can perhaps best be summarized by saying that he gives an account of morality and an account of practical reason, and takes them to arrive at the same place" (Williams 1985: 210n1). It is not that much of a stretch to suggest that Williams's approach may be summarized by saying that his accounts of morality and practical reason can end up arriving at very different places, and "Moral Luck" reinforces this suggestion on a number of different levels. But if such lucky justification truly fails to indemnify Gauguin from recrimination, if his wife remains perfectly justified in considering him a bastard, it seems that Williams's discussion effectively excludes not only circumstantial luck, external luck and incident luck, but moral luck as well.

Nagel was first to make this compelling point: "My disagreement with Williams is that his account fails to explain why such retrospective attitudes can be called moral. If success does not permit Gauguin to justify himself to others, but still determines his most basic feelings, that shows only that his most basic feelings need not be moral. It does not show that morality is subject to luck" (Nagel 1979b: 28n3). Nagel's point may seem vaguely reminiscent of Herman's repeated contention that any philosophical weight attaching to Williams's insistence on the importance of integrity, emotions and personal commitments to our understanding of ethical life proves insufficient to counterbalance the patent unconditionality and overridingness of (Kantian) morality.

In any case, Herman makes virtually the same point in connection with "Moral Luck":

> As Gauguin took success in painting to be the project of his life, the achievement of success gives his life its deepest significance to him, and so constitutes the only standpoint from which he can assess previous choices. But ... [t]he Kantian need not deny the possibility of deeply satisfying lives that have been built on morally impermissible actions. Likewise, he need not deny that in altering his hierarchy of values, Gauguin put his action beyond the reach of moral criticism. What the Kantian must hold is that, despite all of this, it is possible that Gauguin was wrong in acting as he did. (Herman 1993a: 41)

It may in fact be an exceedingly tricky question, certainly one beyond the scope of this discussion, whether, as Herman suggests, Kant need not deny the possibility of deeply satisfying yet immoral lives. More to the point, regardless of what Kant would do, Williams does actually trumpet Gauguin's open-ended exposure to moral criticism, irrespective of his success as an artist. As such, Nagel and Herman do seem warranted in disputing the employment of the term "moral" in connection with Gauguin's luck, something Williams appears at least implicitly to concede in his "Postscript", where the emphasis (and terminology) has pretty clearly shifted from moral to rational justification. But Herman's response also serves to turn attention away from the issue of retrospective justification towards another of Williams's three avowed themes in "Moral Luck", namely the division between the ethical and everything else. Before we conclude this section with some remarks on this division, however, something needs to be said, if only very briefly, about Nagel's reference to the determination of "basic feelings" in the passage quoted above.

Chapter 3 discussed Williams's lament that utilitarianism makes tragedy impossible by providing a theoretical basis for the elimination of one of two competing moral claims, thus eliminating the occasion for regret. Perhaps not surprisingly, Williams believes Kantianism makes tragedy impossible as well. Again the focus is on regret. According to Kant, the rightness or wrongness of actions reflects the quality of the agent's will, as read off the agent's intentions. Blame attaches to intentional action, while a feeling of regret accompanies blame. For Kant, then, it can only make sense, it can only be rational, to blame oneself for, or to regret, actions done intentionally from a bad motive. This, Williams thinks, is part of the general Kantian strategy of safeguarding the purity of morality from pollution by luck. Of course, pollution frequently dominates tragedy, as does luck, as does regret, and so "Moral Luck" paves the way for tragedy by insisting that "The sentiment of agent-regret is by no means restricted to *voluntary* agency. It can extend far beyond what one intentionally did to almost anything for which one was causally responsible in virtue of something one intentionally did" (Williams 1981e: 27–8). There may perhaps be some irony in the fact that, while Williams strongly opposes the morality system's overemphasis on (self-) blame as the sole reaction to failed obligations, he effectively chastises that same system for restricting its scope. Nonetheless, according to Williams, agents may well have cause to regret actions whose ill consequences, the result of ill luck, mock the purity of their original intentions.

Remember the unfortunate lorry driver who accidentally runs over and kills a child. Did he intend the child's death? Of course not. Did he cause it? Of course. Should he feel regret? No, says the Kantian. Quite possibly, says Williams (see Wolf 2004 for valuable discussion). The point is, as with Gauguin earlier, that the focus is on events in which the very identities of agents are at stake, with Williams firmly rejecting any possibility "that we might, if we conducted ourselves clear-headedly enough, entirely detach ourselves from the unintentional aspects of our actions ... and yet still retain our identity and character as agents" (Williams 1981e: 29). As he puts it in a particularly striking image: "One's history as an agent is a web in which anything that is the product of the will is surrounded and held up and partly formed by things that are not ... if one attaches importance to the sense of what one is in terms of what one has done and what in the world one is responsible for, one must accept much that makes its claim in that sense solely in virtue of its being actual" (*ibid.*: 29–30). Williams directly ties recognizing the influence and importance of the "actual" to (ancient Greek) tragedy: "When Oedipus says 'I did not do it' he speaks as one whose exile and blindness proclaim that he did do it" (*ibid.*: 30n2). Williams asks whether we would want "a concept of agency by which what Oedipus said would be simply true, and by which he would be seeing things rightly if for him it was straight off as if he had no part in it?" (*ibid.*). Clearly he thinks not. To the extent that Oedipus's character has been formed by the adverse consequences of well intentioned actions, to the extent that Oedipus is who he is because of those actions, regret for them becomes appropriate, lest he sacrifice his identity by distancing himself from the cause of his misfortune in his own actions.

It is unclear just how great a following Williams's views here, indeed, his views on most aspects of moral luck, have attracted. While an extended consideration of tragedy must be postponed until Chapter 7, it may be useful at this point to cite Rüdiger Bittner's rather acerbic retort that Williams's "far reaching and doubtful thesis" concerning Oedipus's culpability and his warrant for subsequent feelings of regret "is just to frighten the children" (Bittner 1992: 266). Bittner continues by helpfully summarizing Williams's position:

> [Williams's] reasoning is: not to regret the unintended consequences of actions is to detach oneself from them, but in detaching oneself from them one fails to retain one's identity and character as an agent. The reasoning should apply with all the more force to the core area of action, intentional action, which is what is under discussion here. Not to regret what one did, Williams is saying, is to detach oneself from one's actions, but that is to lose one's identity and character as an agent. (*Ibid*.: 268)

Bittner goes on to question the coherence of this picture, particularly the alleged severity and hardship of detachment, understood as a penalty for lack of regret, a lack Williams apparently sees as akin to bad faith. Without following Bittner any further, however, one can surely appreciate the similarity between the tenor of his response on agency and intentionality and Nagel's previously quoted dismissal of Williams's complaint about Kantian detachment and impartiality as "a claim few people could make without bluffing". It is, after all, one thing to argue that a host of incommensurable values form legitimate points around which to form flourishing and personally fulfilling, in a word meaningful, identities, but quite another to argue that this evident quantity of values somehow moots consideration of their quality, or, more extremely, that sacrificing one's project in the face of some clear moral demand need invite literal disintegration. And this Williams certainly does argue.

Again and again, Williams resists any suggestion that deliberative inputs and outputs merit deference, motivational or otherwise, simply in virtue of possessing or reflecting moral character or content. Echoing his earlier concern "about what the distinction between the 'moral' and the 'non-moral' is supposed to do for us" (Williams 1993a: xiii), Williams's "Postscript" refers to "a question that ... still ... needs to be pressed: what is the point of insisting that a certain reaction or attitude or judgment is or is not a *moral* one? What is it that the category is supposed to deliver?" (Williams 1995e: 244). Of course, one of

Williams's principal goals in "Moral Luck" is to undermine such deference by soliciting agreement that "while we are sometimes guided by the notion that it would be the best of worlds in which morality were universally respected and all men were of a disposition to affirm it, we have in fact deep and persistent reasons to be grateful that this is not the world we have" (Williams 1981e: 23). The world has Gauguin's Tahitian paintings, is glad to have them and would not have them had not Gauguin renounced his family obligations. Must one conclude, then, that Gauguin was moral? No, not at all, but one must, Williams thinks, if being honest, conclude that morality represents a value that need not always be required to win, and that the world is somehow better off for that fact.

Perhaps not surprisingly, this last point has been disputed by, among others, Herman:

> [Williams's] argument involves a confusion. Given that Gauguin's paintings exist, that they are objects in our world, we value and enjoy them. It does not follow from this that we are committed to valuing whatever led to their production. Nor even that we have to think that a world with Gauguin's paintings is preferable to one without them. While valuing the work, it would not be irrational to judge that the moral cost of the paintings had been too high.
>
> (Herman 1993a: 40–1)

It is true that it would not be irrational. But Williams can concede that one might judge the cost too high in Gauguin's case simply by allowing a plurality of values and pointing to perennial disagreement as to their ranking. In fact, however, Williams does think Gauguin's paintings worth the cost and seems clearly to expect his readers, at least for the most part, to concur. One prominent moral of moral luck, then, in addition to the idea that assessments of rational deliberation and action can be held hostage by later events, involves a general deflation of the category of the moral, a deflation whose precise nature may become clearer in connection with Williams's overall views on practical reason, the subject of Chapter 5.

Conclusion

One might well view this chapter's preceding sections as confirming the not uncommon impression that Williams tends to advance or defend what might be characterized as negative philosophical positions, in this case anti-theory and anti-morality. On top of that, this book's preceding chapters might suggest a tendency, perhaps even a trend, towards the negative portrayal of philosophical personages, whether Locke on personal identity, Mill on utilitarianism or Kant on the morality system, not to mention more contemporary theorists; for example, Parfit, Smart and Nagel. But Williams's views can also, without much effort, be construed far more positively, at least in the sense that they may be said to recall certain philosophical positions of the past (with the proviso, of course, that these themselves may quite possibly be "negative"). To take an example from the previous section, it seems reasonable to compare Williams's willingness to promote aesthetic value at the expense of morality with similar moves by Nietzsche. Now, it may be no secret that Williams's views owe something to Nietzsche; just how much, and in what ways, will concern much of Chapter 7. But it is perhaps not quite so obvious how much of Williams's argument against the morality system might have been portrayed, positively, as it were, as a restatement of, and elaboration on, themes from Hegel.

What, again, are the bugbears, as Williams sees them, of Kantianism and the morality system? Certainly they include impartiality to the point of abstraction and an enervating ubiquity and overridingness ("morality must win"). Without committing to (indeed, scrupulously avoiding) any extensive analysis of Hegel's texts (but see Wood 1990: Chapter 5), it is still possible to see in Williams's two criticisms of the morality system at least shadows of Hegel's own notorious "formalism" and "rigorism" charges against Kant. According to the former charge, Kant's categorical imperative amounts to little more than a purely formal constraint on inconsistency, rather than a mechanism for substantively vetting maxims on moral grounds: agents purchase universality at the price of emptiness. In Hegel's own words: "However essential it may be to emphasize the pure and unconditional self-determination of the will as the root of duty ... [for Kant] to cling on to a merely moral point of view without making the transition to the concept of ethics reduces this gain to an *empty formalism*, and moral science to an empty rhetoric of *duty for duty's sake*" (Hegel 1991: 162). While Williams's focus may seem somewhat broader, we have seen him repeatedly exercised over the parallel issue of whether the Kantian move towards impartiality, effected through the formulation and "testing" of maxims, allows for the retention of enough personal particularity to produce meaningful results for particular persons. Williams, moreover, explicitly endorses Hegel's first charge: "the purest Kantian view locates the importance of morality in the importance of moral motivation itself. ... This view was relentlessly and correctly attacked by Hegel, on the grounds that it gave moral thought no content" (Williams 1985: 184).

According to Hegel's second charge, Kant's insistence on universality and the rational purity of the agent's will as marks of moral worth makes for too rigorous a view, blinding him to the importance of other salient considerations affecting the rightness of action, particularly an action's context and consequences. (Kant's well known views on lying often come up in this regard, characterized – or caricatured – as they are by inflexibility.) While sharing Hegel's concern here, Williams would no doubt also emphasize another crucial casualty of Kantian rigor: the agent's character. As deep dispositions capitulate to morality's nearly insatiable demands, so too do so many potential grounds for meaningful identities. Effectively running together both of Hegel's (and his own) criticisms, Williams observes that morality "in its more Kantian forms ... is governed by a dream of a community of reason that is too far removed, as Hegel first said it was, from social and historical reality, and from any concrete sense of a particular ethical life" (*ibid.*: 197). Finally, Williams especially applauds Hegel's setting of the problem, in so far as he "asks how a concretely experienced form of life can be extended, rather than considering how a universal program is to be applied" (*ibid.*: 104). That emphasis on concrete particularity, embodied for Hegel in *Sittlichkeit*, Williams similarly consecrates in his own conception of ethics.

To be clear, the comparison between Williams's critique of the Kantian morality system and Hegel's critique of the emptiness and procedural rigour of Kantian morality as universal law is meant to be modest, merely suggestive. For one thing, such a comparison once again raises the issue, never very far in the background, of the accuracy and fairness with which Williams (or Hegel, for that matter) portrays Kant. As Robert Pippin writes, with Williams's critique specifically in mind,

> Kant's moral theory is by no means exhausted by his attempt to formulate the practical law binding on all agents, and by his argument that moral worth, goodness, can only be attributed to acts done from duty alone. ... This means that his moral theory is misrepresented if it is portrayed as primarily concerned with a limiting condition in our pursuit of material ends, or portrayed so negatively. There are things we must do, positively, if we are fully to discharge our duty; there are duties of virtue, not just of right;

> and this should prompt some reconsideration of Hegel's criticism and the Hegelian alternative so deeply motivated by that criticism.
> (Pippin 1997a: 114)

Of course it goes without saying that if we owe thanks to Pippin and Herman and so many others for providing us of late with richer, more philosophically satisfying pictures of Kantian ethics, we frequently owe thanks to Williams for their inspiration.

A less modest point stresses the error in taking Williams to reject the entire history of moral philosophy as merely one mistaken view after another. Indeed, the sympathy with Hegel just shown pales in comparison with Williams's affinity to Aristotle, featured in Chapter 7, while his relationship to Nietzsche, especially in his later years, arguably approaches identification. Aristotle, Hegel, Nietzsche, certainly these three offer, in Williams's view, admirable resources for conceptualizing ethics without recourse to the more philosophically stultifying features of the morality system. To simplify grossly, Williams welcomes Aristotle's emphasis on ethics as a function of dispositions, Hegel's emphasis on ethics as culturally embedded and Nietzsche's emphasis on ethics as a reflection of contingent values. There is, however, one past philosopher of considerable prominence whose views have arguably exerted at least as much influence on Williams's thought as those of the three thinkers just mentioned. That philosopher is David Hume. Remember Williams's pithy observation that Kant takes his accounts of morality and practical reason to arrive at the same place. In other words, precisely the way in which Kant conceptually fuses rational action and moral action results in his privileging of the moral. By contrast, Williams effectively privileges his account of practical reason, to which he gives, as we will see in Chapter 5, a distinctively Humean spin. If morality can find a home in that account, so much the better; if it cannot, so much the worse for morality.

Chapter 5

Practical reason

Introduction

It seems hard to believe that Williams's "Internal and External Reasons" was ever "insufficiently discussed" (McDowell 1995: 68). Indeed, this "agenda-setting" paper, as Elijah Millgram (1996: 197) rightly calls it, lays fair claim to having elicited more responses, by more distinguished philosophers, than any other article or book by Williams in his long and illustrious publishing career. Why this should be so is the subject of this chapter.

"Internal and External Reasons" presents Williams's account of practical reasoning, or, more specifically, his account of reasons for action, or, more specifically still, his account of statements about reasons for action. As Williams puts the issue in "Internal Reasons and the Obscurity of Blame", the first of three follow-up attempts to clarify his initial discussion: "What are the truth conditions for statements of the form 'A has a reason to ϕ', where A is a person and 'ϕ' is some verb of action? What are we saying when we say someone has a reason to do something?" (Williams 1995c: 35). Williams's most recent, as well as his preferred, answer to these questions takes the following form: "A has a reason to ϕ only if there is a *sound deliberative route* from A's subjective motivational set ... to A's ϕ-ing" (Williams 2001: 91). This answer goes to the heart of Williams's internalism about reasons for action; that is, it captures the connection Williams deems necessary between an agent's reason to ϕ and a "motive which will be served or furthered by his ϕ-ing"

(Williams 1981b: 101). By contrast, external reasons statements fail to connect up with an agent's extant motivations and, "when definitely isolated as such, are false, or incoherent, or really something else misleadingly expressed"; in a word, "bluff" (*ibid.*: 111). For Williams, "there are only internal reasons for action" (Williams 1995c: 35).

Although Williams treats this issue quite generally, so that his analysis of how best to characterize reason statements applies equally well to, say, reasons to go surfing or to get married or to eat Thai food, clearly the stakes increase, and the implications of Williams's approach appear, at least to many philosophers, more worrisome, when the actions to which reason statements would apply are ethical in nature. Putting this worry most simply, if the truth of any statement concerning reasons for action necessarily depends on the agent to whom it applies possessing some particular motivation, but at the same time nothing guarantees that the agent will in fact be so motivated, then ethical reasons (reasons, say, to keep a promise or to refrain from harming someone) may seem to be contingent, local, subjective or otherwise lacking in the sort of qualities that many philosophers believe render them *sui generis* and grant them force; for example, necessity, universality or objectivity. In other words, Williams's account of action and its attendant deliberations covers *all* actions. Ethical reasoning, then, becomes an unremarkable instance of the only sort of practical reasoning there is, and so must ultimately involve internal reasons; moreover, this seems to leave perhaps the dominant conception of ethics held hostage to Williams's attack on the possibility of external reasons. (Once again one hears echoes of Williams's concern with "what the distinction between the 'moral' and the 'non-moral' is supposed to do for us" (Williams 1993a: xiii).)

This chapter discusses Williams's case for internalism about reasons for action as presented in "Internal and External Reasons" and subsequent papers. To help to clarify that case, it also discusses three significant responses to Williams's views by three well known philosophers. In "Skepticism about Practical Reason", Korsgaard (1996c) in effect asks Williams whether his account might be able to accommodate Kantian principles of pure practical reason. In "Might there Be External Reasons?", McDowell (1995) in effect asks Williams whether reasons for action must be the product of rational deliberation. And in an appendix to *What We Owe to Each Other*, T. M. Scanlon (1998) in effect asks Williams whether his position fully appreciates the universality that necessarily attaches to reason statements. Not only do these three responses merit consideration independently, owing to their quality and force, but that quality and (to some degree) that force have been recognized by Williams himself, in brief allusions to Korsgaard (see Williams 1995c: 44; 1995e: 220; 2001: 97) and Scanlon (see Williams 2001: 95–6), and in a detailed reply to McDowell (see Williams 1995h: 186–94). Broadening the discussion to include these responses will serve to highlight key issues, while probing certain perceived vulnerabilities, in Williams's important and influential account of practical reasoning.

Internal reasons

As we have seen, Williams believes that statements such as "*A* has a reason to ϕ" or "There is a reason for *A* to ϕ" may be subjected to either of two interpretations, introduced in "Internal and External Reasons" as follows:

> On the first, the truth of the sentence implies, very roughly, that *A* has some motive, which will be served or furthered by his ϕ-ing, and if this turns out not to be so the sentence is false: there is a condition relating to the agent's aims and if this is not satisfied it is not true to say, on this interpretation, that he has a reason to ϕ. On the second interpretation, there is no such condition, and the reason-sentence will not be falsified by the absence of the appropriate motive. I shall call the first the "internal", and the second the "external", interpretation. (Williams 1981b: 101)

While no one disputes that both internal and external *statements* about reasons for actions find wide employment, Williams questions, and here is the focus of the paper, whether both internal and external reasons *themselves* actually exist, or whether, despite the prevalence of external reason statements, the only bona fide reasons for action are internal. His strategy involves: first, setting out a bare-bones model for internal reason statements; secondly, expanding this model by clarifying and refining a number of its implications; and, thirdly, advancing two related arguments designed to rule out the possibility of external reasons.

Williams calls his bare-bones model "sub-Humean", formulating it originally as follows:

> *A* has a reason to ϕ iff *A* has some desire the satisfaction of which will be served by his ϕ-ing. (Williams 1981b: 101)

The model is Humean in as much as it forges and relies on a link between possessing a reason for action and possessing a desire, recalling Hume's famous insistence that "reason alone can never produce any action, or give rise to volition" (Hume 1978: 414); however, it is *sub*-Humean in as much as it lacks many of Hume's own bells and whistles, most notably any explicit role for natural sentiment. Just as it stands, however, "The sub-Humean model is certainly too simple", and Williams's "aim will be, by addition and revision, to work it up into something more adequate" (Williams 1981b: 102). These additions and revisions take the form of four propositions that together fine-tune the connection between internal reasons statements and that to which they "must display a relativity", namely "the agent's *subjective motivational set*", or, as Williams abbreviates it, *S* (*ibid.*). In doing so they spotlight the roles reasons play as both explanations and norms.

The first qualification of the sub-Humean model states:

> (i) An internal reason statement is falsified by the absence of some appropriate element from *S*. (*Ibid.*)

On the one hand, Williams wants to establish a necessary connection between elements of an agent's subjective motivational set and the truthful ascription to that agent of reasons to act. (Actually, Williams believes that the agent's possession of such motivating elements is sufficient for the truth of reason statements, although he has consistently restricted his attention to making good only the claim of necessity (see Williams 1995c: 35).) On the other hand, Williams wants to rule out the possibility that just any element of *S* will justify the attribution of a reason. In particular, he wants to undercut the reason-generating power of motivational elements resting on false belief, illustrating his concerns with the now classic gin/petrol example:

> The agent believes that this stuff is gin, when in fact it is petrol. He wants a gin and tonic. Has he reason, or a reason, to mix this stuff with tonic and drink it? ... On the one hand, it is very odd to say that he has a reason to drink this stuff, and natural to say that he has no reason to drink it, although he thinks that he has. On the other hand, if he does drink it, we not only have an explanation of his doing so (a reason why he did it), but we have such an explanation which is of the reason-for-action form.
> (Williams 1981b: 102)

How should this situation be analysed?

Williams takes seriously the explanatory feature of reasons for action and so takes seriously the second alternative above, that the agent might, in virtue of possessing a reason *why* he drank petrol and tonic (if he did), also have had a reason *to* drink petrol and tonic in the first place, albeit a reason resting on a mistaken belief that the petrol is gin. Certainly reasons do form explanations. As Williams puts it in a key passage, "If there are reasons for action, it must be that people sometimes act for those reasons, and if they do, their reasons must figure in some correct explanation of their action" (Williams 1981b: 102). In this case, if the agent does mix petrol with tonic and drink it, a perfectly straightforward explanation for these actions presents itself; nevertheless, although reasons may invariably beget explanations, Williams balks at the converse. Acknowledging that "The difference between false and true beliefs cannot alter the *form* of the explanation which will be appropriate to his action", Williams nonetheless claims that attributing a reason to the petrol drinker ultimately "looks in the wrong direction, by implying in effect that the internal reason conception is only concerned with explanation, and not at all with the agent's rationality" (*ibid.*: 102–3). While the ability to explain an agent's taking a gulp of petrol and tonic may initially seem to warrant ascribing to that agent a reason to take a gulp of petrol and tonic, in the end Williams believes that other considerations must prevail.

In "Internal and External Reasons", Williams suggests that in as much as "the internal reasons conception is concerned with the agent's rationality" we need to add a second qualification to the sub-Humean model along the following lines:

> (ii) A member of *S*, *D*, will not give *A* a reason for ϕ-ing if either the existence of *D* is dependent on a false belief, or *A*'s belief in the relevance of ϕ-ing to the satisfaction of *D* is false.
>
> (*Ibid.*: 103)

So, to go back to Williams's example, a member of *S*, the desire to drink from the bottle at hand, will not give *A* a reason for mixing the contents of the bottle with tonic and drinking it, since the desire to drink the bottle's contents is based on a false belief. Alternatively, a member of *S*, a desire to drink gin and tonic, will not give *A* a reason for mixing the contents of the bottle with tonic and drinking it, since *A*'s belief in the relevance of mixing the bottle's contents with tonic and drinking it to the satisfaction of the desire to drink a gin and tonic is false. "The claim that somebody can get to the conclusion that he should ϕ (or, the conclusion to ϕ) by a sound deliberative route involves", says Williams, "at least correcting any errors of fact and reasoning involved in the agent's view of the matter" (Williams 1995c: 36). But by explicitly linking rationality with the elimination of false belief, Williams may seem to confuse the issue.

At one point in his discussion, Williams allows the following: "It will, all the same, be true that if he does ϕ in these circumstances, there was not only a reason why he ϕ-ed, but also that that displays him as relative to his false belief, acting rationally" (Williams 1981b: 103). If an agent drinks petrol and tonic owing to a false belief that the petrol is gin, then the agent indeed acts rationally relative to his false belief; that is, one might say, he adopts appropriate means, mixing what he takes to be gin and tonic together and drinking it, to achieve his end, having a gin and tonic. Moreover, there is also the sense in which the agent may be said to possess a reason. But note from previous discussion that any such reason will be merely explanatory in nature, a reason why he acted as he did, why he drank the stuff, since Williams deems the capacity to explain an action, all by itself, insufficient to justify the attribution of a reason to act, claiming that the presence of an explanation may be insufficient to guarantee an agent's rationality. It is for this reason that he apparently stipulates that elements of *S* cannot generate reasons if based on false beliefs. But, and here arises the possible confusion, rationality and reasons are not the same thing; for, as Williams's allowance above clearly indicates, rationality need not be at odds with false belief.

If Williams wants to distinguish reasons *why* from reasons *to*, or explanatory reasons from, as we might call them, justificatory reasons, he can certainly do so, by requiring, as in his second modification to the sub-Humean model above, that reasons of the latter sort be purged of false belief. But he misleads if he equates this concern for eliminating false belief with a concern for ensuring an agent's rationality. Whether an agent has a reason to act is one thing; whether an agent acts rationally is another. This point appears to be at least tacitly acknowledged in Williams's shift in emphasis over the years from rationality to sound deliberation. Just as sound arguments feature both validity and true premises, sound deliberation features both rationality and true beliefs. Williams's second qualification to the sub-Humean model of internal reasons, then, may be best understood as highlighting an important connection, not as much between true belief and rationality as between true belief and sound deliberation.

Williams's third addendum to the sub-Humean model consists of the following two-part "epistemic consequence", drawn from his discussion of the gin/petrol case:

> (iii) (a) *A* may falsely believe an internal reason statement about himself, and (we can add) (b) *A* may not know some true internal reason statement about himself. (Williams 1981b: 103)

The first of these consequences appears straightforward and well illustrated by the agent falsely believing he has a reason to drink petrol, but Williams urges caution in gauging the second sort of consequence, where, but for the cognizance of some fact or other, the agent would have reason to act in a certain way, emphasizing that "the relevance of the unknown fact to his actions has to be fairly close and immediate; otherwise one merely says that *A* would have a reason to ϕ if he knew that fact" (*ibid.*). As to how best to discriminate between these two cases, between the actual and the counterfactual, Williams suggests only, and perhaps not all that helpfully, that the decision "must be closely connected with the question of when the ignorance forms part of the explanation of what *A* actually does" (*ibid.*). Williams further cautions, now concerned with the possibility of unconscious motivation, that elements of *S* must be rationally related to the actions they engender if we are to allow that such actions are performed for a reason. Here we do find a legitimate link between reasons and rationality, for, of course, one classic conception of rationality boils down to the capacity to provide reasons justifying our belief or behaviour on demand, something that unconscious motivational elements might well prevent.

Finally, Williams introduces a fourth qualification to the claim that reasons must be relativized to an agent's subjective motivational set:

> (iv) internal reasons statements can be discovered in deliberative reasoning. (*Ibid.*: 104)

With this qualification Williams moves still further from the Humeanism of the sub-Humean model and from what he sees as its narrow instrumentalism. Now, the issue of just how best to understand instrumentalism about practical reason can be controversial (see Vogler 2002: 11–15), as can, for that matter, the question of whether Hume's *Treatise*, with its famous admonition that "Reason is, and ought only to be the slave of the passions" (Hume 1978: 415), should be regarded as instrumentalism's *locus classicus* (see Millgram 1995; Korsgaard 1997). In a general sense, however, instrumentalism involves bringing means–ends reasoning to bear on decisions about how to act. As Millgram defines it,

> Instrumentalism is the view that all practical reasoning is means–end reasoning. It says that there are various things you want, and the point of practical reasoning is to figure out how to get them. Instrumentalism is an exclusionist view: if it is right, then while you can think about how to get what you want, you can't think about what you want in the first place. (Millgram 1997: 2)

It is not hard to see, then, why some ethicists – and certainly all moralists – might wish to distance themselves from instrumentalism. With reason's role confined to determining efficient means to antecedently given ends, no platform exists for the rational critique of ends themselves, no straightforward way to rationally adjudicate between competing ends, and thus anything may seem permitted.

Although "The sub-Humean model supposes that ϕ-ing has to be related to some element in *S* as causal means to end", for Williams "this is only one case" (Williams 1981b: 104); a sound deliberative route between an agent's subjective motivations and action "does not merely involve perceiving means to an end that has already been formulated" (Williams 1995c: 38). Clearly concerned to escape instrumentalist constraints, Williams urges a more expansive view of the forms practical reasoning or sound deliberation may take: "A clear example of practical reasoning is that leading to the conclusion that one has reason to ϕ because ϕ-ing would be the most convenient, economical, pleasant, etc. way of satisfying some element of *S*. . . . But there are much wider possibilities for deliberation" (Williams 1981b: 104). Such possibilities include: breaking deliberative log-jams through time-ordering or weighting various options; coming up with altogether new courses of action by considering or imagining alternatives; and "finding constitutive solutions" (*ibid.*), by which Williams means "finding a specific form for a project that has been adopted in unspecific terms" (Williams 1995c: 38), such as "deciding what would make for an entertaining evening, granted that one wants entertainment" (Williams 1981b: 104). Reflecting, inventing, comparing, these are just some of the deliberative processes, acting on and through elements of an agent's *S*, that Williams believes can both generate new and undermine old reasons for action.

Obviously what counts as sound deliberation, and so what justifies reasons in the internalist view, may make for a fairly messy business, but we should expect no less:

> Since there are many ways of deliberative thinking, it is not fully determinate in general, even for a given agent at a given time, what may count as "a sound deliberative route"; and from this it follows that the question of what the agent has a reason to do is itself not fully determinate. It is often held against this combination of the internalist view with this broad conception of deliberation that it leaves us with a vague concept of what an agent has a reason to do. But this is not a disadvantage of the position. It *is* often vague what one has a reason to do. (Williams 1995c: 38)

This issue of vagueness will come up again at the conclusion of the chapter. For now, Williams champions not only, as he says, "a broad conception of deliberation", but also a broad conception of an agent's subjective motivational set.

Taking off from what he sees as essential interaction between deliberation and motivation, Williams urges readers not to

> think of *S* as statically given. The process of deliberation can have all sorts of effects on *S*, and this is a fact which a theory of internal reasons should be very happy to accommodate. So also it should be more liberal than some theorists have been about possible elements of *S*. I have discussed *S* primarily in terms of desires, and this term can be used, formally, for all elements in *S*. But this terminology may make one forget that *S* can contain such things as dispositions of evaluation, patterns of emotional reaction, personal loyalties, and various projects, as they may abstractly be called, embodying commitments of the agent.
> (Williams 1981b: 105)

Without question, by adding to the motivational mix such things as virtues and vices, emotional entanglements and personal values and aspirations, and by stirring that mix with deliberation-cum-imagination, Williams winds up with a far more sophisticated, no doubt far truer to life model of practical reasoning than narrow instrumentalism. Nevertheless, just how far this admittedly expanded model goes towards addressing concerns, previously noted, about the lack of any mechanism for critiquing the ends of action remains a bit unclear.

There are actually two overlapping worries here: first, that the ends of action are immune from rational critique; second, that the attachments and commitments that Williams makes room for in the agent's

S are immune from rational critique. These worries overlap, of course, because the ends of action on the internal reasons model must necessarily be related to elements of the agent's *S*, but given Williams's claim that deliberation can both add and subtract elements in *S*, they seem to resist collapsing into one another. Again, these worries get their point from the possibility that either the ends or that which motivates them may be immoral.

Now, Williams himself, no doubt sensitive to this perceived vulnerability of the internal reasons model to immoral influence, goes out of his way to make clear that "there is of course no supposition that the desires or projects of an agent have to be egoistic; he will, one hopes, have non-egoistic projects of various kinds, and these equally can provide internal reasons for action" (Williams 1981b: 105). Still, hoping may not be good enough for some, especially those philosophers who would effectively guarantee moral action by, say, making moral reasoning either a criterion or a component of sound reasoning itself, a move Williams both anticipates and resists:

> But if we are licensed to vary the agent's reasoning and assumptions of fact, it will be asked why we should not vary (for instance, insert) prudential and moral considerations as well. . . . The internalist proposal sticks with its Humean origins to the extent of making correction of fact and reasoning part of the notion of "a sound deliberative route to this act" but not, from outside, prudential and moral considerations. (Williams 1995c: 36–7)

More recently:

> We cannot simply assume that moral considerations, for instance, or long-term prudential concerns must figure in every agent's *S*. For many agents, as we well know, they indeed do so, if not altogether securely; but a philosophical claim that they are necessarily part of rational agency needs argument. (Williams 2001: 92)

Actually, it might be fairer to say that Williams does not as much anticipate this move as respond to Korsgaard's attempt to make room for it, as will be seen below when we discuss her response to "Internal and External Reasons".

So, in Williams's view, the ethical significance of elements in an agent's *S* should not be pre-judged. It may well include, probably will include, a host of ethical dispositions and tendencies towards right conduct, but not necessarily. What is necessary is simply some connection between having a reason to act and a sound deliberative route from elements in an agent's *S*. Williams sees himself improving on the sub-Humean model by liberalizing both what counts as motivation and what counts as deliberation, and in doing so he garners quite a few favourable reactions, such as this one by McDowell: "It is a strength of Williams' argument that he bases it on a subtle and flexible conception of the materials available to the internal interpretation" (McDowell 1995: 68). But, again, has such liberalization really reduced Williams's debt to instrumentalism?

In a discussion of these issues, Candace Vogler argues that Williams is not "strictly" an instrumentalist, for he

> can hold that there may be things in one's character that lead one to forgo short-term gain, private advantage, rewards – in short, opportunities to fare well in the short run – for the sake of acting well in the sense of doing as it ethically or prudentially befits one to do, and that these items do not have the characteristics of the instrumentalist's preferences or desires. For Williams, this happens when one's subjective motivational set contains elements that side with one's long-term private interests or with ethics.
> (Vogler 2002: 190)

Now it is true, as has been shown, that Williams eschews a mode of practical reasoning, *à la* Hume, in which each action bottoms out in the satisfaction of an occurrent passion or desire, and instead develops a more complex model involving a host of deliberative processes ranging over temporally extended projects and commitments, internalized dispositions of character, perhaps even deliberative principles themselves, many of which may be patently ethical. Nevertheless, there may still be some worry that, for Williams, deliberation (no matter how expansively construed) ultimately involves determining the best means to the satisfaction of ends set by elements in *S* (no matter how expansively construed), so that the plausibility of the internal reasons interpretation may not be completely independent of the plausibility of instrumentalism about practical reason (see Millgram 1996: 209–13).

Two arguments against external reasons

In transforming the sub-Humean into the internal reasons model of practical reasoning, Williams, as noted above, believes that reasons must both explain why an action was performed and reflect certain deliberative norms; for example, that deliberation leading to action should avoid inference from false belief. These two features of reasons retain leading roles when Williams comes to argue explicitly against the possibility of external reasons. Unlike the internalist view about reasons for action, which holds that an agent possesses a reason to act just in case some sound deliberative route links the conclusion to act to the subjective motivational set of the agent, the externalist view holds "that it can be true of *A* that he has reason to ϕ even though *A* has no motivation in his motivational set that could, either directly or by some extension through sound deliberation, lead him to ϕ" (Williams 1995c: 35). In attempting to undermine the external reasons account, Williams invokes Owen Wingrave, the titular character of a Henry James short story, by way of a Benjamin Britten opera.

Williams focuses on what to make of the claim that Owen has a reason to join the army: "Owen's family urge on him the necessity and importance of joining the army, since all his male ancestors were soldiers and family pride requires him to do the same" (Williams 1981b: 106). In as much as Owen "has no motivation to join the army at all", "all his desires lead in another direction" and "he hates everything about military life and what it means", the family's claim is suspect and, more to the point, paradigmatically external (*ibid.*). For an internal reasons interpretation to be appropriate, joining the army would have to satisfy or otherwise advance some element of Owen's motivational set, something it most certainly does not do. Yet the family, presumably knowing full well that Owen possesses no motivation whatsoever to enlist, continues to press its case, and to assert that Owen does indeed have a reason to join up. "They mean it in an external sense", observes Williams, who, seeking both to understand and to mitigate the force of that sense, employs two related arguments (*ibid.*).

Williams's first argument takes off from earlier observations, in "Internal and External Reasons", regarding the explanatory capacity of reasons, reiterating that "If something can be a reason for action, then it could be someone's reason for acting on a particular occasion, and it would then figure in an explanation of that action" (*ibid.*: 106). Unfortunately for the externalist interpretation, external reasons are explanatorily impotent or, as Williams puts it, "no external reason statement could *by itself* offer an explanation of anyone's action" (*ibid.*). This impotence appears ultimately conceptual in nature, a combination of the conceptual requirements of explanation and the conceptual inability of external reason statements to meet them.

"The whole point of external reason statements", Williams argues, "is that they can be true independently of the agent's motivations. But nothing can explain an agent's (intentional) actions except something that motivates him so to act" (*ibid.*: 107). This last claim, crucial to Williams's case, has not gone unchallenged by, for example, Rachel Cohon: "This is a controversial claim whose truth is by no means obvious" (Cohon 1986: 549). Williams, however, seems to find the claim not only obvious, but uncontestable: "When the reason is an explanation of his action, then of course it will be, in some form, in his *S*, because certainly – and nobody denies this – what he actually does has to be explained by his *S*" (Williams, 1995c: 39). Moreover, Williams sees Owen's case as lending this explanation/motivation dynamic strong support. (Millgram provocatively suggests that the very uncontestability of the example ill serves a more general understanding of practical reasoning, charging that, with Owen Wingrave, Williams "picks a particularly implausible example of a would-be external reason, one of which we would be inclined to say that the agent *has* no reason, and then proceeds as if all external reasons had to be like *that*" (Millgram 1996: 205).)

McDowell neatly captures the reasoning behind Williams's initial argument against the possibility of external reason statements:

> Any reason for action must be something that *could* explain someone acting in the way for which it is a reason. If a reason did explain an action, the agent *would* have a motivation towards acting in the way in question – a motivation that the reason-giving explanation would spell out. But *ex hypothesi* an external reason statement can be true of someone without his actually having any motive that would be "served or furthered" by his doing what he is said to have a reason to do – not even one whose relevance to his doing that would need to be uncovered by deliberation.
>
> (McDowell 1995: 70)

Given that the external reason offered by his family completely fails to engage Owen's *S*, and given that any explanation of action must somehow relate to elements of an agent's *S*, an external reason for action is not only incapable of explaining action, but, in Williams's account, incapable of being a reason for action in the first place. Having dismissed external reasons on conceptual grounds – that is, based on the failure of external reasons to fulfil an important criterion of reasons for action generally – William turns, and here begins his second argument, to consider just what else might be needed, in the light of this failure, to make external reason statements efficacious.

Recall Owen Wingrave's putative reason to join the army based on considerations of family tradition and honour. Such considerations fail to engage Owen's *S*, making the statement that he has a reason to join the army patently external and, Williams believes, patently false. But suppose Owen were to end up acting for the reason advanced by his family; suppose, that is, Owen were to join the army to uphold tradition and preserve honour; for this to occur something new must be in the picture, something not present in the initial case, something that could now explain, as reasons must be capable of doing, Owen's action. Whatever this new something might be, it cannot be the truth of the external reason statement, for such truth would have attended Owen's previous recalcitrance, would have been on the scene even when Owen was unmotivated to join up. Not the truth itself, but coming to believe that truth, coming to believe that particular external reason statement, constitutes, in Williams's view, the only way Owen might acquire, simultaneously as it were, a motivation, an explanation and a reason for action.

As he says in "Internal and External Reasons", beginning with his earlier link between explanation and motivation:

> But nothing can explain an agent's (intentional) actions except something that motivates him so to act. So something else is needed besides the truth of the external reason statement to explain action, some psychological link; and that psychological link would seem to be belief. *A*'s believing an external reason statement about himself may help to explain his action.
>
> (Williams 1981b: 107)

How could such a belief come about? More to the point, how could a new motivation come about? After all, here is the real challenge for the external reasons position: "The agent does not presently believe the external statement. If he comes to believe it, he will be motivated to act; so coming to believe it must, essentially, involve acquiring a new motivation. How can that be?" (*ibid.*: 108). In formulating an answer to this question, Williams shifts his concern from explanation to deliberation.

Of paramount interest now are constraints on the way in which an agent may come to believe, and so come to be motivated by, an external reason statement. Of course, Hume, upon whose skeletal position Williams's own rests, denies reason the power "to give rise to volition", but Williams, as we have seen, appears more permissive when it comes to reason's reach. Still, the challenge remains formidable: "The basic point lies in recognizing that the external reasons theorist must conceive *in a special way* the connexion between acquiring a motivation and coming to believe the reason statement" (*ibid.*: 108). What special way? "[T]hat the agent should acquire the motivation because he comes to believe the reason statement, and that he should do the latter, moreover, because, in some way, he is considering the matter aright" (*ibid.*: 108–9). Just what might "considering the matter aright" involve? "[T]hat he should deliberate correctly; and the external reason statement itself will have to be taken as roughly equivalent to, or at least as entailing, the claim that if the agent rationally deliberated, then, whatever motivations he originally had, he would come to be motivated to ϕ" (*ibid.*: 109). "But", objects Williams, moving towards the conclusion of his second argument, "if this is correct, there does indeed seem great force in Hume's basic point, and it is very plausible to suppose that all external reasons statements are false" (*ibid.*); false, that is, because of something that a process of considering the matter aright simply cannot provide, that being, to borrow yet another apt term from Millgram, "motivational fuel" (Millgram 1996: 198).

Williams's point here seems to rest, once more, on largely conceptual grounds. Just as external reason statements earlier proved lacking, in as much as their very concept, that of reason statements bearing no relation to an agent's *S*, ruled out, in Williams's view, the explanatory capacity required to fulfil the concept of a reason for action, so they prove lacking once more, in as much as their very concept, that of reason statements, the belief in which can be acquired through correct deliberation, is ruled out by the very concept of correct deliberation itself. Although Williams is willing to grant that rational deliberation might identify some new motivation in one of the ways previously mentioned – say, by imagining or comparing constitutive solutions to some given end – that is merely to grant the identification of an internal reason. But in the case under consideration, where Owen becomes motivated to join the army because he comes to believe, through considering the matter aright, the external reasons statement presented by his family, Williams argues that the conditions for practical deliberation cannot be met:

> For, *ex hypothesi*, there is no motivation for the agent to deliberate from, to reach this new motivation. Given the agent's earlier existing motivations, and this new motivation, what has

> to hold for external reason statements to be true, on this line of interpretation, is that the new motivation could be in some way rationally arrived at, granted the earlier motivations. Yet at the same time it must not bear to the earlier motivations the kind of rational relation we considered in the earlier discussion of deliberation – for in that case an internal reason statement would have been true in the first place. (Williams 1981b: 109)

In effect, Williams offers a *reductio*. Assume the truth of an external reason statement; for example, that there is a reason for Owen to enlist in the army. Assume that Owen, not presently disposed to join up, could only acquire a motivation to do so through coming to believe in the truth of the external reason statement. And, finally, assume that Owen's coming to believe in the truth of the external reason statement, and so acquiring a new motivation, could only come about through rational deliberation, through "considering the matter aright". Now see that this is absurd, for considering the matter aright requires appropriate motivation, which, as known all along, is just what Owen lacks; and, in any case, if he had possessed such motivation, and if he had come to see that he had reason to enlist, then he would also have succeeded in satisfying Williams's model of internal, not external, reasoning.

This conceptual nature of Williams's second argument has elicited a worry, similar to one connected with his first argument, that he may end up begging an important question or questions. Whereas Cohon, for example, objects to the first argument, and to what she sees as Williams's unwarranted assumption that explanation must be cashed out in terms of motivation, Brad Hooker, for example, objects to the second, and to what he sees as Williams's unwarranted assumption that motivation must be cashed out in terms of subjectivity (see Hooker 2001). This sort of objection is considered further below, in connection with articles by Korsgaard, McDowell and Scanlon, as part of a broader examination of the norms Williams imposes on considering the matter aright; that is, as part of an examination of what, for Williams, makes correct deliberation correct. But before we turn to these important responses to Williams's arguments for internal reasons, it is worth considering what might be termed Williams's "error theory" concerning external reason statements. If one adopts Williams's position and grants that an external reason statement cannot truly provide an agent with a reason for action, then (at least) two further questions deserve attention. First, what is really going on, what error is being committed, according to Williams, when people offer external reasons to one another? Secondly, given that reasons must ultimately be validated subjectively, according to the motivational elements agents actually possess, what room remains, if any, to criticize them?

Error theory

Williams suggests that if external reason statements do not in fact provide reasons for the agent, then perhaps they are best accounted for as either implicit accusations of irrationality or tacit exhortations to internal reasoning. Regarding the first of these suggestions, Williams allows that

> There are of course many things that a speaker may say to one who is not disposed to ϕ when the speaker thinks that he should be, as that he is inconsiderate, or cruel, or selfish, or imprudent; or that things, and he, would be a lot nicer if he were so motivated. Any of these can be sensible things to say. But one who makes a great deal out of putting the criticism in the form of an external reason statement seems concerned to say that what is particularly wrong with the agent is that he is *irrational* ... in particular, because he wants any rational agent, as such, to acknowledge the requirement to do the thing in question. (Williams 1981b: 110)

Putting aside for just a moment the many "sensible things" one might say to the undisposed, certainly Williams must believe that if his modifications of the sub-Humean model and his arguments against external reasons succeed at anything, it is in warding off just this charge, that in disregarding external reason claims and acting to satisfy elements of S, agents act irrationally. Indeed, it is precisely in eliminating the grounds for this charge, by identifying practical rationality with internal reasoning, that Williams appears to some to beg the question against the external reasons interpretation.

As to his second suggestion, Williams writes "I suspect what are *taken* for external reason statements are often, in fact, optimistic internal reason statements: we launch them and hope that somewhere in the agent is some motivation that by some deliberative route might issue in the action we seek" (Williams 1995c: 40). Understood in this way – that is, understood as so many attempts to jump-start the recognition of heretofore unrecognized internal reasons – external reasons become an instrument of "prolepsis", which the *Oxford English Dictionary* defines as "the representation or taking of something future as already done or existing". Although Williams gives only "the merest sketch", external reason claims apparently operate proleptically as follows: "the claim that *A* has a reason to ϕ is not strictly true, by internalist standards, at the moment that it is made, but the very fact that it is made, can help to elicit a more general motivation from the agent's *S*" (Williams 2001: 95). What sort of motivation? In the course of exploring certain structural similarities between attributions of external reasons and attributions of blame, Williams points to "a motivation to avoid the disapproval of other people", which may manifest itself as "the ethically important disposition that consists in a desire to be respected by people whom, in turn, one respects" (Williams 1995c: 41). Apparently "this motivation together with the recognition of those people's desire or demand that he should ϕ can indeed bring it about that he (now) has a reason to ϕ" (Williams 2001: 95). A standing desire in Owen's *S* to cultivate or maintain a certain view of himself in the eyes of his family would be activated by their exhortation to join the army, and by such means succeed in underwriting the truth of their (internal) reason statement.

Williams concludes that "it is only by invoking such mechanisms that we can bridge the gap between genuinely internalist reason claims, and externalist claims which, unless they get some help in social or psychological terms, there may be no reason to see as more than bluff and brow-beating" (*ibid.*). But is there no room between external brow-beating and the faux-external generation of internal reasons? What about external reason statements as the appropriate expression of those "many sensible things" one might say to the ethically obtuse?

Williams addresses the issue of what we may justifiably say to those apparently without any motivation (and so any reason) to act ethically in the following case study:

> Suppose, for instance, I think someone ... ought to be nicer to his wife. I say, "You have a reason to be nicer to her." He says, "What reason?" I say, "Because she is your wife." He says – and he is a very hard case – "I don't care. Don't you understand? I really do not care." I try various things on him ... and I find that he really is a hard case: there is nothing in his motivational set that gives him a reason to be nicer to his wife as things are.
>
> (Williams 1995c: 39)

This specific scenario is considered at greater length below, in connection with Scanlon's reaction to Williams's position; for now, recall that Williams readily admits that one may be justified, in the face of such indifference, in chastising the husband as "ungrateful, inconsiderate, hard, sexist, nasty, selfish, brutal, and many other disadvantageous things" (*ibid.*). Furthermore, one can insist that "it would be better if he were nicer to her" (*ibid.*). But, and here we are meant to feel the accumulated weight of Williams's reasoning thus far, even this judgement must fail to justify "the one specific thing the external reasons theorist wants me to say, that the man has a reason to be nicer" (*ibid.*). Criticism of the husband may well reveal a perfect understanding of the ethics of the situation, but the insistence on putting it into the form of a reason statement reveals a perfect misunderstanding of the nature of practical reasoning. As Williams takes his arguments for the internal reasons interpretation to show, reasons failing to muster subjective motivational support simply fail to be reasons, amounting, even when offered in the spirit of moral improvement, to so much bluff. It is time to look at three noteworthy critiques of Williams's interpretation.

Korsgaard: "Skepticism about practical reason"

What are the chances that Williams's Hume-inspired, subjectivist position on practical reasoning winds up compatible with Kant's view of moral action as a function of objective and autonomous principles of pure willing? Excellent, according to Korsgaard's widely admired paper "Skepticism about Practical Reason". By scepticism about practical reason, Korsgaard means "doubts about the extent to which human action is or could possibly be directed by reason" (Korsgaard 1996c: 311), doubts that come in two flavours, "content" and "motivational". Content scepticism "is doubt about the bearing of rational considerations on the activities of deliberation and choice" (*ibid.*). Motivational scepticism "is doubt about the scope of reason as a motive" (*ibid.*). Hume is, famously, sceptical in both senses. Content-wise, reason has only a narrow role in determining appropriate means to given ends. Motivation-wise, only passion, not reason, carries motive force. Kant is, just as famously, sceptical in neither sense. Content-wise, rational principles have broad scope in producing reasons for action through self-legislation. Motivation-wise, such reasons carry motive force regardless of the state of one's passions. Korsgaard does not as much plump for Kant in this paper as argue that, regardless of whether Kant's or Hume's view ultimately prevails, "motivational skepticism must always be based on content skepticism", for "motivational skepticism has no independent force" (*ibid*.: 312). The ramifications of her argument for Williams's position on internal reasons are, she believes, significant.

When it comes to scepticism about practical reason, Korsgaard regards the position advocated in "Internal and External Reasons" as something of a hybrid: "Williams takes up one part of the skeptic's argument: that a piece of practical reasoning must start from something that is capable of motivating you; and drops the other, that the only kind of reasoning is means/end" (*ibid*.: 326). This bears out the earlier discussion in which Williams insists, *à la* Hume, on motivational scepticism, by relativizing reasons for action to subjective elements, while at least claiming, *contra* Hume, to disavow content scepticism, by disavowing the confines of narrow instrumentalism. But if Korsgaard is right, then what can count as motivation may well depend on what can count as deliberation, and Williams's conservatism towards the former may not be justified by his liberalism towards the latter.

Much of Korsgaard's paper involves teasing out the implications of what she calls "the internalism requirement", whereby "Practical-reason claims, if they are really to present us with reasons for action, must be capable of motivating rational persons" (*ibid*.: 317). In fact, it is probably not that great a stretch to say that the main point of "Skepticism about Practical Reason" is the following: "The internalism requirement is correct, but there is probably no moral theory it excludes" (*ibid*.: 329). Williams, as we have seen, effectively sets the internalism requirement with his not uncontroversial claim that "nothing can explain an agent's (intentional) action except something that motivates him to act", a claim that itself reflects his explanatory requirement on reasons (Williams 1981b: 107). He then simply presents the agent's subjective motivational set as the only plausible source of reliable motivational fuel for practical deliberation. Korsgaard points out, however, that, unlike Hume, "Williams can accommodate the case of someone's acting for reasons of principle, and in this case the form the deliberation will take is that of applying the principle or of seeing that the principle applies to the case at hand" (Korsgaard 1996c: 327). Moreover, acting from principle may open up new ways of looking at motivation.

Once Williams claims, for example, that "actions can flow from various elements in the agent's *S* without being means to some separate end" (Williams 2001: 92), he cannot rule out the possibility that some sort of receptivity to principles of pure practical reason is included among the elements of *S*, which is just to say that he cannot rule out the compatibility of pure practical reason with the internalism requirement:

> If one accepts the internalism requirement, it follows that pure practical reason will exist if and only if we are capable of being motivated by the conclusions of the operations of pure practical reason as such. Something in us must make us capable of being motivated by them, and this something will be part of the subjective motivational set. (Korsgaard 1996c: 327–8)

Observing that "Williams seems to think that this is a reason for doubting that pure practical reasons exist", Korsgaard begs to differ: "what seems to follow from the internalism requirement is this: if we can be motivated by considerations stemming from pure practical reason, then that capacity belongs to the set of every rational being" (*ibid.*: 328). Pure practical reason, indifferent to contingent, subjective motivation, may yet find purchase in Williams's internalist model of practical reasoning.

Closed off to Williams, Korsgaard believes, is any move to counter her claims by limiting the candidates for *S*:

> One cannot argue that the subjective motivational set contains only ends or desires; for that would be true only if all reasoning were of the means/ends variety. ... What sorts of items can be found in the set does not limit, but rather depends on, what kinds of reasoning are possible. Nor can one assume that the subjective motivational set consists only of individual or idiosyncratic elements, for that is to close off without argument, the possibility that reason could yield conclusions that every rational being must acknowledge and be capable of being motivated by. As long as it is left open what kinds of rational operations yield conclusions about what to do and what to pursue, it must be left open whether we are capable of being motivated by them. (*Ibid.*: 328)

By limiting the scope of reason in deliberation, Hume limits what can count as motivation. By expanding the scope of reason in deliberation, Williams expands what can count as motivation.

As we have seen, significant aims of Korsgaard's paper include showing that motivational scepticism depends upon content scepticism and showing how few, if any, styles of practical reasoning the internalism requirement actually rules out. One style most definitely not ruled out, she thinks, is Kant's, a conclusion whose striking nature only serves to underscore the general importance of her paper. One might be forgiven, after all, for taking Kant to be a paradigm of external reasoning, in as much as Kant seems to believe, if he believes anything, in the existence of reasons for action that can apply regardless of the contents of an agent's *S*. It is, again, Korsgaard's ambitious conclusion that the form of pure reasoning and the content of subjective motivation need not be strangers, let alone enemies. It is, moreover, as the following passage makes clear, a conclusion that Williams accepts, an acceptance undoubtedly owing something to "Skepticism about Practical Reason":

> Kant thought that a person would recognize the demands of morality if he or she deliberated correctly from his or her existing *S*, whatever that *S* might be, but he thought this because he took those demands to be implicit in a conception of practical reason which he could show to apply to any rational deliberator as such. I think that it best preserves the point of the internalism/externalism distinction to see this as a limiting case of internalism. (Williams 1995h: 220)

But such agreement about the theoretical amenability of the internal reasons model to pure practical reason should in no way mask Williams's significant disagreement, on display throughout Chapter 4, with Kantianism.

In fact, Williams and Korsgaard are at loggerheads. For her part, Korsgaard maintains that "Williams' argument does not show that if there were unconditional principles of reason applying to action we could not be motivated by them. He only thinks that there are none" (Korsgaard 1996c: 329). For his part, and clearly with Korsgaard in mind, Williams maintains that "Someone who claims the constraints of morality are themselves built into the notion of what it is to be a rational deliberator cannot get that conclusion for nothing" (Williams 1995c: 37). Although concurring with Korsgaard that "If it were true that the structure of practical reason yielded reasons of a certain kind as binding on every rational agent, then it would be true of every rational agent that there was a sound deliberative route from his or her *S* to actions required by such reasons" (Williams 2001: 94), Williams does not for a moment consider affirming the antecedent of the conditional. With respect to one another, each makes a concession and a demand. Korsgaard concedes the internalism requirement, but demands an argument from Williams ruling out the possibility that practical reasoning could turn out to be pure in Kant's sense. And Williams does in fact concede to Korsgaard the possibility that practical reasoning might be pure, but demands an argument that it is so. At the end of the day, Kant remains on the table. It is McDowell's contention that Aristotle remains there as well, as does the possibility of external reasons.

McDowell: "Might there be external reasons?"

As McDowell sees it, Williams deserves both praise and blame for the way he reacts to "the only point of believing in external reasons", namely "to be able to bring a charge of *irrationality* against anyone who is not motivated in some direction that the [external reasons] theorist thinks he should be motivated in" (McDowell 1995: 75). On the one hand, McDowell credits Williams for insisting that "an accusation of irrationality ... is nothing but 'bluff'" (*ibid.*). But, on the other hand, McDowell faults Williams for insisting, with equal vigour, "that the external reasons theorist must envisage a transition to considering matters aright that would be effected by reasoning" (*ibid.*), and it is this position he sets out to undermine in "Might there Be External Reasons?"

Remember that Williams presents the advocate of external reason statements with his own version of Hume's challenge: how can reason give rise to volition? McDowell recaps Williams's position:

> The external reasons theorist must envisage a procedure of correct deliberation or reasoning which gives rise to a motivation, but which is not "controlled" by existing motivations, ... for, if the deliberation were thus "controlled" by existing motivations, the reason it brought to light would simply be an internal reason. So the external reasons theorist has to envisage the generation of a new motivation by reason in an exercise in which the directions it can take are not shaped by the shape of the agent's prior motivations – an exercise that would be rationally compelling whatever motivations one started from. (*Ibid.*: 71)

But whereas, Williams concludes "I see no reason to suppose that these conditions could possibly be met" (Williams 1981b: 109), McDowell is not so sure.

McDowell's discussion focuses on the following "crucial claim" in Williams's challenge to the external reasons view: "the external reason statement itself will have to be taken as roughly equivalent to, or at least entailing, that claim that if the agent rationally deliberated, then, whatever motivations he originally had, he would come to be motivated to ϕ" (*ibid.*: 109). In response to this crucial claim, McDowell poses this "crucial question": "why must the external reasons theorist envisage the transition to considering the matter aright as being effected by *correct deliberation*?" (McDowell 1995: 72). Just as Korsgaard concedes the internalism requirement, but accuses Williams of simply assuming that nothing but his quasi-instrumentalist views can meet it, McDowell concedes the challenge facing the external reasons proponent, of acquiring a new motivation without recourse to existing motivational stock, but accuses Williams of simply assuming that the only possible way to effect such transition is though reasoning. And just as Korsgaard argues that Williams's view of the content of practical reasoning leaves indeterminate what can count as motivation, McDowell argues that Williams's view of the transition from being unmoved to moved by the truth of an external reason statement leaves indeterminate what can count as "considering the matter aright".

Of course, "considering" does seem to imply deliberation, but McDowell contends that the work "considering the matter aright" does for Williams only amounts to providing "an *explanation* of the agent's coming to believe the reason statement, suited to reveal the transition as one to a *true* belief" (*ibid.*: 72–3). If so, he continues, "all that the external reasons theorist needs ... is that *in* coming to believe the reason statement, the agent is coming to consider the matter aright" (*ibid.*: 73). Not only rational deliberation will satisfy the implicit terms of that "*in*", but also, McDowell suggests, the decidedly non-deliberative forces of, say, persuasion, inspiration and, most notably, conversion. However, McDowell's preferred stand-in for correct reasoning, and so his preferred response to Williams's challenge, appears to be something like character development, a candidate with ancient philosophical roots. McDowell elaborates:

> If we think of ethical upbringing in a roughly Aristotelian way, as a process of habituation into suitable modes of behaviour, inextricably bound up with the inculcation of suitably related modes of thought, there is no mystery about how the process can be the acquisition, simultaneously, of a way of seeing things and of a collection of motivational directions or practical concern. ... And if

> the upbringing has gone as it should, we shall want to say that the way of seeing things ... involves considering them aright. ... Here talking of having been properly brought up and talking of considering the matter aright are two ways of giving expression to the same assessment. (*Ibid.*)

In McDowell's view, people unremarkably acquire new motivations through habituation, in the form of dispositions to act this way or that, including motivations in no sense derived from previously acquired motivations.

In cases of people raised by wolves, where the result is motivational lassitude in the face of external reason statements (the case of Williams's unsympathetic husband comes to mind), perhaps some sort of conversion experience might rise to the level of considering the matter aright. Although admitting that "the bare idea of conversion points at best to a schema for explanations of shifts of character", McDowell goes on "to suppose that at least sometimes we really might be able to understand on these lines how someone who had slipped through the net might suddenly or gradually become as if he had been properly brought up" (*ibid.*: 74). More importantly, such sudden or gradual becoming would effectively answer Williams's challenge: "The idea of conversion would function here as the idea of an intelligible shift in motivational orientation that is exactly *not* effected by inducing a person to discover, by practical reasoning controlled by existing motivations, some internal reasons that he did not previously recognize he had" (*ibid.*). Most importantly, such sudden or gradual becoming would be tantamount to recognizing the truth of an external reason.

In McDowell's view, although the end of practical reasoning must indeed be correct reasoning, it does not follow that correct reasoning must be the sole means to that end. Rejecting what he sees as Williams's commitment to "a deliberative or rational procedure that would lead anyone from not being so motivated to being so motivated", McDowell advances his own crucial claim: "On the contrary, the transition to being so motivated is a transition *to* deliberating correctly, not one effected *by* deliberating correctly" (*ibid.*: 78). As such, "effecting the transition may need some non-rational alteration like conversion" (*ibid.*). McDowell goes on to locate the ground of Williams's mistake in the "psychologistic" nature of the internal reasons model, with its overreliance on "the mere facts of individual psychology" and its construal of beliefs and desires as "rationally self-contained psychic phenomenon" (*ibid.*: 77). The point seems to be that

Williams errs by implausibly assuming that elements of *S* are readily isolable and identifiable to the agent for purposes of conducting deliberation. But Williams refuses to take the point, or, he takes it only so far, refusing to admit that it leads him to error.

Williams responds to McDowell's paper at some length, denying at the outset that his own argument "presupposes quite what McDowell says that it presupposes" and schematically introducing two statements intended to clarify the matter:

> (R) *A* has reason to ϕ.
> (D) If *A* deliberated correctly, he would be motivated to ϕ.
> (Williams 1995h: 187)

Williams takes it that both he and McDowell agree "that to believe (R) is in some sense to believe (D)", meaning at least that "if someone (for instance *A*) is presented with the statement (R), he must understand it as claiming (roughly) (D)" (*ibid.*: 188). But from this, as far as the relation between correct deliberation and considering the matter aright goes, it does not follow, and here, according to Williams, is where McDowell gets it wrong, that "*A* would have to come to believe *the statement (D)* through deliberation" (*ibid.*). "That", Williams admits, "would be a very implausible idea" (*ibid.*).

Williams, then, contests McDowell's charge that he has failed to appreciate the crucial difference between a transition "*to* deliberating correctly" and a transition "*by* deliberating correctly". Moreover, Williams contests that his argument implies, as McDowell claims, "that there must be a deliberative or rational procedure that would lead *anyone* from not being so motivated to being so motivated" (McDowell 1995: 78, emphasis added). Although Williams admits that his argument both relies on "a connection between (R) and (D)" and "uses the idea of *A*'s arriving at a first personal form of (R) by deliberation", he denies that his argument makes (R) and (D) equivalent; instead, their connection remains eminently defeasible:

> The internalist's idea is that there are some processes that would count, and others that would not count, as deliberately arriving, from one's existing *S*, at the project of ϕ-ing. Granted this, the internalist can give a constrained sense to (D), one which – he claims – matches it to (R). But this does not imply, as McDowell's objection suggests, that the agent should be able to conduct the relevant deliberation in fact. (Williams 1995h: 188)

Interestingly, although Williams works to defend himself against McDowell's charge that he unreasonably interprets the relation between (R) and (D), he seems much less concerned to defend himself against the charge of excessive psychologism, which McDowell posits as the root of those unreasonable internalist demands. For Williams, better excessive psychologism than excessive idealization, which is what he thinks you get with McDowell's version of Aristotelian practical reasoning.

What worries Williams most about McDowell's approach to salvaging external reasons is the unacceptable cost he sees as being attached to any attempt to legitimate (usually ethical) reasons without reference to an agent's *S*, a cost reckoned as the loss of the personal point of view. For one thing, "with an externalist account ... (R) does not emerge as a statement distinctively about the person *A*" (*ibid*.: 191). For another, "from both an ethical and a psychological point of view it is important that (R) and its relatives should say something special about *A*, and not merely invoke in connection with him some general normative judgment" (*ibid*.: 192). But just such a general normative judgement, independent of any particular personal connection, is what Williams sees as the fallout from McDowell's justificatory appeal to being "properly brought up". There are two issues here for Williams. Is McDowell's position plausible? Is McDowell's position plausibly Aristotelian?

Williams finds McDowell's putative externalist position implausible because it seems to guarantee that "statements of the type (R) do not relate actions to persons, but types of actions to types of circumstances" (*ibid*.: 190). In fact, as Williams sees it, on the external reasons interpretation,

> (D) – the claim that if *A* deliberated correctly, he would be motivated to ϕ – means only this: ... if *A* were a correct deliberator, *A* would be motivated in these circumstances to ϕ, where "a correct deliberator" means someone who deliberates as a well informed and well-disposed person would deliberate. (*Ibid*.: 189)

Furthermore, for McDowell, a "correct deliberator" means "someone like Aristotle's *phronimos*, or ... someone who has been properly brought up" (*ibid*.). But then, Williams complains, "It follows that on this account (R) does not make a statement distinctively about *A* at all" (*ibid*.), for "the *phronimos* is an ideal type, and the fact that he is invoked does not make the formula any less impersonal, relative to particular agents" (*ibid*.: 190). Although it is true that, for McDowell, as for Williams, "(R) invokes the person *A*", in McDowell's view "none of its content is distinctively about *A*", or so Williams maintains (*ibid.*). This means that in determining what *A* has reason to do, the extent to which *A* fails, for whatever reason and to whatever extent, to approximate the qualities of the *phronimos* has no bearing. But this is just to ignore the agent's subjectivity, and in doing so to locate the normativity of reasons in an ideal, and so unrealistic, account of practical reasoning.

There remains the question of whether or not Williams thinks McDowell gets Aristotle right. There is a detailed discussion of Williams on Aristotle in Chapter 7, and for now it must suffice to say that, whereas Williams and Korsgaard could apparently agree, whatever the ultimate plausibility of pure practical reason, that Kant's avowed position constitutes a (limiting) case of internalism, Williams disagrees, whatever the ultimate relevance of a *phronimos* to practical reason, with McDowell's attempt to impress Aristotle into the externalist camp. After all, practical wisdom only gains its point in relation to actual contents of actual subjective motivational sets, a relation Williams believes is effectively lost on McDowell's account. As Williams says, "Aristotle's own way of focusing considerations of the good life on to the individual was, if I understand him, internalist" (*ibid.*: 192). But whether we should take Aristotle, however anachronistically, to back an internal or external reasons interpretation, Williams concludes his discussion of McDowell unequivocally: "nothing yet has persuaded me to give up the opinion that internalism in some form is the only view that plausibly represents a statement about *A*'s reasons as a distinctive kind of statement about, distinctively, *A*" (*ibid.*: 194). It is Scanlon's turn to try.

Scanlon: "Williams on internal and external reasons"

Where Korsgaard and McDowell appear particularly keen to critique Williams's position on internal reasons in terms of its perceived compatibility with their own preferred (broadly) Kantian and Aristotelian approaches to practical reasoning, Scanlon at least appears less partisan, concerned only to point out a most general quality of reasons, their universality, which he believes Williams's account largely ignores. Scanlon begins by recalling the example, discussed above, of the brutish husband, whose insensitivity to the claim that he has a reason to treat his wife better may indeed, in Williams's view, warrant all manner of epithets, but not an ascription of truth to the claim. Scanlon points out that, in sanctioning such epithets, Williams effectively concedes that the husband suffers from "a kind of deficiency", in the form of "a failure to be moved by certain considerations that we regard as reasons" (Scanlon 1998: 367). After all, Scanlon asks, "What else is it to be inconsiderate, cruel, insensitive and so on?" (*ibid.*) But "If it is a deficiency for a man to fail to see these considerations as reasons, it would seem that they must be reasons for him", and so, Scanlon wonders, "Why not conclude, then, that the man has a reason to treat his wife better ... ?" (*ibid.*). As might be anticipated, Williams's answer to this question could not be more straightforward: because he doesn't.

Scanlon counters Williams's argument that the very concept of a reason rules out the external reasons interpretation, because, for instance, it fails to meet the explanatory condition on reasons, with conceptual considerations of his own. In a narrow sense, surely if an agent fairly invites opprobrium for failing to appreciate a reason, he must possess the very reason he fails to appreciate (see Williams (1995c) on the relation between external reasons and blame). But much more broadly, Scanlon appeals to "the universality of reason judgements" and the idea that if I judge that I have a reason to take some action, then the very concept of judging that one has a reason dictates that anyone similarly situated will also have a reason to take that same action:

> The universality of reason judgments is a formal consequence of the fact that taking something to be a reason for acting is ... a judgment that takes certain considerations as sufficient grounds for its conclusion. Whenever we make judgments about our own reasons, we are committed to claims about the reasons that other people have, or would have under certain circumstances.
>
> (Scanlon 1998: 74)

Scanlon takes this feature of reasons to be completely uncontroversial and equally applicable to all species of practical reasoning.

The relevance of the universality of reason judgements to Scanlon's critique of Williams becomes obvious with his appeal to first-person experience: "Insofar as we do not think that our own reasons for refraining from being cruel to our spouses are dependent on our having some 'motivation' that is served by so refraining, we cannot regard others' reasons as being so dependent" (*ibid.*: 367). This puts the point negatively, but the thrust seems clear enough: one can see that one has a reason to be kind to one's spouse, a reason that anyone in relevantly similar circumstances should acknowledge and, therefore, a reason that may be confidently ascribed to the lout in Williams's example.

Just why Scanlon should seem so confident about this disconnect between reasons for restraint and one's *S* remains somewhat puzzling. No doubt the answer relates both to his faith in motivational factors independent of an agent's *S* and, as the following passage indicates, to his suspicion concerning Williams's tendency to characterize or illustrate internalism in third person terms:

> Williams' examples are all put in the third person; they concern the claims we can make about the reasons other people have. But his internalism seems to force on us the conclusion that our own reasons, too, are all contingent on the presence of appropriate elements in our subjective motivational sets. This rings false and is, I believe, an important source of the widespread resistance to Williams' claims. (*Ibid.*)

Scanlon seems to believe that even cursory introspection will confirm the existence of motivations bearing no relativity to one's *S*. This confirmation plus the universality of reason judgements equals the downfall of Williams's position.

Now, Scanlon admits that "it does seem to be browbeating to insist that a person has a reason when he denies this, and when he truly could not see the force of the consideration in question no matter how hard he tried" (*ibid.*: 371). In fact, he agrees with Williams that "It *is* browbeating to go on saying this in such a case" (*ibid.*). Nevertheless, Scanlon observes, rightly, of course, that "from the fact that it would be browbeating to go on saying something in such a context it does not follow that that thing is not true" (*ibid.*: 372), and he concludes with the hope that Williams might "relax the requirement that in order for a person to be said to 'have a reason' the argument for it must be linked to some element of the agent's current *S*" (*ibid.*: 373). This, however, Williams will not do. Although Williams applauds Scanlon for his "notably constructive contribution to the discussion" (Williams 2001: 95) and agrees with a couple of key points in Scanlon's analysis, he also believes that Scanlon misses the only point that really matters.

Williams does agree with Scanlon, referring once again to the odious husband, "that the agent's faults can be understood in terms of a failure to see certain considerations as reasons, just as the opposed virtues can be understood as dispositions to see those considerations as reasons" (*ibid.*: 95–6). He further agrees "that if we think of this as a deficiency or fault of this man, then we must think that in some sense these reasons *apply* to him" (*ibid.*: 96). But such agreement falls short of establishing any link between seeing or coming to see certain considerations and the husband's *S*. As Williams puts the point, "But none of this implies that these considerations are already the defective agent's reasons; indeed, the problem is precisely that they are not" (*ibid.*). Although we can frame the matter in terms of *A* remedying a deficiency and so, "as critics, express ourselves by saying 'There is a reason for *A* to behave differently', it does not make that statement ... any more a matter of *A*'s reasons" (*ibid.*). The idea is the by now familiar one that, for Williams, something more than just our ability to formulate a reason statement will be needed to warrant its truth.

Owing to their substantial agreement, Williams maintains that Scanlon's connection between recognizing a deficiency and justifying a reason statement "is not, and is not intended to be, a knock-down argument against the internalist position" (*ibid.*: 95), just as Scanlon maintains that, once their agreement has been acknowledged, "the remaining disagreement over the range of applicability of the locution 'has a reason' does not seem to me to be so important" (Scanlon 1998: 372). In the end, "The issue is not whether it can be a deficiency not to be able to see the force of certain considerations, but rather what the relation is between these judgments and the idea of the reasons that a person has" (*ibid.*: 371). Still, at least for Williams, a gap remains between the applicability of a judgement and the presence of a reason.

Conclusion

If anything unifies the seemingly disparate critiques of Korsgaard, McDowell and Scanlon, it may be a common concern with excessive indeterminacy in Williams's account as far as what counts as a reason; indeed, as far as what counts as practical reasoning. Korsgaard finds such indeterminacy in Williams's view of deliberative "content": "His argument seems to show that only natural extensions of the instrumental principle can meet the internalism requirement, but he is prepared to extend the instrumental principle so far that this turns out to be no limitation at all" (Korsgaard 1997: 216). McDowell finds such indeterminacy in the notion of correct deliberation or "considering the matter aright": when it comes to acquiring belief in external reason statements, Williams "leaves it quite open how the transition is effected" (McDowell 1995: 73). And Scanlon finds such indeterminacy in the idea of "a sound deliberative route": "the variability that internalism provides may be too great", meaning that a lack of uniformity across subjective motivational sets may leave agents indifferent to the worth of certain values (Scanlon 1998: 370). But to Williams, effectively engaging all three philosophers, "it is unclear what the limits are to what an agent might arrive at by rational deliberation from his existing *S*", and any decent view of practical reason "should preserve and account for that unclarity" (Williams 1981b: 110). As his respondents attest, he certainly preserves unclarity, but does he actually account for it?

One's confidence in Williams's account of the "essential indeterminacy" of practical deliberation (Williams 2001: 92) will largely mirror the extent to which one shares his view that "Practical reasoning is a heuristic process, and an imaginative one", or that "there are no fixed boundaries on the road from rational thought to inspiration and conversion" (Williams 1981b: 110). (It is hard to be sure just how this last claim meshes with McDowell's response.) For Williams, "There is indeed a vagueness about '*A* has reason to ϕ', in the internal sense, insofar as the deliberative processes which could lead from *A*'s present *S* to his being motivated to ϕ may be more or less ambitiously conceived" (*ibid.*). However, far from being the liability Korsgaard imagines, Williams's account "merely shows that there is a wider range of states, and a less determinate one, than one might have supposed, which can be counted as *A*'s having a reason to ϕ" (*ibid.*). More importantly, Williams's account demonstrates his ongoing commitment to portraying realistically the psychology of human agency, avoiding heavily idealized models of practical reasoning that rely on such implausibly impersonal devices as Korsgaard's pure practical reason or McDowell's standardized upbringing. Although Korsgaard and McDowell, even Scanlon, may dispute just how hostile Williams's internalism, with its necessary connection between subjective motivation and reasons for action, actually is to the letter of their own preferred accounts, they cannot dispute its hostility in spirit.

This concern to get the psychology right constitutes the primary motive behind Williams's resistance to the suggestion that insusceptibility to an external reasons claim demonstrates irrationality on the part of the agent. As the previous discussion indicates, Williams regards this suggestion as mere "bluff", which in turn prods the following observation from Korsgaard: "But if it is, then we ought to have a lot of respect for bluff. It plays an essential role in our efforts to hold ourselves and each other together, to stay on track of our projects and relationships in the face of the buffeting winds of local temptation and desire" (Korsgaard 1997: 233). Yet this observation, while certainly leaving room for agreement between Korsgaard and Williams, introduces questions of its own, especially concerning the relation between "our projects" and "local temptation and desire". To Korsgaard, it may well point to an important role for objective value in practical deliberation. But for Williams, such a role cannot be guaranteed. For one thing, that which influences deliberation must reside in the agent's *S*, and while values are sure to be found there, their precise composition and distribution remain a contingent matter. For another, there may simply be no such thing as objective value, a possibility now taken up in Chapter 6.

Chapter 6

Truth, objectivity and knowledge

Introduction

Philosophers, no less than others, take comfort in familiar labels. To discover that someone is a physicalist or a compatibilist or a Platonist is to be instantly situated philosophically with regard to that person, and, while such familiarity may well breed contempt, it also orients and, in orienting, comforts. Williams, however, in this as in so many ways, provides little comfort; that is, his views either resist being labelled entirely, or invite only radically attenuated application, particularly in the realm of ethical philosophy. Not surprisingly, Williams's ethical scepticism and anti-theoretical tendencies militate against ascribing to him obvious first-order or normative positions, as his critique of others' answers to Socrates' question (how should one live?) effectively camouflages his own. But what about his positions on second-order, or more meta-ethical, issues? However difficult it may be to label Williams's own custom-made alternative to, say, utilitarianism or Kantianism, surely he must embrace certain ready-to-wear views concerning its philosophical underpinnings; surely he must embrace certain familiar metaphysical and epistemological commitments; and surely these can be labelled.

Metaphysically, such commitments typically invite the labels "realist" or "anti-realist", as they assert or deny, as Williams roughly puts it in *Morality*, "that thought has a subject matter which is independent of the thought" (Williams 1972: 36). They are no doubt best construed along a continuum of gradually intensifying avowals of ethical objectivity; indeed, objectivity constitutes the playing field upon which realists and anti-realists butt heads. Epistemologically, such commitments typically invite the labels "cognitivist" or "anti-cognitivist", as they assert or deny, again, putting it roughly, that the descriptive statements and prescriptive judgements of ethical life can be true and false, or, alternatively, as they assert or deny the existence of ethical knowledge. As objectivity is to realist/anti-realist squabbles, so knowledge is to debates between cognitivists and non-cognitivists, a valuable currency for negotiating competing claims regarding the susceptibility of ethical statements to truth. Still, the prevalence of labels aside, hard and fast distinctions between metaphysical and epistemological aspects of ethical enquiry may be difficult to establish and maintain, because, for example, accounts of ethical objectivity shape accounts of ethical knowledge. But no matter how one sets out to navigate the territory between realism and cognitivism, or between ethical objectivity and knowledge, it can be difficult to locate Williams on the map.

To begin with, although it might seem as though, to take one edge of the continuum, realist metaphysics and cognitivist epistemology would be natural allies, in as much as moral facts track moral properties – that is, in as much as ethical statements might be said to owe their truth or falsity to correspondence with some underlying ethical reality – Williams refuses to endorse the alliance. As he says in the provocatively titled essay "Who Needs Ethical Knowledge?", "I take it that the question whether there can be ethical knowledge is not the same as the question whether ethical outlooks can be objective" (Williams 1995k: 203). Indeed, when it comes to ethics Williams himself combines a consistent anti-realism with a sometimes cognitivist, sometimes anti-cognitivist stance, depending on a fairly complex set of circumstances. Convinced that "the concept of knowledge has only a limited usefulness in ethical matters", Williams believes that "our best candidates for ethical knowledge are local, and this fails to match up such ethical knowledge to the ambitions of cognitivism" (*ibid*.: 203, 209). But if the concept of ethical knowledge provides a less than transparent window on the nature of ethics, objectivity holds greater promise; moreover, the key to understanding the nature and possibility of ethical objectivity, in Williams's view, involves appreciating that a "fundamental difference lies between the ethical and the scientific", a difference explored in the following section (Williams 1985: 135). Still, can Williams really so easily dismiss the relevance and importance of cognitivist concerns, particularly the idea of ethical knowledge as a body of true ethical belief? Can truth be so easily dismissed as a key ethical consideration?

One might be forgiven for thinking that Williams's considered views on truth and its relation to ethics must be ready to hand. His last book, after all, is called *Truth and Truthfulness*. It must be said, however, that although this book contains many interesting and original discussions (two of which, in particular, on Thucydides and genealogy, are taken up in Chapter 7), it is principally concerned with "what may be summarily called 'the value of truth"', and much less, or not at all, concerned with the philosophical conception of truth underlying the value it proposes to consider (Williams 2002: 6). In fact, in *Truth and Truthfulness* Williams seems to call into question the very project of investigating truth as a stand-alone notion:

> we should resist any demand for a definition of truth, principally because truth belongs to a ramifying set of connected notions, such as meaning, reference, belief, and so on, and we are better employed in exploring the relations between these notions than in trying to treat one or some of them as the basis of the others. It is also true that if any of these notions has a claim to be more basic and perspicuous than the others, it is likely to be truth itself.
>
> (*Ibid.*: 63)

Michael Dummett has retorted that "indefinability is not to be confused with inexplicability", and he criticizes Williams for failing to provide more in the way of an account of truth, in particular by failing to provide more in the way of an account of meaning (Dummett 2004: 106). Nevertheless, Williams became increasingly convinced towards the end of his career that "truth in ethics is not itself such an important question, because the question of truth in ethics is not itself any of those questions about objectivity, the possibility of ethical knowledge, and so forth" (Williams 1996a: 19). It was not always so.

In his seminal paper "Consistency and Realism", Williams had argued for "an account of the need for consistency that puts the weight squarely on the consideration that the basic aim of assertions is to be true", and, further, that "if one is going to rely on the notion of truth in giving the account of assertion and consistency, it will have to be a substantial notion of truth" (Williams 1973d: 202). However, although he acknowledged that "the interesting question is what this notion [of truth] is going to be like, and what sort of account can be given of it", he was refreshingly quick to say "I confess that I have not much idea of how to go on with these questions" (*ibid.*: 203). What Williams does hold on to, early and late, is a suspicion of so-called deflationary, disquotational and redundancy theories of truth, as well as various claims made for the material adequacy condition advanced in Alfred Tarski's work on truth in formalized languages (see Tarski 2001; Lynch 2001; Ramsey 2001; and, perhaps especially, Horwich 1998, 2001).

Even as Williams gradually becomes receptive to a more minimalist treatment of truth, in particular Crispin Wright's (see Williams 1996a; Wright 1992, 1996), he remains doubtful that accounts employing disquotation can helpfully illuminate truth, at least for purposes of investigating its value, which, again, seems to be his real interest. Put another way, Williams sees Tarski's equivalences (e.g. "'Snow is white' is true if and only if snow is white") as unhelpfully underdetermining the concept of truth from a philosophical point of view:

> The conclusion that truth in itself isn't much follows from what I take to be an undeniable starting point, namely the soundness of Tarski's equivalence. If we can start from anything in the question of truth, we can start from the idea that "*p*" is true just in case that *p*. ... What is not undeniable is any given philosophical interpretation of what Tarski's equivalence means ... [T]he fact that it's been taken by authoritative and competent commentators to express both the correspondence theory and the redundancy theory seems itself good evidence that it does not express any such theory. (Williams 1996a: 19–20)

Although Williams's scepticism towards theories of truth is clearly rooted in different soil from his scepticism towards theories of ethics, it would be surprising if the former doubts failed to inform the latter. In so far as an ethical theory may, for example, rely upon truthful ethical discourse, and in so far as that truthful discourse in turn relies upon its correspondence to some underlying ethical reality, doubts about the possibility of such correspondence may undermine the discourse and, in turn, the theory itself. As will become clear, Williams himself seems inclined to relegate whatever truth there may be in terms of correspondence to the province of science rather than ethics.

The following sections take up the three most important and best known aspects of Williams's views on the nature and possibility of knowledge and objectivity in the realms of science and ethics. More specifically, they take up: Williams's "absolute conception" of reality and its implications for ethical objectivity; his views on "thick concepts" and their implications for ethical knowledge; and, finally, his position on ethical relativism, taken as a consequence of his views on the absolute conception and thick concepts. Williams backs what may seem a fragile coalition of positions, uniting ethical anti-realism with qualified forms of ethical cognitivism and relativism. This chapter attempts to assemble and to assess the strength of this coalition.

The absolute conception

First hinted at in *Morality* (1972), originally formulated in *Descartes: The Project of Pure Enquiry* (1978a), given its mature articulation in *Ethics and the Limits of Philosophy* (1985) and defended against criticism as recently as "Philosophy as a Humanistic Discipline" (2000b), Williams's position regarding the aspirations of scientific and ethical inquiry to truth, knowledge and objectivity remains remarkably consistent over the years. Anchored in what he at times calls the "absolute conception of reality", and at other times the "absolute conception of the world", this position holds at bottom that "science has some chance of being more or less what it seems, a systematized theoretical account of how the world really is, while ethical thought has no chance of being everything it seems" (Williams 1985: 135).

The absolute conception involves a robust realism, "knowledge of a reality that exists independently of that knowledge"; it further involves, as Williams puts it in one of any number of striking lines on this topic, "Knowledge of what is there *anyway*" (Williams 1978a: 64). It is, in short, a conception "to the maximum degree independent of our perspective and its peculiarities" (Williams 1985: 139). As indicated, Williams first develops the absolute conception of the world in the process of explicating Descartes's views on the nature of knowledge and the possibility of certainty. But Williams does not take the absolute conception to be uniquely Cartesian, as this passage from his essay "Descartes's Use of Skepticism" makes clear:

> a very natural interpretation of what scientific knowledge should be ... takes [it] to be a system which represents the world as it is independently of any inquirer, using terms which to the greatest extent display that independence. This objective of *absolute* knowledge, as it may be called, is not peculiar to Descartes. Indeed, it can be seen as implicit in a natural conception of knowledge itself, and the fact that this ideal is, in particular, an ideal for scientific

> knowledge implies the idea that scientific knowledge peculiarly realizes, or seeks to realize, the ambitions of knowledge *tout court*. (Williams 1983: 344)

Williams's commitment to this "natural interpretation" of a "natural conception" never wavers, cementing his convictions concerning what science can, and, perhaps more importantly, what ethics cannot, accomplish in the realm of knowledge. But the philosophical promise of the absolute conception of the world relies upon two critical, and by no means uncontroversial, assumptions: that scientific beliefs tend to converge ("sheer dogmatism", Hilary Putnam calls it), and that the absolute conception can "nonvacuously explain how it itself, and the various perspectival views of the world, are possible" ("an illusion", says McDowell) (Williams 1985: 139; Putnam 1990a: 171; McDowell 1998a: 123).

It may seem odd for Williams to point to the convergence of scientific belief as support for science's superiority over ethics in representing reality. After all, ethical beliefs tend to display no little convergence themselves. But Williams insists that

> The distinction does not turn on any difference in whether convergence will actually occur, and it is important that this is not what the argument is about. It might well turn out that there will be convergence in ethical outlook. ... The point of the contrast is that, even if this happens, it will not be correct to think it has come about because convergence has been guided by how things actually are, whereas convergence in the sciences might be explained in that way if it does happen. (Williams 1985: 136)

Driven by convergence, guided by reality, the absolute conception owes much, as Williams readily acknowledges, to "that 'final opinion' which C. S. Peirce believed that enquiry would inevitably converge upon, a 'final opinion ... independent not indeed of thought in general, but of all that is arbitrary and individual in thought"' (Williams 1978a: 244; quoting Peirce 1966a: 82). Williams appropriates wholesale this idea of escaping the arbitrary and individual:

> The idea of the world as it really is involves at least a contrast with that of the world *as it seems to us*. ... By the same token, the world as it really is is contrasted to the world as it peculiarly seems to any observer – that is to say, as it seems to any observer in virtue of that observer's peculiarities. In using these notions, we are implying that there can be a conception of reality corrected for

> the special situation or other peculiarity of various observers, and the line of thought leads eventually to the conception of the world as it is independently of the peculiarities of any observers. That, surely, must be identical with a conception which, if we are not idealists, we need: a conception of the world as it is independently of all observers. (Williams 1978a: 241)

Williams finds it helpful to elaborate on the notion of correcting for observational peculiarity in terms of the familiar distinction between primary and secondary qualities.

According to Williams, "There is every reason to think that such a conception should leave out secondary qualities" (*ibid.*). That objects appear coloured depends on visual apparatus and cognitive processes (perhaps) peculiar to humans; but it is just this dependence on a particular perspective that the absolute conception aims to transcend and that, one may argue, science in fact does transcend with an account of colour in terms of, for example, an interaction between light and microphysical structure. That such an interaction is presumably further removed from any peculiarly human perspective than, say, looking green only underscores Williams's earlier insistence on locating the relevant opposition between science and ethics, rather than, say, cognitivism and non-cognitivism:

> It is centrally important that these ideas relate to science, not to all kinds of knowledge. We can *know* things whose content is perspectival: we can know that grass is green, for instance, though *green*, for certain, and probably *grass* are concepts that would not be available to every competent observer of the world and would not figure in the absolute conception. The point is not to give an account of knowledge. ... The aim is to outline the possibility of a convergence characteristic of science, one that could meaningfully be said to be a convergence on how things (anyway) are.
> (Williams 1985: 139)

Moreover, even as it embodies scientific convergence, the absolute conception must, in Williams's view, not only justify itself, but also explain the possibility of each of the more perspectival representations of reality it transcends.

As Williams sees it, "It is an important feature of modern science that it contributes to explaining how creatures with our origins and characteristics can understand a world with properties that this same science ascribes to the world" (*ibid.*: 139–40). Just this important explanatory feature Williams finds conspicuously absent in ethics. In as much as science may, even paradigmatically, involve moving from secondary-quality to primary-quality analyses, one way to frame Williams's science/ethics distinction is in terms of the essentially secondary-quality nature of ethics. Not only can science explain how humans converge upon the belief that grass is green in terms of "how things (anyway) are" – that is, not only can science explain secondary-quality infused representations in terms of primary qualities – but it can explain how humans come naturally to form such representations. In such cases "it is the explanation of the perspectival perceptions that enables us, when we come to reflect on them, to place them in relation to the perceptions of other people and other creatures. ... The question is whether we can find an ethical analogy to that. Here we have to go outside local judgments to a reflective or second-order account of them, and here the analogy gives out" (*ibid*.: 150). Although there certainly may be human convergence upon the belief that torturing cats for fun is wrong, such convergence will not, in Williams's view, be explained by "how things (anyway) are".

As the next section makes clear, the position is nuanced. Williams pointedly embraces the possibility that the belief that killing cats is wrong is *true*, just as he embraces the possibility of *knowing* that truth, but at the same time he rejects the possibility that this belief is true, or that we can possess knowledge of it, *absolutely*. Ethical knowledge, then, retains a parochial, secondary-quality nature, tied as it is to a particular, and particularly human, perspective. Whereas in science "the explanation also justifies, because it can show how the perceptions are related to physical reality and how they can give knowledge of that reality, which is what they purport to do" (*ibid*.), nothing comparable is available to ethics; ethics allows no correction for human perspective.

The idea of an absolute conception of the world, with its claims to capture "the ambitions of knowledge *tout court*" and to undermine the realist credentials of ethics, has attracted no little criticism over the years. Williams himself freely admits in *Truth and Truthfulness* that "It remains controversial whether the idea of an absolute conception is coherent" (Williams 2002: 295n19; cf. Williams 2000b: 481). While some have self-consciously laboured to refine and extend Williams's notion of an absolute conception (see Moore 1997), others have raised serious challenges to the way Williams would distinguish science and ethics (e.g. McDowell 1986, 1998a; Putnam 1990a, 1992, 2001; Rorty 1991a; Hookway 1995; Jardine 1995) Although each critic sings a different verse, their refrains sound remarkably similar: "Science is not like that!" In the remainder of this section, an extremely general objection, advanced by two of Williams's most illustrious and most persistent critics, Putnam and McDowell, will be very briefly taken up, if only better to illuminate Korsgaard's memorable claim that "Williams's realism about science ... is really just a statement of his confidence in the subject" (Korsgaard 1996d: 70–71). Of course, if it does turn out that science is not what it seems, it will not follow that ethics, by that fact alone, improves its chances of being everything *it* seems; for although Williams certainly takes his own brand of scientific realism to suggest and support his ethical anti-realism, the latter position is ultimately independent of the former.

Both Putnam and McDowell fault Williams's absolute conception of the world for relying on a bankrupt notion of correspondence between reality and perspective-free representations thereof. As McDowell sees it, "on the Peircean view that Williams endorses ... [t]he method itself is conceived as intrinsically non-distorting; as a pure or transparent mode of access to reality" (McDowell 1998a: 119). Putnam basically concurs: "The idea that some statements force themselves upon us because 'that is how things are' is taken with extreme seriousness by Williams; indeed, it is the center of his entire metaphysical picture" (Putnam 1990a: 172). But, Putnam continues, "The idea that some statements get recognized as true (if we investigate long enough and carefully enough) because they simply describe the world in a way that is independent of perspective is just a new version of the old 'correspondence theory of truth"' (*ibid.*; cf. McDowell 1998a: 126n17). Ultimately, Williams's inability to address satisfactorily a dilemma involving (roughly) issues of scheme and content leads him to embrace "a philosophical fantasy of truth, and of science as an approach to truth", or so suggests McDowell (McDowell 1986: 380).

In *Ethics and the Limits of Philosophy*, Williams somewhat mysteriously attributes objections involving a potentially devastating dilemma to "Rorty and others", mysteriously in as much as Williams himself had earlier, in *Descartes*, attributed the very same dilemma to "a natural, if very abstract, progression" in the development of the absolute conception (Williams 1978a, 65). In other words, Williams not only anticipates the dilemma, which is, in any case, "a kind of problem which has constantly recurred in the history of Western thought", but succinctly sets forth its terms:

> On the one hand, the absolute conception might be regarded as entirely empty, specified only as "whatever it is these represen-

> tations represent". In this case it ... provides insufficient substance to the conception of an independent reality; it slips out of the picture, leaving us only with a variety of possible representations to be measured against each other, with nothing to mediate between them. On the other hand, we may have some determinate picture of what the world is like independent of any knowledge or representation in thought; but then that is open to the reflection, once more, that that is only one particular representation of it, our own, and that we have no independent point of leverage for raising this into the absolute representation of reality.
>
> (Williams 1978a: 65)

On the one hand, the absolute conception becomes all scheme; on the other, it has content of dubious worth. On the one hand, the absolute conception features strict correspondence between reality and representation, yet no means of triangulating for truth; on the other, it features unregenerate parochialism.

As McDowell and Putnam see it, Williams's obsessive fear of the dilemma's second horn leads him into the clutches of correspondence, whereas a much more reasonable approach would be to embrace the second horn (and reject the absolute conception) by embracing the unavoidable parochialism of science itself. McDowell, for instance, argues that "Surely whatever is substantive in any actual view of scientific method is itself part of a substantive view of what the world is like, which cannot escape being the product of a particular location in the history of science. One's beliefs about which sorts of transactions with the world yield knowledge of it are not prior to, but part of, one's beliefs about what the world is like" (McDowell 1998a: 126). In a similar spirit, Putnam insists that "the notion of absoluteness is incoherent. Mathematics and physics, as well as ethics and history and politics, show our conceptual choices; the world is not going to impose a single language upon us, no matter what we choose to talk about" (Putnam 1990a: 171). And, rather conveniently for present purposes, McDowell's considered view on the topic makes explicit reference to Putnam's own:

> The right response to the claim that all our assessments of truth are made from the standpoint of a "conceptual system" that is inescapably our own is not to despair of our grip on reality but to say, with Hilary Putnam, "Well? We should use someone else's conceptual system?" It is pointless to chafe at the fact that what we believe is what *we* believe. ... Occupation of the second horn of Williams's dilemma, unblunted by the idea of a somehow

> impersonal and ahistorical mode of access to reality, ought not to seem to threaten anything we should want to mean by Williams's thesis "knowledge of what is there *anyway*".
>
> (McDowell 1998a: 128; quoting Putnam 1978: 32; Williams 1978a: 67)

In rejecting perfectly good content, Williams, at least according to Putnam and McDowell, accepts a totally empty scheme.

It bears repeating that this represents only the broadest charge levelled against the absolute conception. Just sticking with Putnam and McDowell one finds a number of more narrow criticisms, including a rejection of the absolute conception's view of scientific theories as destined to converge (see Putnam 1990a), as well as a rejection of the possibility of either truly *explaining* perspectival representations from within a perspective-free absolute conception (see McDowell 1998a) or truly *reducing* semantic or intentional properties to the absolute conception's presumed language of physics (see Putnam 1992). It is beyond the scope of this chapter to engage these or other narrower complaints; however, as far as Williams's ability to respond to the broadest charge goes, two things need to be said. First, Williams takes the absolute conception not as much to provoke the dilemma between empty scheme and unvetted content as to solve it, meaning, secondly, that he rejects outright any characterization of himself as impaled upon the dilemma's first horn.

Williams takes the dilemma to be a fundamental epistemological quandary, arising naturally in attempts to validate knowledge, which the absolute conception ultimately finesses. As he sees it, "Each side of the dilemma takes all our representations of the world together, in the one case putting them all in and in the other leaving them all out. But there is a third and more helpful possibility, that we should form a conception of the world that is 'already there' in terms of some but not all of our beliefs and theories" (Williams 1985: 138). Where Putnam and McDowell see Williams's conception effectively "leaving them all out", resulting in an only trivially absolute correspondence, Williams takes himself to have established conceptual room, not necessarily for an absolute independence from local perspective, but for a maximally independent local perspective, which is to say something like room for a *least local*, or perhaps even an *absolute-for-us*, perspective. Responding directly to Putnam, Williams writes

> My aim in introducing the notion of the absolute conception was precisely to get round the point that one cannot describe the world

> without describing it. ... The idea was that when we reflect on our conceptualization of the world, we might be able to recognize from inside it that some of our concepts and ways of representing the world are more dependent than others on our own perspective, our peculiar and local ways of apprehending things. In contrast, we might be able to identify some concepts and styles of representation which are minimally dependent on our own.
> (Williams 2000b: 482)

Regardless of how plausible this task of identifying minimally dependent styles of representation may seem, it is worth keeping in mind the Cartesian context in which the absolute conception was first introduced.

Williams portrays Descartes as a "pure enquirer", with pure enquiry seen as "the undertaking of someone setting aside all externalities or contingent limitations on the pursuit of truth" (Williams 1978a: 66). Williams further portrays Descartes as "attempting to transcend this dilemma [set out above], and trying to extract an absolute conception of reality from the process of Pure Enquiry" (*ibid.*). In a word, Descartes seeks certainty. But by the exacting standards of pure enquiry, certainty and the absolute conception, Descartes's project ultimately fails; indeed, chronicling this failure is the very task of *Descartes*. Such failure notwithstanding, Williams plainly hesitates to jettison the absolute conception: "To give up the Cartesian search for certainty may seem a fairly easy option, but can we so easily give up the idea of an absolute conception of reality, if there is to be any knowledge at all?" (*ibid.*: 212). As Williams sees it, three options present themselves: first, as Putnam and McDowell urge, reject the absolute conception as a condition of knowledge; secondly, accept the condition, but then also the *de facto* impossibility of knowledge; thirdly, "preserve the connection, and seek to detach the absolute conception from considerations of certainty" (*ibid.*). Not surprisingly, to Williams, "it is this third approach that seems correct, though it involves large difficulties" (*ibid.*).

In the light of such difficulties, perhaps two suggestions might be profitably entertained. First, take Williams's absolute conception to be a valuable heuristic rather than an attainable goal. Secondly, switch the focus from Williams's absolute conception as an in principle realizable aspiration of science to Williams's absolute conception as an in principle unrealizable aspiration of ethics. Whether or not science can capture the world as it is *anyway*, ethics, despite persistent pretensions to perspective-free conceptualization, stands, as Williams says, "no chance" of doing so. For truth, for knowledge, for objectivity, its best hopes lie not in the absolute conception, but in so-called thick concepts.

Thick concepts

Thick concepts and the absolute conception have at least one thing in common: they both represent pre-existing notions shaped by Williams to his own purpose. As we have seen, Williams believes that the freedom from local perspective idealized in the absolute conception simply comes with the territory of (especially Cartesian) epistemology, even as he employs it not as a path to guaranteed certainty, but as a heuristic for elucidating both the ambitions of science and the limitations of ethics. Similarly, thick concepts may not be original with Williams, yet he brings them into heightened relief, exploring their implications for ethical objectivity to a degree far surpassing his predecessors. Thick concepts contrast, naturally enough, with thin, and, although both types play a role in contemporary ethical discourse, only thick concepts, in Williams's view, hold the key (if anything does) to ethical objectivity.

Effectively employed by Williams for the first time in *Morality*, under the rather vague description "more substantial concepts" (see Williams 1972: 32), thick concepts come into their own in *Ethics and the Limits of Philosophy*, where he gives the following examples: "treachery", "promise", "brutality", "courage", "cowardice", "lie" and "gratitude". Uniting factual and evaluative elements, and in doing so tempering contemporary moral philosophy's (the morality system's) overly simplistic and intellectually debilitating obsession with the fact/value distinction, Williams presents thick concepts as simultaneously "world-guided" and "action-guiding" (Williams 1985: 140–41). Williams takes over the term "thick" from Clifford Geertz's notion of "thick description", a vital tool in situations where an ethnographer encounters "a multiplicity of complex conceptual structures, many of them superimposed upon or knotted into one another, which are at once strange, irregular, and inexplicit, and which he must contrive somehow first to grasp and then to render" (Geertz 1973: 10). No doubt it is this image of concepts "knotted into one another" that Williams finds sympathetic to his own designs. (Incidentally, Geertz, for his part, attributes the term's coinage to Gilbert Ryle's distinction between "thin descriptions" of purely physical behaviour and "thick descriptions" that capture both the physical behaviour and its cultural significance.) Although Williams may not have originated the term "thick", a more interesting question concerns whether he should be considered the first philosopher to focus on the phenomenon thick concepts purportedly pick out; that is, the first to focus on terms that unite fact and value.

Certainly he is not the first philosopher to utilize such terms. Aristotle's virtues of character – courage, temperance, generosity and the like – and their corresponding excesses and deficiencies pretty clearly render description and evaluation inseparable (see Aristotle 1999: especially Books II–IV), and Hume lists words – discretion, caution, enterprise, frugality, to name a few – "whose very names force an avowal of their merit, … [and] to which the most determined scepticism cannot for a moment refuse the tribute of praise and approbation" (Hume 1975: 242–3). (See Blackburn 1992, however, for determined scepticism regarding Hume's claim, and much else besides.) Nor does it seem that Williams is the first philosopher to appeal explicitly to the hybrid nature of such terms. In fact, his own Oxford tutor, R. M. Hare, speaks of "secondarily evaluative" words, such as "tidy" and "industrious", that pair descriptive and prescriptive elements, albeit with the former dominant (see Hare 1952: Chapter 7; 1963: Chapter 2), and Murdoch discusses "specialized normative words" or "secondary specialized words", including "bumptious", "vulgar" and "spontaneous", which are, like Williams's thick concepts, essentially "normative-descriptive" (see Murdoch 1970a). So it appears that Williams cannot lay claim to inventing thick concepts; nevertheless, no philosopher has made more detailed and ambitious claims for their role in providing whatever foundation there may be for ethical knowledge.

On the one hand, the world-guidedness of thick concepts ensures that objective features of the world ("what the world is like") determine their application. On the other hand, the action-guidingness of thick concepts ensures that their application provides at least a prima facie reason for action. For example, to apply the thick concept "treacherous" to a proposed action is not only to claim that the act meets certain objective criteria warranting the term's application, that it involves, say, talking about someone behind their back or passing state secrets to another country, but also that there exists a reason, simply in virtue of the act's being treacherous, not to do it; there is, as it were, not-to-be-doneness built right into the "treacherous". Thin concepts, by contrast, include "good", "right" and "ought", and can be defined either positively or negatively: by their generality and abstractness, or by their lack of world-guidedness. They constitute the currency of the sort of reductive, universal and overriding enterprises that make up the much maligned morality system, discussed in Chapter 4.

Before we turn to the specific use Williams makes of thick concepts, perhaps a significant reservation concerning the very coherence of any distinction between thick and thin should be briefly noted. In a powerful review of *Ethics and the Limits of Philosophy*, Scheffler convincingly argues that "any division of ethical concepts into the two categories of the thick and the thin is itself a considerable oversimplification" (Scheffler 1987: 418). To begin with, he encourages the reader to "Consider the following concepts, for example: justice, fairness, and impartiality, to take one cluster of notions; liberty, equality, freedom of expression, to take another; privacy, self-respect, envy, to take a third; needs, well-being, and interests, to take a fourth; and rights, autonomy and consent, for a fifth" (*ibid.*: 417). He then asks, reasonably enough: "Are the concepts on this list thick or thin?" (*ibid.*). Any answer at all, Scheffler believes, proves illuminating:

> If they are all thick, that suggests that contemporary ethical theories are far more concerned with thick concepts than Williams allows, for surely they are all concerned with concepts on this list. If on the other hand these concepts are all thin, that suggests that the class of thin concepts is much more diverse than Williams indicates, so that even if current ethical theories are preoccupied with thin concepts, this preoccupation may not involve the kind of gross oversimplification that was earlier alleged [in *Ethics and the Limits of Philosophy*]. And if some of the concepts on the list are thick while others are thin, then each of the two foregoing conclusions is supported to some extent. (*Ibid.*)

Supposing that Scheffler's own conclusion holds, and that "it is impossible confidently to classify various of the concepts on the list as either thick or thin" (*ibid.*), might not Williams's thick concept driven agenda for ethical objectivity be stymied?

Roughly a decade later, Williams himself appears to acknowledge the force of Scheffler's critique regarding the distinction between thick and thin concepts, yet perhaps without truly appreciating its intended target. Williams writes: "It's worth adding, as Samuel Scheffler has pointed out, that there is an important class of concepts that lie between the thick and the thin ... " (Williams 1996a: 26). But as the quotations above suggest, it is far from clear that Scheffler seeks to identify some third class of concepts, those in some grey zone between thick and thin, as opposed to problematizing the very distinction itself. World-guidedness and action-guidingness are both scalar qualities and, more to the point, may just as well inhere in the vocabulary of the moral theories Williams attacks as in the vocabulary of the pre-theoretical ethical experience he champions, or so Scheffler has it. In any case, Scheffler's analysis seems to warrant a more cautious attitude towards Williams's indictments of the morality system based on the alleged unavailability of thick concepts to theory.

Central to Williams's case for thick concepts is the claim that "a society that relies on very general ethical expressions is a different sort of society from one that puts greater weight on more specific ones" (Williams 1985: 128). To elucidate more fully this latter sort, he introduces the notion of a "hypertraditional society", one that is "maximally homogeneous and minimally given to general reflection" and, not incidentally, one that utilizes thick rather than thin ethical concepts (*ibid.*: 142). Now, depending on what one takes as appropriate epistemological criteria, in utilizing those concepts the members of the hypertraditional society may or may not display ethical knowledge. In *Ethics and the Limits of Philosophy*, Williams relies on "the best available accounts of propositional knowledge" (specifically citing Nozick 1981), so that for a society to manifest ethical knowledge: (a) its members must believe their judgements, (b) their judgements must be true and (c) conditions (a) and (b) must be "non-accidentally linked", which is to say that their beliefs must, in Nozick's terms, "track the truth" (*ibid.*: 142–3). As will be evident, Williams believes there is at least one way of construing the practice of the hypertraditional society such that all three conditions can be met.

It may be worth noting in passing that as far as thick concepts are concerned Williams seems to embrace a rather different model of knowledge in the years following *Ethics and the Limits of Philosophy*, one some distance removed from "truth tracking". Based on Edward Craig's naturalized epistemology, and bearing the not so faint impression of Aristotle, the "advisor model" assumes that "the point of the concept of knowledge is that of helping us to identify reliable informants" (Williams 1996a: 27; see Craig 1990). Taking this point,

> If we concentrate on thick concepts, we do indeed have something like the notion of a helpful informant. We have the notion of a helpful advisor. This is somebody who may be better at seeing that a certain outcome, policy, or way of dealing with the situation falls under a concept of this kind, than we are in our unassisted

> state, and better than other people who are less good at thinking about such matters. (Williams 1996a: 27)

The advisor model preserves the local flavour of the hypertraditional society. As such, Williams believes it can do "very little for the larger concerns of cognitivism" (Williams 1995k: 208), bound as they are to reduction and generality, which is just to say that the advisor model "looks a lot better than a model of ethical knowledge as theoretical" (Williams 1996a: 27). But whether or not thick concepts should be best understood as constituents of reliable advice or on some other epistemological model, the question of objectivity remains.

An important character in Williams's analysis is the "insightful but not totally identified observer", Geertz's ethnographer, say, who "can follow the practice of the people he is observing; he can report, anticipate, and even take part in discussions of the use they make of their concepts. But, as with some other concepts of theirs, . . . he may not be ultimately identified with the use of the concept: it may not really be his" (Williams 1985: 142). This character assumes importance for two reasons. First, he provides needed contrast between a culture based on thick concepts and a more reflective culture employing thin concepts. Second, and more immediately, the outside observer provides Williams with a way to frame the possibility of ethical knowledge through thick concepts. According to Williams,

> The members of the hypertraditional society apply their thick concepts, and in doing so they make various judgments. If any of those judgments can ever properly be said to be true, then their beliefs can track the truth since they can withdraw judgments if the circumstances turn out not to be what was supposed, can make an alternative judgment if it would be more appropriate, and so on. They have, each, mastered these concepts, and they can perceive the personal and social happenings to which the concepts apply. If there is truth here, their beliefs can track it. The question left is whether any of these judgments can be true. (*Ibid*.: 143)

The answer to that question depends on just how the outside observer interprets the practices of the hypertraditional society.

Williams introduces two distinct interpretive frameworks an outside observer might apply to the hypertraditional society, each with distinct implications as far as the ascription of truth to judgements employing thick concepts is concerned. The difference between the two frameworks turns on the degree of reflection imputed to the society's ethical practices. On the first, "objectivist", framework, the members of the society attempt, "in their local way, to find out the truth about values" (*ibid*.: 147). Put most basically, in this view they possess first-order judgements involving values, as well as reflective or second-order practices intended to underwrite the accuracy of such judgements. According to Williams's second framework,

> we shall see their judgments as part of their way of living, a cultural artifact they have come to inhabit (though they have not consciously built it). On this, nonobjectivist, model, we shall take a different view of the relations between that practice and critical reflection. We shall not be disposed to see the level of reflection as implicitly already there, and we shall not want to say that their judgments have, just as they stand, these implications.
> (*Ibid*.: 147)

Williams draws a profound epistemological moral from these duelling interpretive schemes:

> if we take the nonobjectivist view of their ethical activities . . . various members of the society will have knowledge, when they deploy their concepts carefully, use the appropriate criteria, and so on. But on the objectivist view they do not have knowledge, or at least it is most unlikely that they do, since their judgments have extensive implications, which they have never considered, at a reflective level, and we have every reason to believe that, when those implications are considered, the traditional use of ethical concepts will be seriously affected. (*Ibid*.: 148)

In sum, a society whose ethical practices revolve around thick concepts may satisfy Williams's conditions for propositional knowledge, as long as it maintains a minimally reflective character.

This minimally reflective character of the hypertraditional society becomes key, as it is this feature that, on Williams's view, allows ethical beliefs to track the truth. Ethical judgements containing thick concepts may be straightforwardly true within the confines of societal practice, in as much as the concepts themselves and the circumstances inviting their application reflect accepted and deeply internalized forms of collective practice. Once such practice turns reflective and begins to consider both the implications of and the epistemic warrant for the society's ethical beliefs, the conditions for confident application of thick terms, and so the conditions for truth tracking, may evaporate. Most basically, such reflection means evaluating thick concepts in terms of thin, asking, for example, whether it is *right* to believe that sharing state secrets is *treachery*. As Williams says,

> A judgment using a very general concept . . . is essentially a product of reflection, and it comes into question when someone stands back from the practices of the society and its use of these [thick] concepts and asks whether this is the right way to go on, whether these are good ways in which to assess actions, whether the kinds of character that are admired are rightly admired.
>
> (Williams 1985: 146)

Once a society slips into this reflective mode, it becomes more and more difficult for it to retain a firm hold on ethical truth and knowledge. And the prospects for regaining its hold in cases where specific ethical judgments have been compromised by reflection seem rather dim, since Williams maintains (or, as Scheffler has it, since Williams "rather gleefully concludes") that "in ethics, *reflection can destroy knowledge*" (*ibid.*: 148; Scheffler 1987: 419). Indeed, Putnam insists that "*reflection destroys ethical knowledge* . . . could be the motto of [*Ethics and the Limits of Philosophy*]" (Putnam 1994: 188).

Acknowledging that some philosophers have found this motto "confusing or unnecessarily provocative", Williams attempts not only to restate his position, but to refine it in terms of an "elementary theory of truth" (Williams 1996a: 29, 30). First, the restatement:

> All I claimed [in *Ethics and the Limits of Philosophy*] was that reflection can destroy knowledge, not that it must do so. . . . What I had in mind was the situation in which they no longer have the concept with which they used to express a certain class of beliefs. They lose a concept, and so cease to have a disposition that expresses itself in categorizing the world in those terms.
>
> (*Ibid.*: 30)

Now the refinement:

> Statements of the kind "X is chaste" and "X is not chaste" are true, when they're true, in some Language L, which is a certain ethical language but not the same as our ethical language L_0 because the languages differ at least in the respect that one contains the concept of chastity and the other doesn't. . . . Someone can come to understand this ethical language L without its being that person's own language. . . . What he can't do is to generate a Tarski-equivalent right hand side in his own language L_0 for the

> claim that (e.g.) "X is chaste" is true in L. The reason he can't do this is that ... the expressive powers of his own language are different from those of the native language precisely in the respect that the native language contains an ethical concept which his doesn't. ... Granted the fact, which I find undeniable, that different societies' thick ethical concepts are not simply homogeneous, don't simply map on to each other, we have a perfectly coherent account of what truthfulness in L is and what its relation can be to the language of an observer. (*Ibid.*: 30–31)

Also here, of course, is a natural invitation to ethical relativism, the details of which are considered in the next section.

Acknowledgment, restatement and refinement notwithstanding, Williams's attenuated ethical cognitivism has drawn its share of criticism, perhaps most shrilly from Putnam: "Williams' conclusion is right but the argument is terrible!" (Putnam 1994: 189). Instead of taking up that criticism, however, it may be more helpful if we briefly note a certain parallel between Williams's embrace of ethical cognitivism via thick concepts and his rejection of ethical realism via the absolute conception. While the absolute conception is depicted as maximally independent of perspective, thick concepts are depicted as maximally independent of reflection. Both, however, prove inherently unstable. Just as the absolute conception succumbs to instability in practice, occasioned by the fine line between empty absolutism and inevitable localism, so thick concepts cannot but remain vulnerable, given the practical demands of this "pervasively reflective" modern life (Williams 1985: 2). Still, for Williams, "thick concepts provide the most promising area in ethics for delivering more than minimal truth, more than simply the surface facts", even as he concedes that "of course these facts don't remove all disagreement" (Williams 1996a: 31). In as much as relativism may suggest itself as a philosophical approach to ethical disagreement, Williams's influential views on the subject are now canvassed.

A relativism of distance

Williams points out that although "there are limits to the degree of ultimate disagreement that can exist within a society (for without some degree of moral homogeneity it would not be a society); ... there are no limits ... on disagreement between societies" (Williams 1972: 19). Such intersocietal discord proves fertile soil for ethical relativism, in as much as "Its aim is to take views, outlooks, or beliefs that apparently conflict and treat them in such a way that they do not conflict: each of them turns out to be acceptable in its own place" (Williams 1985: 156). Williams's influential views regarding relativism's success in meeting this aim can be found in three principal locations. In *Morality*, Williams rejects "the most distinctive and the most influential form" of ethical relativism (Williams 1972: 20); in "The Truth in Relativism" and in Chapter 9 of *Ethics and the Limits of Philosophy* he identifies a strain of relativism, "the relativism of distance", that he believes passes philosophical muster.

Morality's target is "vulgar relativism", which Williams calls "possibly the most absurd view to have been advanced even in moral philosophy" (Williams 1972: 20). Vulgar relativism as a philosophical position can be captured in two statements thought to be obviously inconsistent (hence the vulgarity): "that 'right' means (can only be coherently understood as meaning) 'right for a given society'; ... and that (therefore) it is wrong for people in one society to condemn, interfere with, etc., the values of another society" (*ibid.*). Clearly employing a non-relative sense of "wrong", Williams sees the "logically unhappy" second statement as undermining the relativist ambitions of the first (*ibid.*: 21). Perhaps this *tu quoque* inconsistency, exceedingly familiar in the wake of postmodernism and end-of-philosophy debates, may have appeared less so in 1972. In any case, Williams summarizes "the central confusion of relativism" as attempting "to conjure out of the fact that societies have differing attitudes and values an *a priori* nonrelative principle to determine the attitude of one society to another" (*ibid.*: 23). Yet, in dismissing the attempt as "impossible", Williams equally rejects any automatic move towards principles of universal toleration.

For one thing, such a move, even assuming some moral justification for it, may be quite implausible as a matter of practical psychology. As Williams remarks, "it is essential ... to morality and its role in any society that certain sorts of reactions and motivations should be strongly internalized, and these cannot merely evaporate because one is confronted with human beings in another society" (*ibid.*: 23). Moreover, inherent universalizing tendencies in any society's moral views militate against the easy adoption of a "When in Rome ... " alternative. From just the fact, if it is one, that different societies or cultures or countries have different moral codes, it does not follow that all such codes must be tolerated or respected. Concluding his discussion of vulgar relativism, Williams observes that "it cannot be a consequence of the nature of morality itself that no society ought ever interfere with another, or that individuals from one society confronted with the practices of another ought, if rational, to react with acceptance" (*ibid.*: 25). Ethical relativism as a factual description of ethical difference can never justify ethical relativism as a moral prescription of universal toleration.

The similarity and complementarity of Williams's discussions of relativism in "The Truth in Relativism" and *Ethics and the Limits of Philosophy* belie their appearance ten years apart. Both begin by distinguishing "real" from "notional" confrontations between two cultures or "systems of belief". As Williams defines them, "A real confrontation between two divergent outlooks occurs at a given time if there is a group of people for whom each of the outlooks is a real option. A notional confrontation, by contrast, occurs when some people know about two divergent outlooks, but at least one of those outlooks does not present a real option" (Williams 1985: 160). Of course this merely shifts the explanatory weight on to "real option": "The idea of a 'real option' is largely, but not entirely, a social notion. An outlook is a real option for a group either if it is already their outlook or if they could go over to it; and they could go over to it if they could live inside it in their actual historical circumstances and retain their hold on reality, not engage in extensive self-deception, and so on" (*ibid.*: 160–61). Williams rounds out the idea of a real option with two further claims. First, an outlook may be a real option for a society without being explicitly conceived as such. It is basically "an objective question" whether an outlook provides a real option: "People can be mistaken about these questions" (Williams 1981j: 140; 1985: 161). Second, options may be "asymmetrically related". While there may be some sense in which meaningful roles in the contemporary information age are available to the Yanamamo, there is no sense, no "real" sense, in which the role of tribal subsistence hunter in the Amazonas is available to members of contemporary society.

Of course, most unreal options (Williams gives "a Bronze Age chief or a medieval samurai" as examples) and, therefore, most notional confrontations will be related diachronically. Although conceding that "The socially and historically remote has always been an important object of self-critical and self-encouraging fantasy", Williams insists that

> to raise seriously questions in the vocabulary of appraisal [e.g. good, bad, right, wrong] about this [remote] culture considered as a concrete historical reality will not be possible for a

> reflective person ... [T]o stand in merely notional confrontation is to lack the relation to our concerns which alone gives any point or substance to appraisal ... [T]he only real questions of appraisal are about real options. (Williams 1981j: 141–2)

In notional confrontations, then, "no judgements are made", which is just to say a sort of relativism applies, a sort Williams, in *Ethics and the Limits of Philosophy*, labels "the relativism of distance" (Williams 1985: 161, 162). In cases where, as one might put it, inhabiting an alternative form of life proves impossible, or where, in familiar terms from the previous section, adopting another culture's use of thick concepts proves impossible, Williams takes it that meaningful ethical criticism also proves impossible: "While the vocabulary [of appraisal] can no doubt be applied without linguistic impropriety, there is so little to this use, so little of what gives content to the appraisals in the context of real confrontations, that we can say that for a reflective person the question of appraisal does not genuinely arise ... in purely notional confrontation" (Williams 1981j: 141). This idea that notional confrontation warrants the suspension of ethical judgement constitutes "the truth in relativism".

Somewhat puzzlingly, however, no sooner has Williams established the pointlessness of ethical judgement in notional confrontations than he seems to waffle a bit, or at least to allow one notable exception. That exception involves justice, specifically the application of the judgements "just" and "unjust" to societies in cases where it would seem the relativism of distance should apply; that is, to societies so removed in space or, especially, time that the language of appraisal gains no purchase. Williams suggests that "It may be that considerations of justice are a central element of ethical thought that transcends the relativism of distance" (Williams 1985: 166). His reasoning goes as follows:

> "Just" and "unjust" are central terms that can be applied to societies as a whole, and in principle, at least, they can be applied to societies concretely and realistically conceived. Moreover, an assessment in terms of justice can, more obviously than others, be conducted without involving the unhelpful question of whether anyone was to blame. The combination of these features makes social justice a special case in relation to relativism. Justice and injustice are certainly ethical notions and arguably can be applied to past societies as a whole, even when we understand a good deal about them. (*Ibid.*: 165)

Williams's willingness to make an exception of justice seems of a pattern with viewing that virtue as straddling the fence between thick concepts and thin. Thick concepts "belong" to a culture, and their very thickness, their particular weaving of fact and value, precludes outsiders from employing their thick terms and, *a fortiori*, evaluating another culture in terms of them. Thin concepts, by contrast, do the bidding of the morality system, their context-transcending generality undermining any serious application at a distance. But, and here simply echoing the point Scheffler insists applies to a host of evaluative terms, justice seems to possess both thick and thin aspects.

Williams himself says of justice: "There is more to it than a concept of 'right': that an action is just is *one reason* it can be right. On the other hand, the content of 'just' is in a certain way indeterminate or disputable or open to a variety of conceptions" (Williams 1996a: 26). Presumably this hybrid nature – arguably action-guiding, yet not quite truth-tracking – empowers its application to remote ethical practices. Certainly Williams believes that "there are strong pressures for the justice or injustice of past societies not merely to evaporate in the relativism of distance ... [S]ome conceptions of justice were used in those societies themselves, and it is not a pun or linguistic error to call them that. ... Earlier conceptions, in some form, are still with us" (Williams 1985: 166). And it is this continuity in conception that warrants the suspension, in the case of justice, at least, of the relativism of distance.

Not that such suspension purchases anything much philosophically, at least according to Scheffler, who, in the same essay cited earlier, suggests that exempting justice from the relativism of distance merely "allows temporally remote societies with divergent conceptions of justice to call each other names, just as societies that are contemporaries do, instead of simply glaring at each other in silence across the temporal divide" (Scheffler 1987: 428). In the absence of the sort of objectivity purchased by a thick concept-backed cognitivism (or any other kind), Williams's concept of transhistorical justice "provides no basis whatsoever for regarding one side's ideas as right or the other's as wrong" (*ibid.*). And Scheffler's is hardly the only voice of dissent as far as Williams's relativism of distance is concerned.

Perhaps not surprisingly, both Putnam and McDowell advance doubts concerning the coherence of the relativism of distance, particularly the idea at its heart, that ethical appraisal in notional confrontations makes no sense; indeed, that to the reflective individual the issue of such appraisal tends not to arise in the first place. For his part, Putnam seriously questions Williams's basic division between real and notional confrontations, astutely, if troublingly, pointing out that even "the confrontation between the Jews and the Nazis would not count as a real confrontation by Williams' definition – because 'going over to' the point of view of the other was not a 'real option' for either the Jews or the Nazis" (Putnam 1992: 104). Furthermore, Putnam finds considerable irony in Williams's position. While much of Williams's point in introducing world-guided and action-guiding thick concepts had to do with dissolving that favourite philosophical fiction, the fact/value distinction, Putnam sees the plausibility of the relativism of distance as heavily dependent on the maintenance of just that distinction, as the very intertwining of fact and value that Williams correctly emphasizes weighs against the suspension of ethical appraisal in notional confrontations.

Take, Putnam urges, a notional confrontation with Aztec culture. The Aztecs believed that their gods required regular human sacrifice. In Williams's view, contemporary observers may straightforwardly reject this belief as false. Science reliably informs us that no such gods exist and, therefore, that there could be no such requirement. At the same time, however, these observers may not, given the relativism of distance, reject this same belief, that the gods require regular human sacrifice, as morally wrong. And Putnam wonders: "If we are not allowed to call the practice wrong, why are we allowed to call the belief false?" (Putnam 1990a: 175). After all, "the feature of the Aztec way of life that troubles us (the massive human sacrifice) and the belief about the world that conflicts with science were interdependent. If we can say that the Aztec belief about the gods was false, why can we not say that the practice to which it led was wrong (although, to be sure, understandable given the false factual belief)?" (*ibid.*). As Putnam sees it, Williams "load[s] the dice in favor of relativism by taking science to consist of individual judgments which may be called true or false, while taking cultures to offer only 'take it as a whole or reject it as a whole' options" (*ibid.*: 176). And where Korsgaard saw in Williams's absolute conception merely an expression of confidence in scientific realism, Putnam sees in the relativism of distance merely "an expression of a mood" (*ibid.*), tantamount, he might well say, to mere confidence in ethical relativism.

McDowell expresses similar concerns. Notwithstanding his hunch that modern reflectiveness might actually be a boon to ethical judgement (see also Jardine 1995 for the claim that reflection *adds* knowledge), McDowell wonders how attractive any view can be that allows observers to appreciate the remote evaluative contexts operative in notional confrontations, but then denies those same observers the right to judge them. As he puts it, "if an outlook does conflict with one's own (a condition of the problem arising to which relativism is supposed to be a response), how can one coherently combine recognizing the conflict and standing by one's own outlook with disclaiming any interest in, or even possibility of, making some negative assessment of the other?" (McDowell 1986: 384). McDowell challenges Williams to explain better just why the impossibility of inhabiting an Aztec form of life precludes ethically appraising that life, assuming, as Williams appears to, that the relativism of distance does not preclude understanding it. That one cannot integrate remote ethical concepts piecemeal into one's own life, given their deeply embedded role in some remote practice, ought not to prevent one from voicing a view on the moral value – the rightness or wrongness – of beliefs employing those concepts.

Williams himself says that "The aim of relativism is to *explain away* a conflict, and this involves two tasks. It has to say why there is no conflict, and also why it looked as if there were one" (Williams 1985: 156–7). And he takes his relativism of distance to achieve both tasks: first, there is no conflict because occupying a distant form of life is not a real option; secondly, it only looked as though there were a conflict because we can understand remote beliefs to be different from our own. But Putnam and McDowell believe that the ground of Williams's own error theory, that we can, in fact, grasp the ethical point of remote beliefs, introduces no small doubt regarding the relevance of distance to questions of appraisal; that is, introduces no small doubt regarding the relativism of distance.

Conclusion

A realist, cognitivist and anti-relativist when it comes to science, all positions to which, he believes, the absolute conception, in one way or other, lends support, Williams adopts a bifurcated stance when it comes to ethics. If one characterizes ethical life "reflectively" in terms of the morality system, particularly in terms of its thin concepts, Williams's by now familiar ethical scepticism takes the form of anti-realism, non-cognitivism and relativism ("of distance"). But if one characterizes ethical practice "traditionally" in terms of thick concepts, Williams's position shifts interestingly and noticeably to pair his unwavering anti-realism with unmistakably cognitivist tendencies.

The rub, of course, is that "the modern world is marked by a peculiar level of reflectiveness" (Williams 1985: 163). As things stand, "the urge to reflective understanding of society and our activities goes deeper and is more widely spread in modern society than it has ever been before", and so "the thicker kinds of ethical concepts have less currency in modern society than they did in more traditional society" (*ibid.*). The question then becomes how to respond to the hopelessly endangered status of thick concepts, and here, despite reflection's relentless destruction of ethical knowledge, Williams resists the temptations of conservatism, refusing to advocate that resources (supposing there are any) should be directed towards the preservation or reclamation of traditional culture (supposing they could be). Instead, Williams sounds positively progressive: "Ethical knowledge, though there is such a thing, is not necessarily the best ethical state. Here we must remember that, in the process of losing ethical knowledge, we may gain knowledge of other kinds, about human nature, history, what the world is like. We gain knowledge about, or around, the ethical" (*ibid.*: 168). Such valorizing of alternative forms of knowledge would seem of a piece with Williams's general tendency to favour the intellectual prospects of, say, psychology and anthropology over those of ethical theory.

In *Morality*, Williams takes his ethical anti-realism, and the idea that "things are with morality not quite as they seemed", to warrant "at most resentment rather than panic" (Williams 1972: 37). In *Ethics and the Limits of Philosophy*, he takes it that "the idea that our values are not 'in the world', that a properly untendentious description of the world would not mention any values", should in no way elicit despair (Williams 1985: 128). Instead, Williams believes that "a radical form of freedom may be found in the fact that we cannot be forced by the world to accept one set of values rather than another" (*ibid.*). Of course, a significant strain of twentieth-century philosophy had no trouble linking radical freedom to despair; nevertheless, for Williams, a kind of "liberation" accompanies a proper metaphysics of morals. And, as far as a proper epistemology is concerned, he "cannot see any convincing theory of knowledge for the convergence of reflective ethical thought on ethical reality in even a distant analogy to the scientific case" (*ibid.*: 152). Taking the absolute conception as the gold standard, convergence remains the critical, and for ethics unrealizable, criterion of objectivity.

Notwithstanding Williams's evident pessimism regarding the prospects for robust ethical objectivity, given the demise of thick concepts and the forms of ethical life they support under the seemingly inevitable assault of modernity's increased reflectiveness, he remains hesitant to rule out completely "the project of trying to give an objective grounding or foundation to ethical life" (*ibid.*). Certainly he rejects, as previous chapters have shown, any suggestion that such grounding will be found in the dictates of practical rationality as such. Still to be considered, however, is the prospect of a foundation anchored in "ideas about human nature", one that might generate "a schema of an ethical life that would be the best ethical life, the most satisfactory for human beings in general" (*ibid.*: 152, 153). This prospect too, however, leaves Williams far from sanguine: "The project of giving to ethical life an objective and determinate grounding in considerations about human nature is not, in my view, very likely to succeed. But it is at any rate a comprehensible project, and I believe it represents the only intelligible form of ethical objectivity at the reflective level" (*ibid.*: 153). As far as determining that nature goes, he believes "the most natural and promising field for this kind of inquiry" involves the virtues (*ibid.*). Such talk of virtues, of course, leads naturally to talk of Aristotle's approach to ethics, an approach Williams elsewhere calls "the only colourable attempt to provide a foundation for ethics" (Williams 1995h: 201), not to mention an approach that has attracted a remarkable amount of attention in the years since being labelled promising in *Ethics and the Limits of Philosophy*. To this approach, and, indeed, to other of Williams's philosophical contributions connected with the ancient world, Chapter 7 now attends.

Chapter 7

The ancient world

Introduction

Like Nietzsche a century before, whose persistent influence on Williams may be as difficult to describe as it is to dismiss, and about which this chapter will have more to say, Williams began his university training as a classicist, evidence of which can be found in the mastery of ancient Greek poets, dramatists, historians and, of course, philosophers that pervades his work from beginning to end. For Williams, the ideas of the ancient world fill a reservoir from which moderns and postmoderns may slake their philosophical thirst; not just in the sense that ancient thought holds inherent intellectual interest, which of course it does, but more importantly in the sense that, as Williams puts it in *Shame and Necessity*, almost certainly his finest book, "our view of [the ancient Greeks] is intimately connected with our view of ourselves" (Williams 1993b: 3). In short, contemporary self-understanding depends upon understanding the Greeks.

Williams displays his own understanding of the Greeks in remarkably varied forms. On the one hand, there are a number of fairly narrow, relatively self-contained analyses of more or less focused topics drawn from classical philosophical texts by Plato and Aristotle, topics such as Plato's treatment of names in the *Cratylus* or Aristotle's conception of justice in the *Nicomachean Ethics* (see Williams 1982b and 1980 respectively). On the other hand, there are instances of memorably ambitious breadth. Who but Williams, one is tempted to ask, would take on Plato for a series on "The Great Philosophers" (Williams 1997), producing a stunningly satisfying account in all of forty-five pages? And who but Williams would be invited to compose the chapter simply entitled "Philosophy" (Williams 1981g) for M. I. Finley's expansive *The Legacy of Greece*? Decidedly not for the intellectually faint of heart, such occasions for turning impenetrable philosophical thickets into well tended gardens seem naturally to attract Williams – or to attract others to him. (He is, after all, the author of the entry "the nature of opera" in the multivolume *New Grove Dictionary of Music and Musicians*.) And then, of course, there are the books: *Ethics and the Limits of Philosophy* (1985), with its extended analysis of Aristotelian ethical theory; *Truth and Truthfulness* (2002), with its account of Herodotus, Thucydides and the origins of "real history"; and the aforementioned *Shame and Necessity*.

This chapter presents four key aspects of Williams's thought concerning the ancient world. First, the section "Aristotle", examines his critique of Aristotle's ethical theory, as well as an impressive response to it by Nussbaum. Just as Williams, as shown in Chapters 3 and 4, rejects utilitarian and deontological theories, he comes to reject Aristotelian approaches, understood as approaches that attempt to ground ethical life in the virtues, while attempting to ground the virtues in a certain conception of human life. Still, as noted at the end of Chapter 6, Williams does credit Aristotle with "the only colourable attempt to provide a foundation for ethics" (Williams 1995h: 201), and, whatever "colourable" may mean precisely, it appears tied up with Aristotle's view of ethical life as "a harmonious culmination of human potentialities, recoverable from an absolute understanding of nature" (Williams 1985: 52), a view Williams seems to find at least satisfying for its coherence.

Closely tied to, indeed, probably inseparable from, any appreciation of Aristotle's ambitions for ethics is the complex issue of ethical naturalism. For Williams, "The question for naturalism is always: can we explain, by some appropriate and relevant criteria of explanation, the phenomenon in question in terms of the *rest* of nature" (Williams 2000a: 150). And he provocatively contends that any adequate answer to this question will depend not as much on the resources of philosophy as on the resources of genealogy, in as much as "Genealogy is intended to serve the aims of naturalism" (Williams 2002: 22). Just what he means by genealogy, how to distinguish it from philosophy and whether and how his version of it differs from Nietzsche's are among the questions considered in the section "Naturalism and genealogy".

"Shame and necessity" develops just a few of the dazzlingly many topics that make up the book of that title, focusing especially on the possibility of combining Williams's conceptions of shame and "necessary identities" to form a robust account of moral agency, an account, moreover, eschewing those features of ethical theory he so harshly criticized before. The details of such an account appear firmly linked to tragedy, and particularly to Williams's reading of Sophocles' *Ajax*. But the philosophical implications of Greek tragedy are certainly nothing new to Williams, having commanded his attention, one way or another, for four decades, from "Ethical Consistency" to *Truth and Truthfulness*. The chapter's conclusion explores Williams's conception of tragedy, ponders its relation to pessimism (another prominent Nietzschean theme) and, finally, perhaps somewhat speculatively, considers whether Williams himself may be said to recommend such views – the tragic and pessimistic – as suitable, indeed warranted, approaches to life.

Aristotle

In *Morality*, Williams speaks of Aristotle adopting "a procedure of trying to elicit unquestionable moral ends or ideals from distinguishing marks of man's nature" (Williams 1972: 59). Such a procedure reflects Aristotle's ethical foundationalism, a faith in, as Williams puts it in *Ethics and the Limits of Philosophy*, "an Archimedean point: something to which even the amoralist or the skeptic is committed" (Williams 1985: 29). This distinguishing mark of man, of course, turns out to be rationality, although Aristotle is hardly the only philosopher to seek an ethical foundation in human reason. As Williams points out, "There are two basic types of philosophical venture that fit this pattern. One of them works from the minimal and most abstract possible conception of rational agency. ... The other ... assumes a richer and more determinate view of what rational agency is, taking it to be expressed in living a specifically human life" (*ibid.*). The richer view belongs to Aristotle, the more abstract view to Kant, with at least some of that richness and determinacy probably coming from the fact that for Aristotle man is a rational *animal*, whereas for Kant man is an animal *rational*; that is to say, very roughly, that for Aristotle humans are essentially animals whose characteristic quality just happens to be reason, whereas for Kant humans are essentially rational beings that just happen to be animals. In any case, Chapter 4 has already documented the many ways Williams would impugn Kant's foundationalist enterprise. It remains to consider the plausibility, by Williams's lights, of Aristotle's project.

In considering and critiquing Aristotle's ethical view, Williams highlights different features in different places. In connection with moral epistemology, for example, and the "advisor model" of truth alluded to in Chapter 6, Williams focuses on Aristotle's concept of the *phronimos*, or practically wise person (see Williams 1995k). Relatedly, Williams at times enters Aristotle's ethics through the window of thick concepts, which he takes the *phronimos* to deploy and the virtues to instantiate (see Williams 1995a, 1995f). But the lion's share of Williams's critical attention has been directed towards the teleological aspects of Aristotle's view, both the *telos* itself and its putative grounding in a natural view of humans, whatever that may turn out to involve. Commentators point out that the picture of Aristotle Williams draws, and then takes as his target, is not particularly original. McDowell, for instance, calls Williams's reading of Aristotle "a version of an orthodoxy", while Nussbaum points to similarities between Williams's interpretation and those of Terence Irwin, Alasdair MacIntyre and David Wiggins (McDowell 1986: 385; Nussbaum 1995: 124n2). This seems fair. The real interest of Williams's critique comes not from what he sees as Aristotle's ultimate weaknesses, but from what he admires as his strengths.

Aristotle's basic approach identifies a certain arrangement of ethical dispositions or character traits or virtues as best suited to attaining, in a certain sense to embodying, whatever it is to be a flourishing human being over the course of a lifetime. As Williams puts it, the Aristotelian agent "could come to understand that the dispositions that gave him his ethical view of the world were a correct or full development of human potentiality" (Williams 1985: 52). In this view, ethical life becomes a function of inculcating certain tendencies to act in certain ways in certain circumstances: the tendency, for example, to put up a courageous fight when fear invites flight, or the tendency to give money generously to those in need. The crucial point is that, whatever these tendencies may turn out to be, they will be neither arbitrary nor relative, but will instead represent "a harmonious culmination of human potentialities, recoverable from an absolute understanding of nature" (*ibid.*). It is this absolute understanding that paves the way for externally grounding internal dispositions.

The basic outline Williams traces does seem familiar. To the question of what natural capacity uniquely defines human beings, Aristotle answers: the capacity to reason. Now, does it seem plausible to tie human happiness or well-being to the highest realization of that natural capacity? Certainly. And does it also seem plausible to identify a unique set of dispositions simply by considering which are best suited, individually and in combination, to produce that highest realization? Again, yes; indeed, Aristotle presumes to delineate just that set in the *Nicomachean Ethics*. So we seem to have derived a patently ethical prescription – an answer to the question of how one should live one's life – from considerations of human nature. In Williams's own words,

> According to Aristotle, there are certain characteristics, in particular certain activities and powers, which are distinctive of man, and the life of the good man will exemplify to the fullest degree the development of those powers and activities. Or, more accurately, there is one distinctive feature of man – his ability to shape his actions and dispositions by reason – which will be manifested in the highest degree. (Williams 1972: 55)

Again, it is this claim to have identified, externally, so to speak, and in nature, a characteristic of humans sufficient to underwrite a particular vision of human flourishing that Williams finds so powerful and, at least prima facie, so promising. However, although Aristotle might be right that ethical life is a matter of acquiring some correct set of dispositions (in fact, Williams is sure that he is), and although he might be right to find his own preferred set of dispositions sufficient for happiness, is Aristotle right to find that same set necessary for happiness? Even more importantly, can Aristotle rightfully ground that necessity in some one particular conception of human nature? Williams's scepticism on this point fuels a three-pronged attack.

First, Williams doubts current prospects for identifying in human nature the sort of uncontroversial and definitive characteristic Aristotle needs to ground a univocal *telos*. Secondly, even if some unquestioned distinguishing mark could be read off human nature, he doubts it would recommend any very determinate *telos*. Thirdly, even if the first two conditions could be met – that is, even if human nature plausibly sets up a universal conception of human flourishing as a target for all humans to aim at – Williams doubts that such a target can underwrite or effectively prescribe any very determinate or very harmonious set of virtues. In the first case, externality evaporates; in the second case, teleology proves fuzzy; in the third case, ethical guidance appears too diffuse, perhaps even absent altogether.

In the first case, Williams wonders why Aristotle should take rationality as the distinguishing mark. As he puts it in *Morality*, somewhat darkly, it must be admitted:

> If one approached without preconceptions the question of finding characteristics which differentiate men from other animals, one could as well, on these principles, end up with a morality which exhorted men to spend as much time as possible making fire; or developing peculiarly human physical characteristics; or having sexual intercourse without regard to season; or despoiling the environment and upsetting the balance of nature; or killing things for fun. (Williams 1972: 59)

Here Williams's reservations regarding Aristotle's depiction of the essence of human nature no doubt align with doubts, to be considered in the following section, concerning the ambitions of ethical naturalism more generally.

In the second case, Williams wonders why rationality, assuming it does uniquely define human nature, should be taken to determine a unique *telos*, given that rational powers admit of multiple realizations, even in, or especially in, the *Nicomachean Ethics* itself. Aristotle's appeal to "intelligence and capacity for rational thought" as the "distinguishing mark of man" gives rise to "a weakness that can be seen in the following light, that the pure or creative aspects of intelligence would seem to be the highest form of these capacities, yet a total commitment to their expression is ruled out, and a less than total commitment is not represented as something that practical thought can rationally arrive at" (Williams 1972: 56–7). Offering no textual support on this point, Williams seems merely to be gesturing at the well known interpretive challenge posed by the *Nicomachean Ethics* of reconciling what might be seen as Aristotle's instrumental, practical valorization of intellectual virtues in Book VI with their more intrinsic, theoretical valorization in Book X. The basic issue, however, can be neatly summarized: given the various ways in which humans can develop and manifest intelligence, wisdom, cleverness, creativity and all the other features of their distinctive rationality, there seems little prospect of identifying some single manner or mode of existence that represents the highest or best or most satisfying culmination or balance of such features. But, even more importantly for Williams, no matter how dim such prospects may be, there remains still less reason to think that if such a manner or mode of life were successfully identified, the dispositions or virtues best suited to its realization would prove to be ethical.

This leads directly to the third case, and the idea that whatever guidance the picture of flourishing (itself derived from taking rationality as the quintessentially human characteristic) offers may be at cross purposes or otherwise ineffective in terms of singling out and recommending some particular set of character traits or ethical dispositions for development. As Williams observes in *Morality*,

> A moralist who wants to base a conception of the right sort of life for man on considerations about the high and distinctive powers of man can scarcely disregard the claims of creative genius in the arts or sciences to be included pre-eminently among such powers; yet he will find it hard to elicit from, or even reconcile with, an ideal of development and expression of such genius, many of the virtues and commitments which belong to morality, some of which are more everyday, while most make demands on one's relations to other people which are quite different from those made by creative work. (Williams 1972: 57)

Similarly, running together all three cases somewhat in *Ethics and the Limits of Philosophy*:

> Our present understanding gives us no reason to expect that ethical dispositions can be fully harmonized with other cultural and personal aspirations that have as good a claim to represent human development ... [I]t is hard to believe that an account of human nature – if it is not already an ethical theory itself – will adequately determine one kind of ethical life as against others.
> (Williams 1985: 52)

In point of fact, Williams does accuse Aristotle of adopting an overly ethicized account of human nature, an accusation further explored below in connection with "Thucydidean impartiality". For now, it may be useful to see Williams's critique of the project of extracting patently ethical guidance from peculiarly human traits as he himself does, as of a piece with his earlier observations pertaining to moral luck and the vital lesson Gauguin's life teaches regarding the relative importance of the ethical versus everything else. Focusing on the fullest and highest development of human reason as a guide to the development of character may well result in privileging dispositions possessing scant ethical qualifications, a situation that recalls yet again Williams's "prior question, about what the distinction between the 'moral' and the 'non-moral' is supposed to do for us" (Williams 1993a: xiii).

Williams's various doubts concerning the Aristotelian project of, first, determining a distinctively human characteristic, secondly, determining a distinctive conception of human flourishing based on that distinctively human characteristic and, thirdly, determining a distinctive set of ethical dispositions based on that distinctive conception of human flourishing lead him to dismiss the possibility that "an absolute understanding of human nature" can provide the sort of external foundation sufficient to satisfy, in terms of determinacy and scope, not to mention content, the ambitions of ethical theory. As a consequence of this dismissal,

> a potential gap opens up between the agent's perspective and the outside view. We understand – and, most important, the agent can come to understand – that the agent's perspective is only one of many that are equally compatible with human nature, all open to various conflicts with themselves and with other cultural aims . . . [W]e must admit that the Aristotelian assumptions which fitted together the agent's perspective and the outside view have collapsed. (Williams 1985: 52–3)

But some philosophers question whether the assumptions Williams attributes to Aristotle, and that he so readily dismisses, truly capture Aristotle's project in the first place, whether, that is, what really collapses, in Williams's view, might not be more straw than theory.

Nussbaum, for example, in Altham and Harrison's valuable *Festschrift*, argues that "some of Williams's criticisms of Aristotle fail because the account he gives of Aristotle's human nature project . . . is, in some important respects, inaccurate" (Nussbaum 1995: 87). Not surprisingly, then, she believes that "Aristotle's actual position is stronger than the position Williams describes and then attacks" (*ibid.*). And just as other philosophers share Williams's reservations regarding Aristotle, others share Nussbaum's reservations regarding Williams (see, for example, McDowell 1986; Annas 1993), although it seems safe to say that no other response matches Nussbaum's for depth and focus. Just what inaccuracy does Nussbaum allude to, and how might it affect Williams's rejection of Aristotelian ethical theory, however "colourable" it may be, as a healthy alternative to Kantianism and utilitarianism?

Rankling Nussbaum is the picture Williams draws of Aristotle "recovering" a determinate conception of ethical life from "an absolute understanding of nature" (Williams 1985: 52). According to this picture, Aristotle moves towards ethical conclusions concerning how best to arrange internal virtues of character from external, effectively scientific premises concerning the sort of creatures humans essentially are. When the scientific or external picture begins to break down, under sceptical pressure concerning such essentialism, or concerning the idea of a univocal human *telos* or that *telos*'s prescriptive adequacy, so does the possibility of seeing ethical life as "a harmonious culmination of human potentialities" (*ibid.*: 57). But Williams's picture gets Aristotle wrong, Nussbaum insists, in as much as

> Aristotle's metaphysics of nature, and his biology, are neither value-free nor external. There is nothing anywhere in Aristotle's work precisely corresponding to a modern distinction between fact and value, and, furthermore, science, as well as ethics, is "internal" for Aristotle in the sense that it is the attempt to give an intelligent account of human experience in the world.
>
> (Nussbaum 1995: 102)

Most basically, Nussbaum takes Williams to read illegitimately his own sharp (and, she thinks, sharply questionable) science–ethics distinction into Aristotle, when, she argues, Aristotle himself would have found such a distinction incoherent (see also McDowell 1986: 385).

Rather than seeing Aristotle's elevation of rationality as the most distinctive human attribute as resulting from some objective, value-free scientific investigation, Nussbaum sees Aristotle as simply relying "on the method he uses in all other areas: to preserve the greatest number and the most basic of the 'appearances' – human perceptions and beliefs – on the subject" (Nussbaum 1995: 102). As such, Aristotle's elevation of rationality should be seen as a straightforward reflection of "the importance of practical reasoning in a human life"; that is, Aristotle's elevation of rationality should be seen as reflecting society's *endoxa*, "our firmest convictions concerning who we are" (*ibid.*: 117). As Nussbaum sums up her analysis of Aristotle (and Williams): "Human nature cannot, and need not, be validated from the outside, because human nature just is an inside perspective, not a thing at all, but rather the most fundamental and broadly shared experiences of human beings living and reasoning together" (*ibid.*: 121). In Nussbaum's view, admittedly much condensed, Aristotle's ethics is not the product of bringing independently arrived at conclusions about human nature to bear on questions of how one should live one's life and relate to others, but the product of coming to answer those questions through the very process of trying on, and subsequently interpreting, various possibilities for human development.

Williams responds to Nussbaum's criticism and interpretation at some length in his "Replies", arguably giving ground as far as Aristotelian exegesis goes, yet holding firm regarding what he sees as the foggy prospects for contemporary ethical theories drawn on Aristotelian lines. To begin with, Williams admits "I do not now want to claim that the Aristotelian enterprise requires a 'top-down' derivation of ethical conclusions from a scientifically respectable account of human beings", conceding that "In some things I have written I have suggested that this would be necessary" (Williams 1995h: 200). At the same time, however, he suggests that "Nussbaum tends to ascribe to me a more positivist account of the Aristotelian enterprise than I wanted to give" (*ibid.*: 195). Taking Nussbaum's analysis to heart, Williams agrees that "in inquiring into human nature Aristotle thought he could rely on *endoxa*". Williams points out, however, that "Aristotle thought that he could rely on *endoxa* in all areas of natural inquiry", emphasizing that "the presuppositions of that method have not survived the emergence of what we call the 'natural' as opposed to the human sciences" (*ibid.*: 194). In other words, the "well-established opinions shared by responsible and experienced thinkers" concerning human nature may well have proven sufficient to underwrite a set of virtues in ancient Greek society, but would hardly do as well today.

As Williams sees it, Nussbaum's hopes for a viable contemporary Aristotelianism commit her to the following view: "if one approaches the business of understanding human nature in a sufficiently hermeneutical and non-reductive way, the materials one needs to nourish ethical understanding will be obvious, and not of a kind that could be undercut by more specific or more technical inquiries" (*ibid.*: 195). But although the materials may be obvious, Williams doubts their ultimate ethical efficacy. On the one hand, Williams repeatedly pushes the point that, "as opposed to the emphasis of Martha Nussbaum … it makes a big difference to accepting Aristotle's ethical outlook that we cannot accept his cosmology" (*ibid.*: 199). Without *ergon*, without *telos*, the inherent indeterminacy in *eudaimonia* and the virtues it would underwrite will overwhelm the capacity of theory.

On the other hand, to formulate a conception of human nature for ethical purposes without recourse to more "technical inquiries", as seems to be Nussbaum's intention, strikes Williams as equally misguided. Although evolutionary psychology, say, may have thus far produced more heat than light on questions of human nature, any account of ethical life that ignores its findings risks implausibility, by ignoring what (perhaps someday) could be "the richest account available of human powers and social arrangements" (*ibid.*: 201). In sum, what Williams gives to Aristotle's own project in Aristotle's own time, he takes from attempts, such as Nussbaum's, to retool Aristotle for the twenty-first century, as this rather lengthy passage makes clear:

> I grant that the [Aristotelian] enterprise may be understood in coherentist or hermeneutical terms. I also grant that we can understand Aristotle himself as having seen it in some such terms. However, I do not think that we should infer from those two points that, because we can see it in such terms, and so did Aristotle, we can see it just as Aristotle saw it. This is because our understanding of nature and of what is "natural" does not bear the same relation to (what we call) hermeneutical or social understandings as Aristotle did, and that is why, even granted these points, I still think that, in leaving behind Aristotle's cosmology, the modern world has left behind elements necessary to making his style of ethical theory as a whole plausible, no matter how many useful thoughts we can, quite certainly, gain from it. (*Ibid.*: 201)

Furthermore, at the end of the day, many, if not most, of these useful thoughts appear tied, in Williams's view, to Aristotle's role as a template for some of the more general ambitions of ethical naturalism.

Naturalism and genealogy

Although usually brief, and to some extent overlapping, discussions of ethical naturalism appear with some frequency in Williams's work, and not always in connection with Aristotle (e.g. Williams 1995b, f, h, 2000a, 2002). Certainly a definition of naturalism as "the project of thinking out, from what human beings are like, how they might best and most appropriately live" seems of a piece with the Aristotelian concerns just examined (Williams 1995b: 109), but often Williams appears to prefer an even simpler, yet more sweeping conception: "The question for naturalism is always: can we explain ... the phenomenon in question in terms of the *rest* of nature?" (Williams 2000a: 150) This latter conception, however, tends to raise "a well-known difficulty in stabilizing the idea of 'nature' so that naturalism is not either trivially true or implausible to such an extent as to be uninteresting" (Williams 2002: 22). On the one hand, "nature" may become vacuous, a vessel for "whatever there is"; on the other hand, attempts to delimit "nature" may become restrictively reductionist, turning nature into whatever jibes with contemporary physics. In fact, the dispute touched upon earlier in "Aristotle", between what Williams takes to be Nussbaum's hermeneutical aspirations for Aristotle and what Nussbaum takes to be Williams's rather scientistic ones, in some ways reflects this "well-known difficulty".

Besides these two characterizations of the naturalist's project, the one using (human) nature's alphabet to spell out ethical considerations, the other determining (again, human) nature in terms of some broader nature, Williams also investigates what might be involved in a naturalistic moral psychology, even while conceding "I do not pretend this notion is at all perspicuous", in as much as "no one knows what it involves" (Williams 1995h: 203; 1993b: 67). Nonetheless, he points to an "extensive consensus" whereby a naturalistic moral psychology "means something to the effect that our view of moral capacities should be consistent with, even perhaps in the spirit of, our understanding of human beings as part of nature" (Williams 1993b: 67). Presumably some distinction exists, then, between a conception of how human beings should live, consistent with nature, and a conception of the psychology pertinent to human beings determining how they should live, consistent with nature, with the idea that the latter will have no small impact on the former. However this may be, Williams takes it that the attractions of naturalism in ethics are obvious: "It does not, in any obvious way, require any supernatural warrant, while it is less arbitrary or relativistic than other secular ways of looking at the content of morality. It seems to offer some promise of being both well-founded and contentful" (Williams 1995b: 109). Perhaps that promise may be best assessed, if not fully redeemed, in connection with Williams's views on a practice, genealogy, and a person, Thucidydes.

In *Truth and Truthfulness*, Williams asserts that "Genealogy is intended to serve the aims of naturalism"; moreover, "it was understood to do so by Nietzsche, who first applied the term 'genealogy' in this sense" (Williams 2002: 22). But how best to conceive the project of Nietzschean genealogy, so as to clarify our view of naturalism, let alone how to conceive Williams's own genealogical designs, remains far from obvious. Just what does Nietzschean genealogy involve? Fortunately, Williams specifically addresses this question in an important footnote to his article "Nietzsche's Minimalist Moral Psychology", ultimately providing two memorable conceptions of genealogy. And even if the second of these, "Davidson plus interpretation", may infuriate, the first seems quite helpful in illuminating both Nietzsche's and Williams's views on genealogy as a method, perhaps *the* method, for illuminating ethical life.

According to Williams's first conception, "A Nietzschean genealogy typically combines, in a way that analytical philosophy finds embarrassing, history, phenomenology, 'realistic' psychology, and conceptual interpretation" (Williams 1995f: 75n12). Certainly in the context of *On the Genealogy of Morality*, what Williams must mean by Nietzsche's use of phenomenology and conceptual interpretation seems clear enough, in connection with, say, asceticism or guilt or a comparison of *schlecht* (bad) and *böse* (evil). By contrast, the concepts of "realistic" psychology and history may require a bit more unpacking. Taking history first, a subject about which Williams has always had much to say concerning its vital role in ethical philosophy, its contribution to genealogy stems from its ability to identify past influences on current ethical conceptions, while, at the same time, underscoring their contingency:

> our ethical [life] ... is a complex deposit of many different traditions and social forces, and ... it has itself been shaped by self-conscious representations of those facts. ... Moreover, it is likely to be true ... that the impact of these historical processes will be to some extent concealed by the ways in which their product conceals itself. There is more than one reason for this, but the most general, perhaps, is that a truthful historical account is going to reveal a radical contingency in our current ethical conceptions, both in the sense that they are what they are rather than some others, and also in the sense that the historical changes which brought them about are not obviously related in a grounding or epistemically favorable way to the ethical ideas they encouraged.
> (Williams 2000a: 155)

This emphasis on the radical contingency imbuing ethical life marks a constant, crucial theme throughout Williams's writings. As far as *On the Genealogy of Morality* goes, there history uncovers the stark tension between modern society's most cherished ethical concepts and practices and the violence and cruelty, often the bloodlust, Nietzsche sees at their root.

As for "realistic" psychology, it involves "a perspective, and to some extent a tradition ... in which what seems to demand more moral material makes sense in terms of what demands less" (Williams 1995f: 68). Here, clearly, if not elsewhere, a strong connection between genealogy and the interests of ethical naturalism asserts itself. In fact, "realistic" psychology appears to line up pretty well with what Williams identifies elsewhere as "an appropriately suspicious rule of method", a rule that he believes probably comes as close as is possible to giving a general condition for naturalism: "never explain the ethical in terms of something special to ethics if you can explain it in terms that apply to the non-ethical as well" (Williams 1995h: 204). In *On the Genealogy of Morality*, Nietzsche, displaying his undisputed credentials as a realistic psychologist, takes this rule to heart, explaining, say, moralized guilt ("bad conscience") in terms of internalized *ressentiment*, or retributive punishment in terms of debt–debtor relations. This premium on non-ethicized, yet, importantly, non-reductive, explanations of moral life as the task of genealogy once more reflects the importance of answering "the recurrent naturalist question", one version of which Williams puts as: "how does the phenomenon in question intelligibly relate to the rest of nature, and how, in particular, might it have come about?" (Williams 2002: 26) Expanding on the challenge posed, Williams suggests that

> If we can make sense of this undertaking, of explaining the ethical in terms of an account of human beings which is to the greatest possible extent prior to the ideas of the ethical, then there is a project of ethical naturalism which is intelligible, non-vacuous, and not committed to a general physicalistic reductionism that is (to put it mildly) dubious and anyway ought to be a separate issue. (*Ibid.*: 27; cf. Williams 2000a: 154)

The prospects for ethical naturalism, then, in so far as its aims can be identified with, if not wholly assimilated to, those of realistic psychology, appear indissolubly linked to the prospects for Nietzschean genealogy.

Williams claims that Nietzsche's melding of history and psychology in *On the Genealogy of Morality* "surely owes something to Hegel's *Phenomenology*: there is a set of relations between ideas or outlooks or attitudes which express themselves both psychologically and historically, such that there is an essential connection between the two expressions" (Williams 2000a: 158; cf. Williams 1993b: 75n12). This seem plausible, but only if one acknowledges, as Williams in fact does (Williams 2000a: 155), an important difference between the two, owing to Hegel's manifest teleological commitments or, alternatively, to Nietzsche's focus on contingency. In any case, neither Nietzsche nor Hegel serves as Williams's poster child, whether for genealogy or realistic psychology or ethical naturalism. That honour belongs to Thucydides. Before we turn to ancient Greece from nineteenth-century Germany, it may be worthwhile to note briefly the ways in which Williams differentiates his own employment of genealogical method in *Truth and Truthfulness* from Nietzsche's in *On the Genealogy of Morality*.

The very subtitle of *Truth and Truthfulness*, "An Essay in Genealogy", goes some distance towards demonstrating Williams's faith in Nietzsche's method. The book, characteristically wide-ranging and occasionally frustrating, a collection of interesting intellectual tributaries feeding a somewhat elusive main channel, takes off from a seemingly ineluctable tension in modern life:

> On the one hand, there is an intense commitment to truthfulness. ... Together with this demand for truthfulness, however, ... there is an equally pervasive skepticism about truth itself: whether there is such a thing; if there is, whether it can be more than relative or subjective or something of that kind. ... These two things, the devotion to truthfulness and the suspicion directed to the idea of truth, are connected to one another. The desire for truthfulness drives a process of criticism which weakens the assurance that there is any secure or unqualifiedly stateable truth.
>
> (Williams 2002: 1)

This tension sets out "a basic problem for present-day philosophy", which *Truth and Truthfulness* proposes to solve: "Can the notions of truth and truthfulness be intellectually stabilized, in such a way that what we understand about truth and our chances of arriving at it can be made to fit with our need for truthfulness?" (*ibid*.: 3). As noted in Chapter 6, Williams's solution involves very little engagement with philosophical notions of truth, and considerable engagement with "what may be summarily called 'the value of truth"' (*ibid*.: 6), this value itself seen as derivative of "the "virtues of truth", in particular accuracy and sincerity. It is these virtues of truth that Williams proposes to identify, investigate and, ultimately, stabilize, in no small measure through the practice of genealogy.

Williams's conception of genealogy, however, although considerably indebted, as should be clear, to Nietzsche's own, differs in at least one and perhaps two significant ways. The hesitancy here relates to the character of Williams's genealogical picture as avowedly fictional, and uncertainty about the character of Nietzsche's picture, whether, that is, he takes his story of, say, the slave revolt and the subsequent revaluation of values to represent fact, fiction or some composite of the two. For Williams, at least as concerns the virtues of truthfulness, genealogy involves a "state of nature" story, "a fictional narrative, an imagined developmental story, which helps to explain a concept or value or institution by showing ways in which it could have come about in a simplified environment containing certain kinds of human interests or capacities, which, relative to the story, are taken as given" (*ibid*.: 21). Again, whether some or all of the various genealogical threads comprising *On the Genealogy of Morality* should be viewed as state of nature stories in Williams's sense makes for a difficult question. What makes for a much easier question, and also allows for much clearer differentiation between Williams and Nietzsche, is whether or not a given genealogy, fictional or otherwise, is "vindicatory".

Williams fails to oppose any one specific term to his own vindicatory genealogy, but one that might fairly apply to genealogy *à la* Nietzsche is "enervating". Enervating genealogy bleeds certain ethical concepts or categories or practices of force and vitality, sapping their strength by attacking and undermining their history or their phenomenology, or by applying realistic psychology to expose their decidedly non-ethical antecedents. Moreover, as Williams points out, in so far as Nietzsche sees "blood and cruelty . . . at the bottom of all 'good things'!" (Nietzsche 1967: 498), whatever historical or psychological or conceptual processes lead from such blood and cruelty to morality must resist transparency, on pain of dissolution. In sum, enervating genealogy, Nietzsche's genealogy, tends to be "unsettling or destructive" (Williams 2002: 37). By contrast, vindicatory genealogy, Williams's genealogy for the purposes of *Truth and Truthfulness*, takes its cue not from Nietzsche's analysis of, say, the ascetic ideal, but from Hume's genealogical analysis of justice. One can easily appreciate the vindicatory variety of genealogy, however, without considering a single detail of Hume's account. The main idea is that, as Williams sees it, one can accept Hume's genealogical explanation of justice, whatever that may be, "and still give justice, its motivations and reasons for action, much the same respect as one did before one encountered the explanation – or perhaps more respect" (*ibid*.: 36). Hume's genealogy vindicates the virtue of justice. Similarly, Williams would have genealogy, his own state of nature genealogy, vindicate sincerity and accuracy, the virtues of truthfulness, by considering in the abstract how a basic human need for cooperation might be linked to the value of truth, such value, then, having been transparently preserved, rather than subconsciously destroyed.

Whether or not Williams's fictional, vindicatory genealogical project succeeds in valorizing truthfulness is difficult to say; Williams himself admits that it will require significant supplementation by history. Even assuming that Williams does succeed in establishing the value of truth and truthfulness, through genealogical or other means, it may be even more difficult to say whether such success effectively counters the pervasive, cannibalizing suspicion towards truth that gives rise to the project in the first place. What does seem clear is that Williams, in pursuing genealogy, pursues the goals of ethical naturalism, in as much as "there is a looser sense in which genealogical explanations may be said to be reductive, to the extent that they explain the 'higher' in terms of the 'lower' – knowledge in terms of beliefs and everyday needs, the moral in terms of the non-moral" (*ibid.*). Truly to appreciate this looser sense, however, one must truly appreciate just who Williams trusts as his preferred guide to naturalism: not Hume, not Nietzsche, not Aristotle but, as mentioned above, Thucydides.

In *Shame and Necessity*, Williams, citing Nietzsche's own enthusiasm for Thucydides, embarks on a series of discussions, continuing through *Truth and Truthfulness*, all of which express admiration for the great Greek historian. In fact, it is probably fair to say that no intellectual figure, ancient or modern, throughout all of Williams's writing comes in for as much praise as Thucydides. What Williams finds so deserving of praise in Thucydides is twofold: first, a certain tragic sensibility, about which more will be said in this chapter's concluding section; secondly, a certain impartiality, by which Williams means "that the psychology he deploys in his explanations is not in the service of his ethical beliefs" (Williams 1993b: 161). Such impartiality resonates with both realistic psychology and ethical naturalism – that is, with explaining both moral phenomena in terms of less moral phenomena, and nature in terms of the rest of nature – and is best understood in contrast to what Williams perceives as the overethicized moral psychologies of Plato and Aristotle.

Not that Thucydidean impartiality or, for that matter, Thucydidean history should be seen as value neutral. Instead, Thucydides attempts, in Williams's view, to "*make sense* of social events, and that involves relating them intelligibly to human motivations, and to the ways in which situations appear to agents" (*ibid.*). Still, "Thucydides' conception of an intelligible and typically human motivation is broader and less committed to a distinctive ethical outlook than Plato's; or rather – the distinction is important – it is broader than the conception acknowledged in Plato's psychological theories" (*ibid.*: 161–2). Moreover, "The same is true, if less obviously, in relation to Aristotle" (*ibid.*: 162). Williams sees Plato succumbing to, and Thucydides resisting, the idea of a characterless moral self: "In Plato's case . . . it is precisely because the rational powers of the mind are supposed to be distinctively linked to desirable conduct that no other, contingent, features of the agent, such as character, need come into the account of what the agent must be like in order to lead an ethical life" (*ibid.*: 160). Aristotle resists a similar charge, since considerations of character dominate his ethics. Nevertheless, according to Williams, "when Aristotle describes the formation of character and tells us how the desires are controlled by reason we are led back to a psychology that is still structured, if more subtly [than Plato's], in ethical terms" (*ibid.*). In sum, "The criticism of Plato and Aristotle is not so much that they took psychological explanation to involve values as that they incorporated into it a particular set of ethically and socially desirable values" (*ibid.*: 183n50). Not so with Thucydides.

Perhaps the impartiality Williams finds in Thucydides' writing echoes the impersonality Murdoch finds in the greatest art. As she argues in one of her best known essays, great artists manifest an "exactness and good vision" that permits them "unsentimental, detached, unselfish, objective attention" (Murdoch 1970b: 66). More to the point, "It is also clear that in moral situations a similar exactness is called for" (*ibid.*). Thucydides' take on events in the world, more especially his take on the motivations of agents in those events, remains remarkably free of personal animus, proof to Nietzsche, whose view Williams approvingly cites, of a "willingness to find good sense in all types of people" (Williams 1993b: 161). Again, this allows Thucydides to explain agents (and so events) in less moralized, more realistic, more naturalistic terms than either Plato or Aristotle, whose interpretive frameworks Williams sees as ethically front-loaded: Plato's in so far as it unrealistically rules out contingencies of character; Aristotle's in so far as the teleological considerations structuring the formation of character may themselves be ethically saturated. For Williams, "A non-moralized, or less-moralized, psychology uses the categories of meaning, reasons, and value, but leaves it open, or even problematical, in what way moral reasons and ethical values fit with other motives and desires, how far they express those other motives, and how far they are in conflict with them" (Williams 1995h: 202). History provides few examples of psychology so practised, and so few examples of successful naturalism. Besides Thucydides, Williams singles out in this regard Sophocles and Freud, both of whom are discussed in the following section in connection with Williams's important views on shame and necessity.

Shame and necessity

In a thoughtful review of *Shame and Necessity*, volume fifty-seven of the prestigious Sather Classical Lectures, which Williams delivered at Berkeley in 1989 and reworked for publication in 1993, Richard Kraut identifies no fewer than eleven themes in a "remarkably wide" discussion: Homer's conception of agency; Plato's ethicized psychology; the ancient Greek's conception of responsibility; practical necessity; shame and guilt cultures; the ancient Greek's lack of any hard moral/non-moral distinction; Aristotle on slavery; fate; Plato's characterless self; the need to live without lies in a world without authoritative ethical truth; and the sense in which contemporary ethical life, with its crossed-out God and suspicion of teleology, mirrors that of archaic Greece (Kraut 1994: 178–9). Of course, many of these themes overlap; for example, as shown in the previous section, for Williams, Plato's characterless self and his ethicized psychology cannot be cleanly separated. Still, Kraut is surely right to emphasize Williams's amazing facility with manifold aspects of ancient Greek philosophy and, especially, literature.

As is unfortunately not always the case in *Truth and Truthfulness*, in *Shame and Necessity* Williams's main argumentative thread remains accessible throughout. That thread may be summarized as follows: customary "progressivist" interpretations of archaic Greek ethical life could not be more mistaken, being implicitly refuted at every turn by period literature. According to progressivists, "the Greeks had primitive ideas of action, responsibility, ethical motivation, and justice, which in the course of history have been replaced by a more complex and refined set of conceptions that define a more mature form of ethical experience" (Williams 1993b: 5). According to Williams, the Greeks had perfectly adequate ideas of action, responsibility and ethical motivation, though perhaps not justice, even if they lacked, or precisely because they lacked, the radical reflectiveness so characteristic of modernity and, of course, so characteristic of the morality system. Moreover, in Williams's view, "it is not true that there has been as big a shift in underlying conceptions as the progressivists suppose" (*ibid.*: 7). In other words, there simply has not been all that much progress. As Williams puts his task: "if we can come to understand the ethical concepts of the Greeks, we shall recognize them in ourselves ... [I]f we can liberate the Greeks from patronizing misunderstandings of them, then the same process may help to free us from misunderstandings of ourselves" (*ibid.*: 10–11).

Although this chapter cannot possibly do justice to Williams's investigations into each and every one of these ethical concepts, it can focus on the eponymous and crucial concepts of shame and necessity. Furthermore, it can attempt to do so in a manner that addresses, however tentatively, a familiar and forceful criticism, levelled against much of Williams's work, that it fails to provide any real alternative to the morality system he would undermine. To that end, the remainder of this section considers whether it is possible to cultivate a positive model of ethical practice from *Shame and Necessity*; that is, an account of how ethical considerations come to influence deliberation, motivation and action. Any such model must accomplish at the very least two separate tasks: it must identify the source of the grip that ethical considerations undeniably exert on people's lives, and establish the legitimacy of that grip in the light of, or perhaps despite, the contingency of that practice. *Shame and Necessity* certainly takes on these tasks, the first of which involves Williams's conceptions of shame and an "internalized other", the second his conception of "necessary identities".

Williams begins his analysis of shame along familiar lines: "The basic experience connected with shame is that of being seen, inappropriately, by the wrong people, in the wrong situation" (Williams 1993b: 78). In this view, images of nakedness and exposure, of being caught out, of having disappointed, predominate. Shame speaks not as much to actions as to agents, not as much to what they have done as to what they are, and what they are is somehow deficient, having failed to meet expectations; moreover, such expectations constitute the social glue of a "shame *culture*", understood as "a coherent system for the regulation of conduct" (*ibid.*: 81–2). Shame cultures have frequently been contrasted with guilt cultures, not least by two scholars with whom Williams self-consciously engages in *Shame and Necessity*: E. R. Dodds (one of Williams's teachers at Oxford), author of his own collection of Sather Lectures, *The Greeks and the Irrational*, and A. W. H. Adkins, of *Merit and Responsibility* fame, against whose theses not a little of *Shame and Necessity* is pointedly aimed. All things considered, Williams appears to endorse the view that Greek, especially Homeric, culture substantially embodies shame, but also argues for a more nuanced appreciation of the extent to which shame and guilt overlap (see also G. Taylor 1985, upon which Williams's account to some degree relies, and Cairns 1993).

For Williams, a shame culture depends on "shared sentiments with similar objects [that] serve to bind people together in a community of feeling" (Williams 1993b: 80). Prominent among such shared sentiments are indignation, resentment and anger. Prominent among such similar objects are violations of, or threats to, one's own or another's honour. People are ashamed of themselves or of others in so far as they are angry at themselves or at others in response to compromised honour. To the extent that occasions for such anger – that is, the circumstances that threaten honour – are predictable and patterned rather than haphazard and idiosyncratic, a basis exists for behaviour in conformity with expectations at once public and reliable. Williams cautions, however, against attributing such conformity to agents consciously aligning their own private mores with public ones, for that sort of deliberate adjustment to external standards would fail to account for their tenacious grip. Instead, Williams sees conformity as resulting from internalization.

Although shame is paradigmatically associated with the gaze of another, Williams emphasizes that "for many of its operations the imagined gaze of an imagined other will do" (*ibid.*: 82). Moreover, the "imaginary observer", or, as Williams sometimes says, the "internalized other", "can enter very early in the progression towards more generalized social shame" (*ibid.*). The basic idea seems simple enough: actions tending towards an agent's dishonour, were he or she discovered committing them, become self-proscribed on pain of experiencing shame. Just what actions those happen to be owes something to contingent historical, political, economic, religious – in a word, cultural – facts. But what makes shame such a particularly efficacious ethical consideration, what accounts for its grip, depends upon self-discovery displacing discovery by another. If one wishes to avoid dishonour in another's eyes, one clear strategy is to avoid those eyes; however, such a strategy founders once those eyes have been internalized. To the extent that agents are continuously susceptible to observation, they are continuously susceptible to shame, and thus find themselves continuously pressured to steer their behaviour down an honourable path.

However, it gets trickier, for Williams insists that "The internalization of shame does not simply internalize an other who is a representative of the neighbors" (*ibid.*: 83).

On the one hand, a shame culture binds together its members via a common sensitivity to attacks on its members' honour and a common indignation in response to such attacks. As Williams says, "An agent will be motivated by prospective shame in the face of people who would be angered by conduct that, in turn, they would avoid for those same reasons" (*ibid.*). But, on the other hand,

> It is not merely a structure by which I know that you will be annoyed with me because you know that I will be annoyed at you. These reciprocal attitudes have a content: some kinds of behavior are admired, others accepted, others despised, and it is those attitudes that are internalized, not simply the prospect of hostile reactions. If that were not so, there would be, once more, no shame culture, no shared ethical attitudes at all. (*Ibid.*: 83–4)

The internalized other comes to be "identified in ethical terms" (*ibid.*: 84), and so comes to be a focal point for ethical motivation and appraisal. Embodying a culture's values, the internalized other represents not just a sense of what ought not be done for fear of reprisal, but a sense of what is, say, charitable and gracious and so worthy of praise and pursuit, pettifogging or avaricious and so worthy of opprobrium and avoidance. Yet it remains more than a little obscure how this other is actually internalized and, for that matter, why it should be considered an other at all.

Take this last point first. If agents are the ones internalizing values, and the ideals they approximate or fall short of, that occasion pride or shame, are, in fact, their own, in what sense does anything *other* invade their deliberations? Put another way, what underwrites the independence and authority of the other? Remember that the issue is the grip exerted by ethical considerations. Shame seems promising as both manifestation and explanation of that grip, in the form of constraints imposed upon people's lives by external ethical values – unless, that is, such constraints turn out to be internal. In fact, Williams himself questions whether the internalized other can have "any independent part in my psychology if he is constructed out of my own local materials", conceding that if the other "is imagined to react simply in terms of what I think is the right thing to do, surely he must cancel out; he is not an *other* at all" (*ibid.*: 84). Indeed, in such circumstances the other might be better characterized in terms of, as Williams memorably puts it, "an echo chamber for my solitary moral voice" (*ibid*.).

To such worries Williams responds that attempts to reduce the alternatives to two – other as neighbour or other as oneself – "leave out much of the substance of actual ethical life", presumably by ignoring the fact that although "The internalized other is indeed abstracted and generalized and idealized, he is potentially somebody rather than nobody, and somebody other than me" (*ibid*.). More to the point as far as its grip is concerned, "[the internalized other] can provide the focus of real social expectations, of how I shall live if I act in one way rather than another, of how my actions and reactions will alter my relations to the world about me" (*ibid*.). Since shame, at least in Williams's view, results from anger directed at oneself by oneself, it may certainly be characterized as internal. But since the anger itself results from failure to meet cultural expectations, shame may also be characterized as external. Granted this hybrid nature, Williams's caution against exclusive attention to either aspect appears reasonable.

Unfortunately, Williams's attempt to elucidate the psychological model underlying shame, according to which an observer or other becomes internalized, seems to come up short. He begins by considering the quintessential experience of shame: being seen naked by another. The question is, how can shame be triggered by nakedness under the gaze of an *internalized* other? The short answer is: since "nakedness before an imagined watcher is no exposure", it probably cannot (*ibid*.: 220). Therefore, Williams tries a different tack: not observed nakedness *per se*, but the feelings that accompany it – vulnerability and impotence, inadequacy and diminished prestige – serve as the primitive foundation for shame. The uneasiness or anxiety attaching to such feelings incites anger, and it is the experience of this anger that constitutes shame. Yet it remains more than a little vague just how an imaginary observer enters the picture, although it seems clear that Williams takes that entrance to involve "bootstrapping", a process involving "an increasingly ethical content given to the occasions of shame" (*ibid*.: 221).

A person or society evidently bootstraps by injecting occasions for shame with more and more significant "social, ethical, or moral notions", so that over time loss of face, say, replaces nakedness as shame's precipitating predicament (*ibid*.: 219). In Williams's account, "The farther that 'bootstrapping' has proceeded and ethical considerations are involved, the less a watcher needs to be in the actual offing; the idealized other will do" (*ibid*.: 221). However, this idealized other "still performs a function, of recalling to the subject a person in the eyes of whom the subject has failed, has lost power, is at a disadvantage" (*ibid.*). Still, it is one thing to gesture towards shame's increasingly ethical content, or to reiterate the role of an internalized figure as a catalyst for feelings of shame, and quite another to delineate cleanly the specific events or processes responsible for establishing the psychological reality of this imaginary other, a task that *Shame and Necessity* leaves largely incomplete.

In his defence, however, it should be noted that Williams never promises to unveil the mysteries of individual psychology. Instead, he claims that "The discussion ... is directed to an historical interpretation from which we can ethically learn something, and I have included psychological materials in it only to the extent that it may help to focus that discussion" (*ibid.*: 90). *Shame and Necessity*, then, seems to put psychological analysis squarely in the service of, say, anthropology, or perhaps better, following the lead of the previous section, and as Maudemarie Clark (2001) has argued, genealogy, in a way that stresses the importance of internalization but eshews many of the attendant psychological details. Indeed, Richard Wollheim contends that Williams "would be the first to concede" the "de-psychologized" or "pre-psychologized" nature of his account (Wollheim 1999: 259n27). At the same time, however, Williams's account does bear resemblance to more avowedly psychological accounts of similar ethical phenomena, not least Freud's.

Other than a passing, yet undoubtedly approving, reference to his "realistic" psychology, Williams has virtually nothing to say, in *Shame and Necessity* or elsewhere, about Freud (see Williams 1995h: 202). Yet Williams's sociohistorical, genealogical or quasi-psychological account of the ethical grip exerted by an internalized other does echo to some degree Freud's account of conscience and the emergence of the superego. Very roughly, for Williams, the ability to develop and adopt similar ethical responses to similar ethical stimuli depends upon joining a "community of feeling" through identifying with and internalizing someone else, an other, albeit in a highly abstract and idealized fashion. Even more roughly, for Freud, the ability to develop and adopt similar ethical responses to similar ethical stimuli depends ultimately upon identifying with and internalizing an abstracted and idealized parent (see, for example, Freud 1960; 1961: especially Chapter VII; 1965: especially Lecture XXXI). Certainly Williams's and Freud's mechanisms of internalization take different forms, as, for example, Williams's shame results from indignation, while Freud's conscience results from anxiety. Such differences, however, need preclude neither comparison, nor even alliance (see Jenkins 2001; Lear 2003).

Putting to one side affinities between Williams and Freud, a danger remains that Williams's account of shame may leave matters precariously perched on the boundary of the ethical, or perhaps even outside it altogether. Williams himself points out that "Everyone knows that simply to pursue what you want and to avoid what you fear is not the stuff of any morality; if those are your only motives, then you are not within morality, and you do not have – in a broader phrase – any ethical life" (Williams 1993b: 77). Yet Williams's version of ethical life, at least to this point, does seem to consist of a motive of desire (along the lines of the theory of internal reasons discussed in Chapter 4) and a motive of fear (associated with failing to meet societal expectations), and so perhaps it fails to describe any ethical life at all. The problem is that while Williams's account of shame and internalization manages to capture the way in which ethical considerations infiltrate people's lives, it fails to capture fully the authority ascribed to them, a problem no doubt stemming from the fact that although the process of internalization may be in some sense (psychologically, sociologically, biologically) necessary, in Williams's view the actual values internalized remain in some sense (historically, culturally) contingent.

Entrée into ethical life appears to owe little to alleged form (as God's children, as rational creatures, as happiness maximizers) and much to the actual content internalized. And this content, consisting of inherited norms buttressed by mechanisms of shame, may be damaged, along with the process of internalization itself, by contingencies associated with psychological or social development. In other words, identification with and internalization of an other capable of transmitting values and enforcing standards of conduct represent by no means necessary accomplishments. As such, Williams's account of ethical life appears to require some element of necessity capable of addressing worries raised by the contingent pedigrees of internal reasons and internalized norms. *Shame and Necessity*'s conception of "necessary identities" tries, with questionable success, to meet this requirement. Internalization and subjective motivation, despite their contingent provenance, contribute to the formation, maintenance and expression of character and identity, and Williams sees that character and identity affecting ethical practice necessarily, by promoting or prohibiting certain courses of conduct. He discusses this sort of necessity in connection with Sophocles' tragic figure Ajax.

Ajax embodies critical features of a shame culture, particularly its notion of ethical bounds imposed by considerations of honour, of respect and of what one owes oneself and others through having internalized the predominant values of society. Enraged by perceived injustice, befuddled by divine intervention, humiliated by the futility of his grisly retaliation ("Oh! What a mockery I have come to! What indignity!"), Ajax represents a failed hero, even as he also represents, somewhat paradoxically, a classically heroic response to that failing, to his craven and pusillanimous acts (Sophocles 1957: 233). Oblivious to Athena's machinations, butchering livestock instead of Odysseus, Ajax acts, in the deepest sense of the word, uncharacteristically. He is out of sorts, no longer himself ("All that I was has perished with these poor creatures here"), and he experiences the consequences of this loss of self as shame; that is, in keeping with Williams's account, as self-directed anger in response to the chasm exposed between his actions and his ideals (*ibid.*: 235). Yet Ajax's reaction to his disgrace, his choice of suicide as expiation, seems nothing short of heroic. He responds to his uncharacteristically unheroic actions with characteristic heroism, once again manifesting the values appropriate to the various roles he inhabits and identifies with – noble, Greek, son, warrior, lover – as constituted and transmitted by his society. "Now I am going where my way must go", says Ajax, with that "must" effectively circumscribing Williams's account of necessity (*ibid.*: 245).

Obviously Ajax is ashamed of himself, but a certain tension appears to surround shame and the distinction between self and other, with Williams reluctant to draw firm boundaries between them. On the one hand, shame understood as originating in an external audience seems to allow the possibility that one might remain largely unaffected by its judgement. On the other hand, shame understood as originating in "an echo chamber for my solitary moral voice" may seem unable to provide sufficient authority or externality. Williams's internalized other means to bridge these extremes, and it is illuminating to see this conception operating in Ajax, who sees but two options: "Let a man nobly live or nobly die" (*ibid.*: 237). In forfeiting the first option through his madness, he has made himself abhorrent to himself, he has lost his self-respect: "But now in dishonor I lie abject" (*ibid.*: 235). As Williams summarizes the situation, "[Ajax] has no way of living that anyone he respects would respect – which means that he cannot live with any self-respect" (Williams 1993b: 85). In other words, the capacity for self-respect cannot be neatly severed from the capacity to live according to values that others respect. Still, the source of Ajax's loss of self-respect lies not, or at least not mainly, in any fear of what his compatriots or wife or father or son (one day) may think of him, but in his own failed expectations for himself. Remember that "The internalization of shame does not simply internalize an other who is a representative of the neighbors" (*ibid*.: 83). And having set shame and loss of self-respect as the penalty for acting out of character, Ajax's internalized other prescribes rehabilitation via one final dramatic act: a noble death.

The very same internalized values whose transgression ushered in a crisis of shame and loss of self-respect now provide crisis management. Principal among those values is, of course, courage, precisely the value or virtue most glaringly absent in Ajax's somnambulant slaughter, and precisely the one most visible in his suicidal response. "You have a foolish thought", Ajax admonishes his wife, "if you think at this late date to school my nature" (Sophocles 1957: 242). With these words Ajax forecloses the possibility of a radical shift in character and so forecloses the possibility of adopting new ways of appraising or reacting to his situation. Ajax has no choice but to act "in character"; that is, to act from a character steeped in the heroic virtue of courage. More to the point, with these words, and, especially, their invocation of "nature", Ajax appears to ascribe a certain necessity to his course of action.

Williams has this to say about the necessity – that is, the practical necessity – encumbering Ajax:

> At the extreme, the sense of this necessity lies in the thought that one could not live and look others in the eye if one did certain things, a thought which may be to varying degrees figurative but can also be in a deadly sense literal, as it was with Ajax. These necessities are internal, grounded in the ethos, the projects, the individual nature of the agent, and in the way he conceives the relation of his life to other people's. (Williams 1993b: 103)

Indeed, as Williams notes some years prior to *Shame and Necessity*, also in connection with Ajax, "The recognition of practical necessity must involve an understanding of one's own powers and incapacities, and of what the world permits, and the recognition of a limit which is neither simply external to the self, nor yet a product of the will, is what can lend a special authority or dignity to such decisions", such as, in this case, the decision to take one's own life (Williams 1981h: 130–31).

It is, however, one thing to acknowledge the important role shame plays in ethical life, largely as a sign of betrayed ideals, and another to demonstrate the degree to which, given those ideals, an agent could not have acted otherwise. It is one thing to appeal to the preservation of identity in refusing to perform some action, and another to make clear the authority of that appeal. And it is one thing to be told that the necessity infusing Ajax's behaviour is "grounded in his own identity", and another to elucidate the philosophical picture underlying that grounding. Moreover, there is more at stake here than simply whether Williams can successfully explain the "must" in Ajax's "Now I am going where my way must go" (Sophocles 1957: 245). There is also a worry akin to that arising in Chapter 5 in connection with Williams's account of internal reasons.

That worry focused on the necessary connection Williams tries to establish between ethical action and the agent's subjective motivational set, a connection that seems to license the possibility of unresponsiveness in the face of ethical demands, a disconcerting possibility for those believing that moral demands must pack an overriding motivational punch. Similarly, Williams's account of necessity may seem disconcertingly internal in the sense that nothing ensures that the "must" of practical necessity must be in any sense moral. Kraut does a good job of enunciating this worry: "Williams approves of the hero's thought, 'This is what I must do.' . . . But an agent's feeling that he must act in a certain way does not render his action invulnerable to reasoned criticism. Even if one's project reflects one's character, cannot one's character itself be self-destructive or destructive of others?" (Kraut 1994: 181). As Kraut sees it, Williams illegitimately inserts a relatively modern value, authenticity, being true to oneself come what may or regardless of what others may think, back into Greek ethical life, and he provocatively wonders, "Did Ajax have a project?" (*ibid.*)

Without question, as the discussion of integrity and utilitarianism in Chapter 3 makes clear, a certain romantic flavour does infuse Williams's project-talk; that is, his talk of projects sufficient to ground identity, confer meaning, give one a reason to get up in the morning or, in Ajax's case, a reason not to. But just as clearly, Williams wants the agent's authenticity to reflect values and commitments and projects that, although certainly the agent's own, at the same time reflect values and commitments and projects in some sense external to the agent. It is not, then, a case of worrying about agents being true to possibly unethical characters forged by radical existential choice (as if character and such choice were even compatible). Instead, it is a case of worrying that the wider, external values that do plausibly contribute to the formation of character may themselves lack ethical content. Williams perhaps demonstrates that some sort of necessity attaches to ethical situations, but has he demonstrated that the actions emanating from that necessity need be ethical? One might think that all Williams's account of shame, internalization and practical necessity succeeds in doing in terms of expanding his earlier internal reasons model is to shift concern over the potential lack of ethical content in practical deliberation from the individual's set of subjective motivations to the society from which they have been acquired.

For his part, Williams might well resurrect the by now familiar refrain from *Morality* regarding "what the distinction between the 'moral' and the 'non-moral' is supposed to do for us", reminding critics that, as far as he is concerned, "considerations of the moral kind only make sense if they are related to other reasons for action that human beings use, and generally to their desires, needs and projects" (Williams 1993a: xiii). In fact, *Shame and Necessity* does join this chorus: "we make a lot of the distinction between the moral and the nonmoral and emphasize the importance of the moral. But how far, and in what ways, is this really true of our life, as opposed to what moralists say about our life? Do we even understand what the distinction is, or how deep it really goes?" (Williams 1993b: 92). Yet the claim that moral considerations only gain point when linked with projects hardly amounts to the claim that all projects have a moral point. At the end of the day, *Shame and Necessity* comes up short, at least as far as establishing the legitimacy or authority of ethical considerations tied to shame and necessity is concerned. Still, "shame continues to work for us, as it worked for the Greeks, in essential ways. By giving through the emotions a sense of who one is and of what one hopes to be, it mediates between act, character, and consequence, and also between ethical demands and the rest of life" (*ibid.*: 102). Sophocles' "stark fictions" continue to provide a powerful glimpse of a continuingly relevant moral psychology.

Conclusion

In an intriguing paper, "*The Women of Trachis*: Fictions, Pessimism, Ethics", delivered on the occasion of A. W. H. Adkins's retirement, Williams draws on many of the themes thus far addressed in this chapter and, indeed, the entire book, while taking moral philosophy to task for essentially operating as if the manifest horrors of the world were of little or no relevance to their enterprise. Underlying so many of these horrors one finds "uncontrollable necessity and chance", and it is these forces that Williams believes moral philosophers ignore in taking the moment of rational decision as paradigmatic for ethical philosophy. As Williams puts things:

> [moral philosophy] tries to withdraw our ethical interest from both chance and necessity, except inasmuch as the necessity sets the parameters of effective action. . . . When in addition morality itself is disconnected historically and psychologically from the rest of life, as it often is by moral philosophy, . . . then necessity and chance and the bad news they bring with them are deliberately excluded.
> (Williams 1996b: 48)

This diagnosis is followed by a discussion of "the ways the defective consciousness of moral philosophy can be extended by appeal to fiction", in the course of which Williams comes to introduce a distinction between "dense" and "stark" fictions.

Although dense fiction, a fine specimen of which Williams takes to be Dickens's *Bleak House*, "provides a depth of characterization and social background which gives substance to the moral situation and brings it nearer to everyday experience", it cannot do full justice to the world's bad news without risking "comedy and farce" (Williams 1996b: 49). By contrast, stark fiction, of which Williams believes virtually all of Sophocles' tragedies make excellent examples, does not merely, as with dense fiction, "yield salutary *exempla* of virtue and vice" (*ibid.*: 48), but is instead "typically directed in a concentrated way to displaying the operations of chance and necessity" (*ibid.*: 50). *The Women of Trachis*, says Williams, "is particularly relevant to the present discussion because its display of undeserved and uncompensated suffering is so entirely unrelieved" (*ibid.*). One interesting issue, sketched further below in connection with a remark by Nussbaum, is whether Williams takes undeserved, uncompensated and unrelieved suffering to be what anyone ought to expect of life. In any event, this article marks yet another occasion upon which Williams exploits the philosophically rich, if dramatically or narratively or thematically stark, resources of tragedy.

In *Shame and Necessity*, Williams discusses the relation between Sophocles and Thucydides, whereby both succeed admirably in capturing various aspects of human endeavour against the backdrop of an indifferent, even hostile, universe: "Each of them represents human beings as dealing sensibly, foolishly, sometimes catastrophically, sometimes nobly, with a world that is only partially intelligible to human agency and in itself is not well adjusted to ethical aspirations" (Williams 1993b: 163). In "*The Women of Trachis*", Williams discusses the relation between Sophocles and Nietzsche, whereby both succeed admirably in capturing various aspects of pessimism: the dramatist by starkly displaying its conditions, the philosopher by pointing out ways in which that very display might enable an audience to cope better with those conditions; that is, in "enabling us to contemplate such things in honesty without being crushed by them" (Williams 1996b: 52). According to Williams, "The point of tragedy", something he claims Nietzsche himself came to appreciate, lies "in the fact that it lays its fictional horrors before us in a way that elicits attitudes we cannot take towards real horrors" (*ibid.*). Just what attitudes those are, and just why we cannot take them, Williams fails to say. Presumably at least one such attitude, however, will involve acknowledging a certain metaphysical reality – a horror-filled reality chock-full of necessity and chance – that Williams sees most moral philosophers effectively denying. As the paper's concluding line puts it: "One of [stark fiction's] most obvious achievements . . . is to offer a necessary supplement and a suitable limitation to the tireless aim of moral philosophy to make the world safe for well-disposed people" (*ibid.*).

Nussbaum, herself a pioneer in interpreting ancient Greek literature with a philosophical eye, draws rather different lessons from Sophocles' stark fiction. Specifically, she rejects what she sees as Williams's passivity in the face of tragic human limitation. As she puts it, "Williams does not exactly counsel resignation, but it is hard to know what other moral attitude his perspective suggests" (Nussbaum 2003: 38). She goes on to say:

> The news that the suffering we witness is the result of distant, implacable, unintelligent necessity would in a sense be bad news: for it would mean that it would have to happen, and that similar things will go on happening no matter what we do. That is what Williams means by saying that such news is a corrective to overly optimistic offers of "good news". But I think that there is another sense in which that kind of news is good: it means that there is nobody to blame and nothing more to do. We can sit back and resign ourselves to the world as it is, knowing that its horrors lie outside our control. (*Ibid.*)

Nussbaum insists, however, that Greek tragedies as often represent the horrors of the world as the product of "malice, ignorance, and callousness", as of blind necessity and chance. And horror so understood demands action rather than resignation, even if such action, directed, after all, against the gods, proves largely futile.

In Nussbaum's view, tragedy performs a great service in so far as it prods audiences to determine, of some great horror, on the one hand, its causes and conditions, and, on the other, its susceptibility to human intervention. She sums up her argument as follows:

> In short, instead of conceding the part of ethical space within which tragic events occur to implacable necessity of fate, tragedies often challenge their audience to inhabit it actively, as a contested space of moral struggle, a place in which virtue might possibly in some cases prevail over the caprices of amoral power and in which, even if it does not prevail, it may still shine through for its own sake. (*Ibid.*: 39)

Williams might be excused for taking this last line, with its implicit invocation of Kant's jewel of a good will, as aspiring to be just the sort of good news to which stark fictions are meant as counterpoint.

Of course, one is also free to find in Nussbaum's reservations regarding Williams on tragedy signs of a much larger reservation regarding what might be simply termed his missing politics, understood as a concern that his serial critiques of moral theory have left him without adequate resources to address at least those horrors featuring all too human sources. As Nicholas White memorably puts it: "The question is not simply whether [Williams] can produce something *better* than modern moral philosophy, but whether he can produce something *different* from it" (White 1994: 621). And here, amid all this discussion of the world's horrors and our limited capacity to understand, let alone address, them, one may also be tempted to recall Murdoch's wonderfully fertile observation that "It is frequently difficult in philosophy to tell whether one is saying something reasonably public and objective, or whether one is merely erecting a barrier, special to one's own temperament, against one's own personal fears. (It is always a significant question to ask about any philosopher: what is he afraid of?)" (Murdoch 1970b: 72). Adopting a strikingly personal tone, Nussbaum suggests that "doing good for a bad world did not energize [Williams], because his attitude to the world was at some deep level without hope" (Nussbaum 2003: 39). Perhaps what Nussbaum calls Williams's "world-weary attitude" (*ibid.*) simply reflects his fears, as, of course, Nussbaum's own good news may reflect hers.

Of the many factors – philosophical, historical, literary – compelling Williams's sustained attention to the ancient world, the ethical stands pre-eminent. Whether sympathetically investigating the plausibility of Aristotelian naturalism, extolling the merits of Thucydidean impartiality or vindicating archaic notions of agency and responsibility, Williams consistently champions the relevance of Greek ethical life to our own. But in championing such relevance, he means to do more than simply point out ways in which certain Greek ethical notions might clarify or even enhance more modern notions; instead he means to point out that the underlying ethical framework of the Greeks can be seen as quite modern or, no doubt better, the modern ethical framework quite Greek. In so far as the modern ethical condition lies "beyond Christianity", it lies to some extent before Christianity (Williams 1993b: 166). With or without the benefit of stark fiction, "We know that the world was not made for us, or we for the world, that our history tells no purposive story, and that there is no position outside the world or outside history from which we might hope to authenticate our activities", and so we know much the same ethical landscape the ancient Greeks knew, before the ethicized psychologies of Plato and Aristotle, before Christian metaphysics, before Kantian rationalism, before the world-historical narratives of Hegel and Marx and before the good news of modern moral philosophy. Whatever its implications for pessimism, Williams's view that "In important ways, we are, in our ethical situation, more like human beings in antiquity than any Western people have been in the meantime" (*ibid.*) may evince a rather refreshing realism.

Chapter 8

Conclusion: "a pessimism of strength?"

Although certainly his contributions to metaphysics, epistemology and the history of philosophy continue to repay close attention, speaking now of, say, papers on personal identity or the book on Descartes, Williams's reputation rightly remains most closely tied to ethics, specifically his critique(s) of moral theory and his work in moral psychology. Such contributions, however, and no one seems more sensitive to this than Williams himself, may strike some readers as fragmentary, decentralized, ad hoc. The foregoing chapters have tried to combat this impression, assuming it even merits combating, in two ways. The first is by pointing up certain themes or, perhaps better, guiding principles on display in almost all Williams's writing. Three in number, spelled out in Chapter 1, these principles reflect his constant push, especially in ethics, for psychology adequate to moral phenomena, history adequate to contemporary values and philosophy adequate to the contingency of life. The second is by sketching, in connection with *Shame and Necessity*, at least the outline of a positive account of ethical practice, based largely on the internalization of norms and the necessity of acting in conformity with the character or identity those norms infuse.

Still, perhaps more may be expected by way of a positive programme, and in *Ethics and the Limits of Philosophy* Williams may seem to oblige such expectations, at least initially, when talking up a model of ethical conviction based not on certainty, nor on decision, but on "confidence". After dismissing the possibility of ethical certainty – that is, after dismissing, for reasons considered in Chapter 6, the possibility of epistemological authority along the lines of science, capturing an ethical world "that is there *anyway*" – and after dismissing the possibility that the notorious value-creating decisions of existentialism might suffice, lacking, as they do, the "aspect of passivity" morality requires, Williams concludes that hopes for ethical conviction might best be harnessed to confidence (Williams 1985: 169). In other words, where absolute knowledge and radical will fail, confidence just might succeed.

The question for Williams – really the question *to* Williams – boils down to whether or not, having undercut the possibility of ethical objectivity, ethical knowledge or ethical certainty, owing to his various attacks on everything from Kantianism and utilitarianism to modern (hyper)reflectiveness, he has anything programmatic (short of moral theory, of course) to put in its place. This is where ethical confidence comes in. But despite admirable attempts to make sense of Williams here (see, for example, Jardine 1995 and, especially, Altham 1995), it remains very, very hazy just what ethical confidence amounts to. "It is a social and psychological question what kinds of institutions, upbringing and public discourse help to foster it" (Williams 1985: 170). Ethical confidence appears to reflect and to reinforce "practical convergence, on a shared way of life", a convergence ideally "explained in terms of basic desires and interests" (*ibid.*: 171). Furthermore, confidence must be uncoerced; it must "come from strength and not from the weakness of self deception and dogmatism" (*ibid.*). Williams adds, however, lest readers find his conception overly optimistic, that ethical confidence "could rest on what Nietzsche called the pessimism of strength" (*ibid.*). Is this allusion helpful?

In his "Attempt at a Self-criticism", added many years after the initial publication of *The Birth of Tragedy*, Nietzsche writes:

> Is pessimism *necessarily* a sign of decline, decay, degeneration, weary and weak instincts – as it once was in India and now is, to all appearances, among us, "modern" men and Europeans? Is there a pessimism of *strength*? An intellectual predilection for the hard, gruesome, evil, problematic aspect of existence, prompted by well-being, by overflowing health, by the *fullness* of existence?
>
> (Nietzsche 1967: 17)

Here Nietzsche speaks to Williams's eyes-wide-open appreciation of life's tragic dimension, simultaneously introducing the possibility of enthusiastically – that is, confidently – embracing the very values such a dimension inspires, as it shapes human needs and interests. Indeed, a number of Williams's ideas, familiar from earlier chapters, now seem quite close at hand: life's ineradicable tragic elements; ethics as a set of internalized dispositions imbued by largely contingent social norms; the vulnerability of such dispositions and their attendant thick concepts to modernity's pervasive reflection; the resultant loss of ethical conviction or, perhaps better, the resultant pessimism of weakness; and, now, the call for ethical confidence.

Williams tries to clarify the need for confidence a decade after its debut, first, in relation to thin concepts: "granted the nature of modern societies, we ... face a good number of ethical tasks with the help of unsupported thin concepts, and, since there [is] not going to be any knowledge in that connection, it would be as well if we had confidence" (Williams 1995h: 207). This appears pretty straightforward and to mesh with his original remarks: where knowledge ends, confidence begins. But when Williams goes on to relate confidence to thick concepts, things get a bit trickier: "The thick concepts under which we can have some pieces of ethical knowledge are not themselves sustained by ethical knowledge, but by confidence" (*ibid.*: 208). But why should thick concepts, in so far as they still exist in contemporary culture(s), and in so far as they underwrite bits of genuine ethical knowledge, require confidence to sustain them, a question astutely raised by Altham in his contribution to Williams's *Festschrift* (Altham 1995: 164). In response, Williams ascribes something like quasi- or semi-reflective, rather than strictly pre-reflective, status to the modern usage of "brutality" and "coward" and "lie":

> While we shall have the knowledge that comes with the deployment of our surviving thick concepts, we shall still not have any knowledge to the effect that we have a definitively desirable set of such concepts. However, unlike the inhabitants of the fictionally pre-reflective society, we do have the thought that other people have had different concepts, and that people may come to do so in the future. (Williams 1995h: 208)

Confidence, then, fills the gap between elusive certainty and pervasive contingency, or needs to.

Just how does one acquire confidence in society's all-there-is or meets-our-needs values and institutions? And where does confidence end and faith, or fanaticism for that matter, begin? "Confidence", Williams asserts, "is both a social state and related to discussion, theorizing, and reflection" (Williams 1985h: 170). But these last two activities in particular have picked up fairly suspect associations along the way, and their eleventh hour juxtaposition with confidence may strike one as forced or volatile or just plain confusing. Although it is not particularly hard to see what Williams wants confidence to do, namely to undergird ethical conviction in a world without ethical certainty, it is much harder to see how confidence gets going or at least stays going in contemporary life. If reflection can destroy knowledge, surely it can destroy confidence. Regretfully, this may just be a place where Williams's views invite his own criticism of Nietzsche, as being at once both "extremely compelling" and "infuriatingly vague" (Williams 2000a: 157).

Perhaps Williams simply tries too hard to resolve a fundamentally irresolvable tension between ethical conviction and contingency, with confidence a conceptual casualty of the attempt. Surely he cannot be faulted for failing to meet an unreasonable demand. If, as he suggests, the "rapid and immense development of symbolic and cultural capacities has left humans as beings for which no form of life is likely to prove entirely satisfactory, either individually or socially", or if, more bluntly, "human beings are to some degree a mess", why should anyone expect philosophically satisfying support for such ethical conviction as humans possess? (Williams 1995b: 109). And why should one be confident? Once more, pessimism makes sense.

It may be worth noting here that, in a memorable footnote that could well spawn a (different) book, orienting his thought with reference to two other distinguished contemporary philosophers, Williams self-identifies as a pessimist: "If Taylor and MacIntyre will forgive my putting them into a mere cartoon sketch, one set of relations between our positions might perhaps be put like this: Taylor and MacIntyre are Catholic, and I am not; Taylor and I are liberals, and MacIntyre is not; MacIntyre and I are pessimists, and Taylor is not (not really)" (Williams 1995h: 222n19). The specific occasion for Williams's comparison here is a certain similarity he detects between the approaches of these other two thinkers to the notoriously problematic fact/value distinction and his own culturally and historically sensitive thick concept approach. Certainly Alasdair MacIntyre and Charles Taylor share Williams's faith in the relevance of philosophy's history to its present predicaments, as well as a suspicion of modern moral theory as the very disease it purports to cure. Still, their differences eclipse similarities.

Where Williams might agree with MacIntyre's diagnosis that, with the failure of the "Enlightenment project", "the integral structure of morality has to a large degree been fragmented and then in part destroyed" (MacIntyre 1984: 5), Chapter 7 underscores his disagreement with MacIntyre's prescription: a rejection of Nietzschean "liberal individualism" and a belief that "the Aristotelian tradition can be restated in a way that restores intelligibility and rationality to our moral and social attitudes and commitments" (*ibid.*: 259). Never mind the arguably odd juxtaposition of Nietzsche and "liberal", MacIntyre's own philosophical conservatism and his commitment to (re)establishing an authoritative, rationally justified, virtue-fixing *telos* places him at no small distance from Williams.

Taylor may seem closer, as his idea of "strong evaluation", initially sketched in "Responsibility for Self", appears quite sympathetic to Williams's talk of identity conferring projects in "Persons, Character and Morality". (Remarkably, both of these important papers first appeared in Rorty 1976.) Indeed, taking off from Harry Frankfurt's notion of second-order desires (see Frankfurt 1988a), Taylor's characterization of strong evaluations vividly recalls Williams's characterization of categorical desires and ground projects: "the concept of identity is bound up with that of certain strong evaluations which are inseparable from myself ... [S]horn of these we would lose the very possibility of being an agent who evaluates; ... we would break down as persons, be incapable of being persons in the full sense" (Taylor 1985c: 34–5; see also Taylor 1976, 1985b; for comparison of Williams and Taylor on selfhood, see Walker 1998: Chapter 6). But while striking formal similarities no doubt exist between the capacity, really the necessity, of both ground projects and strong evaluations to constitute the self, Taylor ultimately moves to legitimate strong evaluations via their link to external, overarching, objective, "constitutive" goods, thus eschewing Williams's much more subjective approach (see Taylor 1989: Chapter 4). In this way, Taylor's Catholic faith (and resultant optimism?) appears somewhat more germane than MacIntyre's to the issue of their respective philosophical distance from Williams.

Needless to say, the task of comparing Williams with other important contemporary philosophers, kindred spirits or not, along a host of philosophical axes, remains formidable and necessarily incomplete, although previous chapters have tried to make a beginning. Besides MacIntyre and Taylor, and sticking just with the topic of selfhood, intriguing affinities, differences of degree, might be profitably explored among Williams and Frankfurt, Korsgaard, Nagel, Rawls and Richard Rorty. Certainly Williams keeps good company on at least some issues, at least part of the way. In fact, the above philosophers might be taken to occupy distinct points on a sort of spectrum of subjective tendencies, with Rorty (arguably Frankfurt) and Taylor (arguably Nagel) marking the limits, and Williams located somewhere to the subjective side of, say, Korsgaard. Establishing the soundness of such a scheme would require more detailed argument than present circumstances permit; still, just the rough outline suggests that some philosophers may have even more to answer for than Williams when it come to justifying identity along the lines of personal projects, strong evaluations, life plans, second-order desires or whatever; others, of course, much less.

In the end, however, regardless of where one chooses to situate Williams with regard to his peers, the demand for more continues unabated: more in the way of practical reliability, more in the way of a determinate good, more in the way of ethical cognitivism, more in the way of a politics, finally, more in the way of confidence, or optimism. While philosophers often effusively praise Williams for imaginatively reconceiving and brilliantly refreshing a number of stale philosophical issues, it is no doubt safe to say they remain largely dissatisfied with his own ways of resolving those same issues. Perhaps no issue better illustrates this dissatisfaction than William's repudiation of ethical theory, where critics have been quick to embrace certain aspects of his critique (by paying more attention to emotions, say, or to personal relationships), but slow to reject outright the need for robust ethical theory. And it is in this connection that probably the most insightful observation ever made of Williams occurs, an observation, moreover, well fitted to conclude to this book.

The observation belongs to Nussbaum, a lifelong, but far from uncritical, student of Williams's work, who, as previous chapters record, memorably responds to her teacher on a number of key topics, including Aristotle, tragedy and the possibility of ethical theory. In "Why Practice Needs Ethical Theory", she offers the following analysis:

> Williams conveys the strong impression that when we do away with theory we will be left with people like Bernard Williams: they will lack philosophical theory, but they will still be energetically critical and self-critical, not captive to any other theory either, and alive to the possibility of distortion and hierarchy in the experiences that are the basis for their judgements.
>
> (Nussbaum 2000: 248)

Exactly. Although Williams consistently endorses a world freed from theory, prejudice and bad faith, it does seem that his confidence (that word again) in realizing such a world, while giving ethical subjectivity and the personal point of view their due, depends upon individuals adopting projects and commitments quite like (one imagines) Williams's own projects and commitments, such as exemplary scholarship, aesthetic engagement, civic duty, stirring romance.

Admittedly, as Nussbaum implies, a population of reduplicated Bernard Williams's might have little need of theory, but, in reality, much of the "hard, gruesome, evil, problematic aspect of existence" consists of precisely the fact that the world is *not* exclusively populated by Williams-like people. His own integrity, his own ethical values, his own selfless desires are just that, his own. In sum, the conditions giving rise to pessimism, even construed as a pessimism of strength, may seem invariably to call into question people's (not to say Williams's) capacity to meet them, at least when armed only with the resources he provides. Nonetheless, Williams's influence on philosophy remains intense, not only because any number of debates are still best articulated in his terms, but also because he has taught a new generation the important lesson that philosophy dismisses psychology, history and contingency at its peril.

Bibliography

Selected works by Bernard Williams

1972 *Morality: An Introduction to Ethics*. Cambridge: Cambridge University Press.
1973a "A Critique of Utilitarianism". See Smart & Williams (1973).
1973b "Are Persons Bodies?" See Williams (1973h).
1973c "Bodily Continuity and Personal Identity". See Williams (1973h).
1973d "Consistency and Realism". See Williams (1973h).
1973e "Ethical Consistency". See Williams (1973h).
1973f "Morality and the Emotions". See Williams (1973h).
1973g "Personal Identity and Individuation". See Williams (1973h).
1973h *Problems of the Self*. Cambridge: Cambridge University Press.
1973i "The Self and the Future". See Williams (1973h).
1978a *Descartes: The Project of Pure Enquiry*. Harmondsworth: Penguin.
1978b "Introduction to *Concepts and Categories*". See Berlin (1978).
1980 "Justice as a Virtue". See Rorty (1980).
1981a "Conflicts of Values". See Williams (1981d).
1981b "Internal and External Reasons". See Williams (1981d).
1981c "Justice as a Virtue". See Williams (1981d).
1981d *Moral Luck*. Cambridge: Cambridge University Press.
1981e "Moral Luck". See Williams (1981d).
1981f "Persons, Character and Morality". See Williams (1981d).
1981g "Philosophy". See Finley (1981).
1981h "Practical Necessity". See Williams (1981d).
1981i "Preface to *Moral Luck*". See Williams (1981d).
1981j "The Truth in Relativism". See Williams (1981d).
1981k "Utilitarianism and Moral Self-Indulgence". See Williams (1981d).
1982a "Cosmic Philosopher". *New York Review of Books* **29** (2/18), 32–4.
1982b "Cratylus' Theory of Names and Its Refutations". See Everson (1994).
1982c *Utilitarianism and Beyond*, with A. Sen (eds). New York: Cambridge University Press.

1983 "Descartes' Use of Skepticism". See Burnyeat (1983).
1985 *Ethics and the Limits of Philosophy*. Cambridge, MA: Harvard University Press.
1993a "Preface to the Canto Edition of *Morality: An Introduction to Ethics*". Cambridge: Cambridge University Press.
1993b *Shame and Necessity*. Berkeley, CA: University of California Press.
1995a "Acting as the Virtuous Person Acts". See Heinaman (1995).
1995b "Evolution, Ethics and the Representation Problem". See Williams (1995d).
1995c "Internal Reasons and the Obscurity of Blame". See Williams (1995d).
1995d *Making Sense of Humanity*. Cambridge: Cambridge University Press.
1995e "Moral Luck: A Postscript". See Williams (1995d).
1995f "Nietzsche's Minimalist Moral Philosophy". See Williams (1995d).
1995g "The Point of View of the Universe: Sidgwick and the Ambitions of Ethics". See Williams (1995d).
1995h "Replies". See Altham & Harrison (1995).
1995i "Saint-Just's Illusion". See Williams (1995d).
1995j "What Does Intuitionism Imply?" See Williams (1995d).
1995k "Who Needs Ethical Knowledge?" See Williams (1995d).
1996a "Truth in Ethics". See Hooker (1996).
1996b "*The Women of Trachis*: Fictions, Pessimism, Ethics". See Louden & Schollmeier (1996).
1997 "The Analogy of City and State in Plato's *Republic*". See Kraut (1997).
1999 *Plato: The Invention of Philosophy*. New York: Routledge.
2000a "Naturalism and Genealogy". See Harcourt (2000).
2000b "Philosophy as a Humanistic Discipline". *Philosophy* **75**, 477–96.
2001 "Postscript: Some Further Notes on Internal and External Reasons". See Millgram (2001).
2002 *Truth and Truthfulness: An Essay in Genealogy*. Princeton, NJ: Princeton University Press.
2005 *In the Beginning Was the Deed: Realism and Moralism in Political Argument*, G. Hawthorn (ed.). Princeton, NJ: Princeton University Press.
2006a *Philosophy as a Humanistic Discipline*, A. W. Moore (ed.). Princeton, NJ: Princeton University Press.
2006b *The Sense of the Past*, M. Burnyeat (ed.). Princeton, NJ: Princeton University Press.

References

Altham, J. E. J. 1995. "Reflection and Confidence". See Altham & Harrison (1995).
Altham, J. E. J. & R. Harrison (eds) 1995. *World, Mind, and Ethics*. Cambridge: Cambridge University Press.
Annas, J. 1993. *The Morality of Happiness*. New York: Clarendon Press.
Anscombe, G. E. M. 1997. "Modern Moral Philosophy". See Crisp & Slote (1997).
Aristotle 1999. *Nicomachean Ethics*, 2nd edn, T. Irwin (trans.). Indianapolis, IN: Hackett.
Baron, M. 1995. *Kantian Ethics Almost without Apology*. Ithaca, NY: Cornell University Press.
Berlin, I. 1978. *Concepts and Categories*, H. Hardy (ed.). New York: Viking.

Bittner, R. 1992. "Is It Reasonable to Regret Things One Did?" *Journal of Philosophy* **89**, 262–73.
Blackburn, S. 1992. "Through Thick and Thin". *Proceedings of the Aristotelian Society* (supp. vol.) **66**, 285–99.
Blackburn, S. 1996. *The Oxford Dictionary of Philosophy*. Oxford: Oxford University Press.
Brink, D. O. 1986. "Utilitarianism and the Personal Point of View". *Journal of Philosophy* **83**, 417–38.
Burnyeat, M. (ed.) 1983. *The Skeptical Tradition*. Berkeley, CA: University of California Press.
Cairns, D. L. 1993. *Aidos: The Psychology and Ethics of Honour and Shame in Ancient Greek Literature*. Oxford: Clarendon Press.
Calhoun, C. 2004. *Setting the Moral Compass*. Oxford: Oxford University Press.
Clark, M. 2001. "On the Rejection of Morality: Bernard Williams' Debt to Nietzsche". See Schacht (2001).
Clarke, S. G. & E. Simpson (eds) 1989. *Anti-Theory in Ethics and Moral Conservatism*. Albany, NY: SUNY Press.
Cohon, R. 1986. "Are External Reasons Impossible?" *Ethics* **96**, 545–56.
Craig, E. 1990. *Knowledge and the State of Nature*. Oxford: Clarendon Press.
Crisp, R. & M. Slote (eds) 1997. *Virtue Ethics*. Oxford: Oxford University Press.
Cullity, G. & B. Gaut (eds) 1997. *Ethics and Practical Reason*. Oxford: Oxford University Press.
Dancy, J. (ed.) 1997. *Reading Parfit*. Oxford: Blackwell.
Davis, N. 1980. "Utilitarianism and Responsibility". *Ratio* **22**, 15–35.
Dummett, M. 2004. *Truth and the Past*. New York: Columbia University Press.
Edwards, P. (ed.) 1967. *The Encyclopedia of Philosophy*. New York: Macmillan.
Everson, S. (ed.) 1994. *Companions to Ancient Thought, Vol. 3. Language*. Cambridge: Cambridge University Press.
Finley, M. I. 1981. *The Legacy of Greece: A New Appraisal*. Oxford: Clarendon Press.
Flanagan, O. 1991. *Varieties of Moral Personality*. Cambridge, MA: Harvard University Press.
Förster, E. (ed.) 1989. *Kant's Transcendental Deductions*. Stanford, CA: Stanford University Press.
Frankfurt, H. 1988a. "Freedom of the Will and the Concept of a Person". See Frankfurt (1988b).
Frankfurt, H. 1988b. *The Importance of What We Care About*. Cambridge: Cambridge University Press.
Freud, S. 1960. *The Ego and the Id*, J. Riviere (trans.). New York: Norton.
Freud, S. 1961. *Civilization and Its Discontents*, J. Strachey (trans.). New York: Norton.
Freud, S. 1965. *New Introductory Lectures on Psycho-Analysis*, J. Strachey (trans.). New York: Norton.
Geertz, C. 1973. *The Interpretation of Cultures*. New York: Basic Books.
Grene, D. & R. Lattimore (eds) 1957. *The Complete Greek Tragedies, Vol. II*. Chicago, IL: University of Chicago Press.
Harcourt, E. (ed.) 2000. *Morality, Reflection and Ideology*. Oxford: Oxford University Press.
Hare, R. M. 1952. *The Language of Morals*. Oxford: Clarendon Press.
Hare, R. M. 1963. *Freedom and Reason*. Oxford: Clarendon Press.
Hare, R. M. 1981. *Moral Thinking*. Oxford: Clarendon Press.

Hegel, G. W. F. 1991. *Elements of the Philosophy of Right*, H. B. Nisbet (trans.), A. W. Wood (ed.). Cambridge: Cambridge University Press.
Heinaman, R. (ed.) 1995. *Aristotle and Moral Realism*. London: UCL Press.
Herman, B. 1993a. "Integrity and Impartiality", rev. edn. See Herman (1993b).
Herman, B. 1993b. *The Practice of Moral Judgment*. Cambridge, MA: Harvard University Press.
Hooker, B. (ed.) 1996. *Truth in Ethics*. Oxford: Blackwell.
Hooker, B. 2001. "Williams' Argument against External Reasons". See Millgram (2001).
Hooker, B. & M. Little (eds) 2000. *Moral Particularism*. Oxford: Oxford University Press.
Hookway, C. 1995. "Fallibilism and Objectivity: Science and Ethics". See Altham & Harrison (1995).
Horwich, P. 1998. *Truth*, 2nd edn. Oxford: Oxford University Press.
Horwich, P. 2001. "A Defense of Minimalism". See Lynch (2001).
Hume, D. 1975. *An Enquiry Concerning the Principles of Morals*, L. A. Selby-Bigge (ed.), revised by P. H. Nidditch. Oxford: Oxford University Press.
Hume, D. 1978. *A Treatise of Human Nature*, L. A. Selby-Bigge (ed.), revised by P. H. Nidditch. Oxford: Oxford University Press.
Jardine, N. 1995. "Science, Ethics and Objectivity". See Altham & Harrison (1995).
Jenkins, M. 2001. *The Ethical Philosophy of Bernard Williams: Between the Everyday and the Eternal*. PhD dissertation, University of Chicago.
Kolak, D. & R. Martin (eds) 1991. *Self and Identity: Contemporary Philosophical Issues*. New York: Macmillan.
Korsgaard, C. 1996a. *Creating the Kingdom of Ends*. Cambridge: Cambridge University Press.
Korsgaard, C. 1996b. "Personal Identity and the Unity of Agency: A Kantian Response to Parfit". See Korsgaard (1996a).
Korsgaard, C. 1996c. "Skepticism about Practical Reason". See Korsgaard (1996a).
Korsgaard, C. 1996d. *The Sources of Normativity*. Cambridge: Cambridge University Press.
Korsgaard, C. 1997. "The Normativity of Instrumental Reason". See Cullity & Gaut (1997).
Kraut, R. 1994. "Review of Bernard Williams' *Shame and Necessity*". *Ethics* **105**, 178–81.
Kraut, R. (ed.) 1997. *Plato's Republic: Critical Essays*. Lanham, MD: Rowman and Littlefield.
Lear, J. 2003. "The Idea of Moral Psychology: The Impact of Psychoanalysis on Philosophy in Britain". *International Journal of Psychoanalysis* **84**, 1351–61.
Lewis, D. 1983a. *Philosophical Papers, Vol. I*. New York: Oxford University Press.
Lewis, D. 1983b. "Postscripts to 'Survival and Identity'". See Lewis (1983a).
Lewis, D. 1983c. "Survival and Identity". See Lewis (1983a).
Locke, J. 1975. *An Essay Concerning Human Understanding*, P. H. Nidditch (ed.). Oxford: Clarendon Press.
Louden, R. B. & P. Schollmeier (eds) 1996. *The Greeks and Us: Essays in Honor of Arthur W. H. Adkins*. Chicago, IL: University of Chicago Press.
Lynch, M. (ed.) 2001. *The Nature of Truth*. Cambridge, MA: MIT Press.
MacIntyre, A. 1984. *After Virtue*, 2nd edn. Notre Dame, IN: University of Notre Dame Press.

McDowell, J. 1986. "Critical Notice of *Ethics and the Limits of Philosophy*". *Mind* **95**, 379–86.
McDowell, J. 1995. "Might there Be External Reasons?" See Altham & Harrison (1995).
McDowell, J. 1998a. "Aesthetic Value, Objectivity, and the Fabric of the World". See McDowell (1998b).
McDowell, J. 1998b. *Mind, Value, and Reality*. Cambridge, MA: Harvard University Press.
Martin, R. & J. Barresi 2002a. "Introduction: Personal Identity and What Matters in Survival: An Historical Overview". See Martin & Barresi (2002b).
Martin, R. & J. Barresi (eds) 2002b. *Personal Identity*. Oxford: Blackwell.
Midgley, M. 1984. *Wickedness*. London: Routledge.
Millgram, E. 1995. "Was Hume a Humean?" *Hume Studies* **21**, 75–93.
Millgram, E. 1996. "Williams' Argument Against External Reasons". *Noûs* **30**, 197–220.
Millgram, E. 1997. *Practical Induction*. Cambridge, MA: Harvard University Press.
Millgram, E. (ed.) 2001. *Varieties of Practical Reasoning*. Cambridge, MA: MIT Press.
Moore, A. W. 1997. *Points of View*. Oxford: Oxford University Press.
Murdoch, I. 1970a. "The Idea of Perfection". See Murdoch (1970c).
Murdoch, I. 1970b. "On 'God' and 'Good' ". See Murdoch (1970c).
Murdoch, I. 1970c. *The Sovereignty of Good*. London: Routledge.
Nagel, T. 1979a. "Brain Bisection and the Unity of Consciousness". See Nagel (1979c).
Nagel, T. 1979b. "Moral Luck". See Nagel (1979c).
Nagel, T. 1979c. *Mortal Questions*. Cambridge: Cambridge University Press.
Nagel, T. 1995a. "Introduction: The Philosophical Culture". See Nagel (1995b).
Nagel, T. 1995b. *Other Minds*. New York: Oxford University Press.
Nagel, T. 1995c. "Williams: One Thought Too Many". See Nagel (1995b).
Nietzsche, F. 1967. *Basic Writings of Nietzsche*, W. Kaufmann (trans.). New York: The Modern Library.
Nietzsche, F. 1986. *Human, All Too Human*, R. J. Hollingdale (trans.). Cambridge: Cambridge University Press.
Nietzsche, F. 2001. *The Gay Science*, J. Nauckhoff & A. Del Caro (trans.), B. Williams (ed.). Cambridge: Cambridge University Press.
Noonan, H. 1991. *Personal Identity*. London: Routledge.
Nozick, R. 1981. *Philosophical Explanations*. Cambridge, MA: Harvard University Press.
Nussbaum, M. 1995. "Aristotle on Human Nature and the Foundation of Ethics". See Altham & Harrison (1995).
Nussbaum, M. 2000. "Why Practice Needs Ethical Theory". See Hooker & Little (2000).
Nussbaum, M. 2003. "Tragedy and Justice: Bernard Williams Remembered". *Boston Review* Oct./Nov., 35–9.
Olson, E. 1997. *The Human Animal: Personal Identity without Psychology*. New York: Oxford University Press.
Parfit, D. 1984. *Reasons and Persons*. Oxford: Clarendon Press.
Peirce, C. S. 1966a. "A Critical Review of Berkeley's Idealism". See Peirce (1966b).
Peirce, C. S. 1966b. *Selected Writings*, P. P. Wiener (ed.). New York: Dover.
Perry, J. 1972. "Can the Self Divide?" *Journal of Philosophy* **69**, 463–88.

Perry, J. 1975a. "The Problem of Personal Identity". See Perry (1975b).
Perry, J. (ed.) 1975b. *Personal Identity*. Berkeley, CA: University of California Press.
Perry, J. 1976. "The Mind and the Self". *Journal of Philosophy* **73**, 417–28.
Pippin, R. B. 1997a. "Hegel, Ethical Reasons, Kantian Rejoinders". See Pippin (1997b).
Pippin, R. B. 1997b. *Idealism as Modernism: Hegelian Variations*. Cambridge: Cambridge University Press.
Putnam, H. 1978. *Meaning and the Moral Sciences*. London: Routledge & Kegan Paul.
Putnam, H. 1990a. "Objectivity and the Science/Ethics Distinction". See Putnam (1990b).
Putnam, H. 1990b. *Realism with a Human Face*, J. Conant (ed.). Cambridge, MA: Harvard University Press.
Putnam, H. 1992. *Renewing Philosophy*. Cambridge, MA: Harvard University Press.
Putnam, H. 1994. *Words and Life*, J. Conant (ed.). Cambridge, MA: Harvard University Press.
Putnam, H. 2001. "Reply to Bernard Williams' *Philosophy as a Humanistic Discipline*". *Philosophy* **76**, 605–14.
Railton, P. 1988. "Alienation, Consequentialism, and the Demands of Morality". See Scheffler (1988).
Ramsey, F. P. 2001. "The Nature of Truth". See Lynch (2001).
Rawls, J. 1971. *A Theory of Justice*. Cambridge, MA: Harvard University Press.
Rawls, J. 1989. "Themes in Kant's Moral Philosophy". See Förster (1989).
Rorty, A. O. (ed.) 1976. *The Identities of Persons*. Berkeley, CA: University of California Press.
Rorty, A. O. (ed.) 1980. *Essays on Aristotle's Ethics*. Berkeley, CA: University of California Press.
Rorty, R. 1991a. "Is Natural Science a Natural Kind?" See Rorty (1991b).
Rorty, R. 1991b. *Objectivity, Relativism and Truth*. Cambridge: Cambridge University Press.
Ross, W. D. 1930. *The Right and the Good*. Oxford: Clarendon Press.
Scanlon, T. M. 1998. *What We Owe to Each Other*. Cambridge, MA: Harvard University Press.
Schacht, R. (ed.) 2001. *Nietzsche's Postmoralism*. Cambridge: Cambridge University Press.
Schechtman, M. 1996. *The Constitution of Selves*. Ithaca, NY: Cornell University Press.
Scheffler, S. 1987. "Morality through Thick and Thin: A Critical Notice of *Ethics and the Limits of Philosophy*". *Philosophical Review* **96**, 411–34.
Scheffler, S. (ed.) 1988. *Consequentialism and Its Critics*. Oxford: Oxford University Press.
Scheffler, S. 1992. *Human Morality*. New York: Oxford University Press.
Scheffler, S. 1994. *The Rejection of Consequentialism*, rev. edn. Oxford: Clarendon Press.
Shoemaker, S. 1997. "Parfit on Identity". See Dancy (1997).
Shoemaker, S. & R. Swinburne 1984. *Personal Identity*. Oxford: Blackwell.
Sidgwick, H. 1981. *The Methods of Ethics*, 7th edn. Indianapolis, IN: Hackett.
Smart, J. J. C. and B. Williams 1973. *Utilitarianism: For and Against*. Cambridge: Cambridge University Press.

Sophocles 1957. *Ajax*, J. Moore (trans.). See Grene & Lattimore 1957.
Statman, D. (ed.) 1993. *Moral Luck*. Albany, NY: SUNY Press.
Swinburne, R. 1984. "Personal Identity: The Dualist Theory". See Shoemaker & Swinburne (1984).
Tarski, A. 2001. "The Semantic Conception of Truth and the Foundations of Semantics". See Lynch (2001).
Taylor, C. 1976. "Responsibility for Self". See Rorty (1976).
Taylor, C. 1985a. *Human Agency and Language: Philosophical Papers I*. Cambridge: Cambridge University Press.
Taylor, C. 1985b. "Self-interpreting Animals". See Taylor (1985a).
Taylor, C. 1985c. "What Is Human Agency?" See Taylor (1985a).
Taylor, C. 1989. *Sources of the Self*. Cambridge, MA: Harvard University Press.
Taylor, G. 1985. *Pride, Shame and Guilt: Emotions of Self-Assessment*. Oxford: Clarendon Press.
Unger, P. 1990. *Identity, Consciousness and Value*. New York: Oxford University Press.
Vogler, C. 2002. *Reasonably Vicious*. Cambridge, MA: Harvard University Press.
Walker, M. U. 1998. *Moral Understandings*. New York: Routledge.
White, N. 1994. "Review of *Shame and Necessity*". *Journal of Philosophy* **91**, 619–22.
Wolf, S. 2004. "The Moral of Moral Luck". See Calhoun (2004).
Wollheim, R. 1999. *On The Emotions*. New Haven, CT: Yale University Press.
Wood, A. W. 1990. *Hegel's Ethical Thought*. Cambridge: Cambridge University Press.
Wright, C. 1992. *Truth and Objectivity*. Cambridge, MA: Harvard University Press.
Wright, C. 1996. "Truth in Ethics". See Hooker (1996).

Index